WITNESSING INSANITY

WITNESSING *INSANITY*

Madness and Mad-Doctors in the English Court

JOEL PETER EIGEN

FOREWORD BY
NIGEL WALKER

YALE UNIVERSITY PRESS
New Haven and London

Designed by Jill Breitbarth and set in Simoncini Garamond type
by Rainsford Type, Danbury, Connecticut.
Printed in the United States of America by Edwards Brothers,
Inc., Ann Arbor, Michigan.

Library of Congress Cataloging-in-Publication Data

Eigen, Joel Peter, 1947–
    Witnessing insanity : madness and mad-doctors in the
    English court / Joel Peter Eigen : foreword by Nigel
    Walker.
        p.   cm.
    Includes bibliographical references and index.
    ISBN 0-300-06289-3

    1. Insanity—Jurisprudence—Great Britain—His-
tory. 2. Forensic psychiatry—Great Britain—
History. I. Title.
KD7897.E36 1995
345.41'04—dc20
[344.1051]   94-31785
                                                          CIP

*A catalogue record for this book is available from the British
Library.*

*The paper in this book meets the guidelines for permanence and
durability of the Committee on Production Guidelines for Book
Longevity of the Council on Library Resources.*

10 9 8 7 6 5 4 3 2 1

*To the memory of Herman and Sadie Eigen
and Dean Bradley Dewey*

Contents

Foreword

It is both an honor and a pleasure to be invited to write a foreword for this important book. The historiography of the English insanity defense, though far from bulky, has produced enough misinterpretations, over-simplifications and dramaturgies. One famous historian thought that the M'Naughten Rules had been anticipated by the Code Napoléon, although their legal effect is about as different as it could be. Another wrote that before the nineteenth century insane persons who committed crimes were held fully responsible: a belief that would have been false even in the Middle Ages. Social historians—or at least historically inclined sociologists—have dramatized the case-histories of lunatics to divert their readers. Modestinus once said that madmen were punished enough by their madness; but Bedlam exposed them to the ridicule of sightseers, and even today there are writers who, while deploring this, are not above cashing in on the gruesome or bizarre.

Joel Eigen neither oversimplifies nor dramatizes; and he certainly does not misinterpret. To my mind this book makes major contributions to the history of the subject. One example is the way it gives the lie to social historians who have represented mad-doctors of the eighteenth and nineteenth centuries as infiltrating the English criminal courts in a campaign of empire-building. Eigen rejects this dramaturgy, and clearly establishes that their appearances in courts were a response to the felt needs of judges as well as defendants.

Another example is his demonstration that twentieth-century English lawyers were mistaken when they assumed that "irresistible impulse" had never been an acceptable version of the insanity defense. They may have been encouraged understandably in this by what have come to be called the M'Naughten Rules (a spelling of his name, by the way, which Daniel McNaughtan himself never used), but which ought to be called the Tindal Rules, after the lord chief of justice who drafted them. Yet even

Tindal's young contemporary Fitzjames Stephen, who later wrote a history of English criminal law, doubted whether the rules reflected the common law exhaustively. Eigen has shown that "lesion of the will" was by no means unheard of as the basis for successful insanity defenses before McNaughtan's case.

Readers will find many other examples of Eigen's accuracy and insight in this milestone of a book.

NIGEL WALKER

Preface

After spending the greater part of the past ten years consumed with one issue in the history of madness, rooting around in dusty medical and legal archives, trying to convince anyone who would listen that I could see things that had eluded all others, I concluded that there were easier things in this world than writing a book about delusion. The capacity to become convinced that what one wants (or fears) to be true actually *is* true does not, after all, distinguish the sane from the insane. Perfectly rational people indulge in delusions of grandeur, and all sorts of purportedly sane people receive daily missives from God. Supposedly it is the *persistence* of delusory belief in the face of contradictory evidence—the inability or refusal to recognize a delusion for what it is—that separates the mad from the merely wishful. And yet, after having spent so much time thinking about the thought-world of the distracted, I have begun to suspect that the difference between the two deluded populations is perhaps more one of degree than one of kind. We all construct worlds that mirror deeply held beliefs, and this is no less true for the historian of psychiatry than for the subjects of such a study.

This book is an effort to provide a reality check to the thought-world that historians and sociologists of medicine have constructed for ourselves and our readers. Over the past twenty years or so, the history of psychiatry has become a growth industry for the social sciences. Researchers have sought historical evidence to examine evolving rationales for the cure and management of the insane, the creation of innovative classification terms for various forms of madness, and jurisdictional rivalries among members of powerful professions, each claiming to be the rightful caretakers of the deranged. The significance of historical evidence, however, is seldom self-evident. Medical texts and professional claims to expertise can be read in a number of ways, symptoms of madness listed in asylum registers afford numerous interpretations, and verdicts in celebrated trials rarely provide unequivocal insight into the definition and implications of severe mental states in law. This ambiguity is especially troublesome in historical studies of insanity because the cast of characters presents a "triple threat" of delusion. There is the afflicted individual, whose language reflects haunting fears, monomaniacal possession, and illusory voices impelling him or her to acts of atrocious barbarity. These fears and visions are then classified by a clinical observer, eager to bring coherence to aberrant experience, and perhaps also to secure a professional niche in the "lunacy-trade." And the classifications of the nosologist are in turn scrutinized by the historian of psychiatry, whose notions about professionalization and power lead to a particular view of clinical classification in a particular light. All three are convinced that the world they see is real. Each defines, acts, and reacts to it as if it were. If what separates the delusional from the sane is indeed the willingness to entertain contradictory evidence, it is essential to search for elements in the historical puzzle that may allow us to examine beliefs anew and to be mindful of the seductive allure of the worlds we create.

Through a stroke of fortune, I came across an unusual and valuable piece of that puzzle during a sabbatical year at the Institute of Criminology at Cambridge University in 1982–83. I had not realized when I read Nigel Walker's magisterial *Crime and Insanity in England* (1968) in graduate school that the hundreds of insanity trials mentioned in the text not only offered an opportunity to observe shifts in the incidence of the insanity plea and its relative success over time but could be retrieved and would yield a wealth of evidence regarding how ordinary people, jurors, and mad-doctors discovered madness. Contained within these verbatim trial accounts was the contemporary language of late eighteenth- and early nineteenth-century Londoners who witnessed madness in its various forms and considered its implication for questions of criminal responsibility. Hundreds of juries in the eighty-year period examined in this volume contemplated the question of the prisoner's impaired mental state, hearing testimony from prisoners' neighbors, prisoners themselves, and mad-doctors. Their language and images of derangement are the subject of this book, particularly those employed by the first forensic-psychiatric witnesses. When and how did this testimony diverge from the ordinary person's? How did the concerns of law inform medical testimony and shape professional opinion? Perhaps most important, what was the source of medical claims to expert ways of knowing, and what externally driven cultural concerns are revealed in medical conceptualization?

My research received its start when Nigel Walker generously shared with me his original notes on the trial narratives that comprised his volume. I gratefully acknowledge his kind assistance and continuing support. Also in that sabbatical year I met Roy Porter, who took an early interest in my work and inspired me to complete this book, not only through direct suggestions and encouragement but also through his amazingly productive pen, which has shaped historical research in psychiatry and madness for a generation of scholars. To both these singularly insightful scholars I owe a massive debt that I can only hope to repay through encouraging other students of eighteenth-century law and psychiatry to treat historical materials with the care and sober reflection they deserve. I should also like to acknowledge a debt to two scholars whose role in directing my graduate career has found resonance in the current study, completed some years after my time at the University of Pennsylvania. Professor Marvin E. Wolfgang nurtured both my interest in historical criminology through his study of crime in Renaissance Florence and my curiosity about quantitative criminology through his analysis of delinquency in a birth cohort. Franklin E. Zimring, then of the University of Chicago Law School, gave me my first taste for examining how the law works in practice, quite apart from its avowed rationale. Looking over this book I am reminded of, and grateful for, the lasting effect of such truly inspiring teachers and scholars.

I have been the fortunate recipient of several fellowships and grants. A Legal History Fellowship from the American Bar Foundation supported a return trip to Cambridge in the summer of 1984, and a Life Membership voted by the Fellows of Clare Hall gave me a college affiliation and residence over visits in the next seven years. I am also grateful to my American college, Franklin and Marshall, whose support through summer research grants permitted the examination of diaries, handwritten medical texts, and records available only in England. I took a second sabbatical year at the University of Durham, where I enjoyed the privileges attendant to the Leonard Slater Fellowship, bestowed by the Fellows of University College, and I gratefully acknowledge their support. The National Endowment for the Humanities granted four fellowships that afforded me the luxury to pace this research and to write it up through an extended leave in 1992–93. I remain indebted to Lynne Cheney and the NEH staff for administering their programs so conscientiously and well.

The mechanics of this research and its varied archival sources also mean that a host of librarians and archivists deserve thanks. The staff at the Guildhall Library in London allowed me to photocopy hundreds of trial narratives, without which I could never have lived with the documents throughout the past ten years. The librarians at the Royal College of Surgeons in London and the Royal College of Physicians in Edinburgh were similarly helpful in securing materials. Mary Shelly of Franklin and

Marshall's Fackenthal Library cheerfully filled every interlibrary loan request, and I salute her ingenuity in tracking down obscure texts.

I owe a great debt to scholars in several disciplines who have guided me toward an understanding of the materials and listened patiently as I expounded on the ideas represented here. G. E. Berrios, Michael Clark, Catherine Crawford, John Langbein, Jacques Quen, and Roger Smith have offered important insight into the history of psychiatry and law, and I thank them warmly. Erica Haimes and Robin Williams have been irreplaceable sounding-boards, *hoteliers,* and unflagging supporters. Annette Aronowicz has been especially helpful in suggesting that I search for the narrative as well as the quantitative in the historical record. During an NEH-sponsored seminar at Cornell University, Sander Gilman offered cogent advice on aspects of this work that eventually were published in *Medical History,* and I thank him heartily for the guidance. Through that seminar I met Phyllis Freeman, who has remained my closest soul-mate in questions of medicine and culture and a patient listener during successive reworkings of this book. I treasure her friendship and am deeply thankful for her interest and kind regard. Other colleagues who lent intellectual support include Carol Böhmer, Maria Höhn, and a former student, Lisa Bonchek, who has embarked on a brilliant graduate career. Lisa's help in the summer of 1991 is reflected in the quantitative displays in chapters 4 and 6. I am grateful to her and take obvious pride in her postgraduate accomplishment. I also thank another former student, Gregory Andoll, who in the summer of 1985 helped me discover how the prisoner met the doctor. One of the great delights of teaching at a small liberal arts college is the opportunity to work directly with bright, imaginative students. Gregory's assistance was made possible through the Hackman Scholars Program, which brings faculty and students together for shared summer research projects. He and I are both grateful to the Hackman family for making this fruitful partnership possible.

There remains only to acknowledge steadfast friends and family members whose encouragement and incessant insistence that I complete this book were every bit as critical as scholarly and library assistance. Jonathan Rosenbloom, Robert Friedrich, Sam Martin, and Anne Mitchell have been very patient with me, especially in the past year. Maurice and Judy Kaplow opened their house and hearts to me through good times and bad, providing a haven in Philadelphia and a measure of love that is all too rare. Caroline Mason afforded shelter and succor at a critical time and has my undying gratitude. I am also grateful to stalwart friend Roger Harris, who provided invaluable plain-speaking wisdom, limitless patience, and a steadying influence throughout. My greatest source of inspiration remains my sister, Mikki Eigen Rocker, whose pride in my work was a beacon in the dark days. I hope each of those named above knows how deeply they are held in my affection and esteem.

This book is dedicated to the memory of three whose influence transcends this project. My parents' love of learning and valuing of scholarship left an unequivocal legacy of how a life should be lived. I deeply regret that I am unable to share this work with them. Another formative influence in my academic life was the former dean of the college at Franklin and Marshall, Bradley Rau Dewey. With others who joined the faculty in the 1970s and 1980s, I experienced firsthand the exemplary influence of this peerless teacher-scholar. His clear-eyed determination, devotion to rigorous thought, and sheer joy in the life of the mind inspired a generation of faculty colleagues. My life has been given direction and added purpose by all three; I am grateful for their wise counsel and inspiring example.

Introduction

$\mathcal{J}_{N}$ *1760, EARL FERRERS'S ATTEMPT TO CONVINCE HIS* peers in the House of Lords that he suffered from "occasional insanity" on the day he killed his servant resulted in a murder conviction and a very public hanging, memorialized in well-circulated engravings and centuries of legal commentary. In the same year, Francis David Stirn, a man of decidedly less celebrity, also tried unsuccessfully to persuade a jury of his occasional madness. Although Stirn was convicted, dissected, and impaled on a stake near Black Mary's Hole, no artwork or legal comment attended his execution. In fact, medical historians have all but ignored his trial, despite clear and compelling parallels with the notorious Earl Ferrers: in both cases the crime was murder, the defense atypical, and the prisoner himself addressed the court. The two prosecutions shared one further feature, which would alter the direction and focus of insanity trials for centuries: the participation of a mad-doctor. In Ferrers's trial, the redoubtable Dr. John Monro, physician to Bethlem Hospital, testified about the symptoms of lunacy. At Stirn's prosecution, a Mr. Chapman, surgeon to Nothing-in-Particular, testified about the prisoner's periodic madness: "I believe it is often the way with mad people that they have intervals [of lucidity]—sometimes of very long duration." In his cross-examination he acknowledged the prisoner's "flighty fits [that] frequently happened at full and change of the moon." Although the year 1760 has become the conventional date for the entrance of expert witnesses on insanity into the English courtroom, only the Ferrers verdict has found its way into legal lore. Francis David Stirn—whose witnesses may well have carried greater significance for the ordinary juror's understanding of insanity—lies buried not only on the outskirts of London but beyond the consideration of insanity-defense historians.[1]

Standard attempts to investigate the evolution of the medical jurisprudence of madness in England have exhaustively considered the courtroom dynamics and jury verdicts of several famous eighteenth- and nineteenth-century trials—specific judicial instructions to the jury, summary statements made by prosecuting counsel, and recorded cross-examination of witnesses. Thus the trials of "Mad Ned Arnold" (1723), Earl Ferrers (1760), James Hadfield (1800), Edward Oxford (1840), and, of course, Daniel McNaughtan (1843) have taken their place in legal texts and histories of psychiatry. But the very exceptionality and notoriety of these crimes—an assault on the sovereign, an intemperate killing by a member of the House of Lords—should give the medico-legal historian pause. The confluence of class, politics, and atypical legal representation immediately elevated these trials to a level of significance not shared by those of the Francis Stirns of London. One wonders whether the acquittal of a deranged assassin necessarily reveals the law's conception of madness at any particular moment in history. Is the same construction of insanity likely to apply to the trial of a deranged defendant who stole spoons or forged checks? Would a mad-doctor in charge of supervising London's largest public asylum be likely to share a professional vocabulary and clinical orientation with a general practitioner who saw only one or two insane persons a year? Ultimately, which trial would the ordinary lay juror be likely to remember and transport into courtroom deliberations: a neighbor's, or Earl Ferrers's? The trials of the notorious provide at best a skeletal outline of the evolution of the medical jurisprudence of mental derangement. How did juries in the much more numerous, though decidedly less posh, insanity trials approach the question of criminal responsibility when allegations of madness constituted the prisoner's defense?

In 1968, Nigel Walker published *Crime and Insanity in England,* and it remains the definitive treatment of common law's historical experience with states of mental derangement. In addition to providing the most thorough analysis we are likely to have of the evolution of English legal thinking on madness, Walker alerted researchers to the existence of hundreds of insanity trials in the eighteenth and nineteenth centuries. His empirical analysis of the incidence and success rates of insanity pleas contains references to peculiar features of some of the trials, including the occasional appearance of medical witnesses. It was the infrequent appearance of a medical man in the eighteenth century that caught my eye. Why should medical witnesses come to constitute a regular feature of insanity prosecutions in the early to mid-1800s when less than a century earlier they were practically unheard of? What did alienists say to the court that distinguished their testimony from that of other witnesses, and how did the court respond to the assertion of medical opinion in an area of human behavior that only decades earlier required no formal explication? Ultimately, I was eager to address the effect of medical testimony on legal conceptions of intent and responsibility. Could an investigation of *all* the insanity trials in these years of rapid growth in medical participation reveal the conceptual maneuvers employed by medical witnesses to address the law's fundamental concern—criminal responsibility and blameworthiness—within the framework of disease? Using Walker's data as a starting point, I decided to extend his survey of insanity trials to complete the years 1760 to 1843: dates that bracket the first appearance of an expert witness to testify about insanity *medically* and the formalization of the insanity plea during the trial of Daniel McNaughtan. This effort entailed scanning the testimony of tens of thousands of trials because it was necessary to consider the examination of all witnesses and prisoners for the mention of mental derangement; a simple "guilty" verdict could easily hide an unsuccessful plea of insanity. The mechanics of that search are discussed below.

As it turns out, finding the cases was the easy part. To unravel the courtroom dynamics that shaped insanity prosecutions both historically and in their eighteenth-century context, I had to trace the English approach to mental derangement to its origin in the writings of Henri de Bracton, legal scribe to Henry II, and then forward through selected legal cases up to the mid-1700s. Walker's volume and a number of supplementary legal texts were invaluable for historical reconstruction. Quite apart from the atypical insanity prosecution, the English courtroom had to be scrutinized for its own peculiarities. The role of the judiciary and the curious evolution of the defense attorney have been skillfully elucidated by John Langbein in his pathbreaking work with the *Old Bailey Sessions Papers,* verbatim narratives of the trials heard in London's central criminal court. In surveying these papers, Walker discovered that although the court's acceptance of a plea of insanity varied considerably depending on the features of the trial under review, one element present in every insanity prosecution was the need to determine the prisoner's intent. Whether phrased as an inability to "tell right from wrong" or an incapacity to "know what one was about," the law's concern was not with how deranged, how raving, or how delirious the prisoner was but rather whether the accused's disturbance precluded a capacity to form intent: "a will to harm." Only intentional behavior was punishable by law: the perpetrator who failed to understand the wrongfulness of an action could not be said to have acted with criminal intent.

No standard element characterized medicine's conception of madness in early modern England. One looks in vain for clear and consistent definitions of lunacy and delirium; indeed, the terms "madness" and "insanity" were often used interchangeably. Medical authors' attempts to discern the essence of madness often overlap, each trying to stake out territory for his own "school." The only thing most writers could agree on was that they themselves were firmly situated in the realm of the sane and the reasonable. Rival authors were thus free to differ about the cause, nature, and cure of the "objects" of derangement.

Few topics in the history of the human sciences have generated as much debate as this consignment of the mad to the status of clinical object, fit for rational, systematic classification. With the publication of *Folie et déraison: Histoire de la folie à l'âge classique* (1961), Michel Foucault moved the spotlight to the classifiers themselves, inaugurating a lively discussion of the motives that generated the medical and moral management of the insane and, by implication, a medical specialty devoted entirely to the mad. In the process, the nature of scientific knowledge and the status of professional expertise—two issues of monumental importance to the rise of forensic-psychiatric testimony—have become bound up in dispute. In fact, the terminology surrounding eighteenth- and nineteenth-century responses to derangement has become as contentious as the elusive essence of madness. Although Foucault's imaginative reconstruction of the fate of madness in the Age of Reason has generated a cottage industry in history and sociology, many elements of his central thesis concerning the Great Confinement—the supposed wholesale incarceration of the "unreasonable" of Europe—have come under intense critical scrutiny and have been substantially qualified when not rejected outright.

The extrapolation of Foucault's version of Continental medical practice to the English experience with madness turns out to be not terribly illuminating and in fact frankly misleading. Much like the growing profession in keeping private madhouses, the evolving specialization in forensic witnessing seems to have been consumer-driven, fragmentary, and perhaps even more court-inspired than professionally generated. Of much greater help has been Roy Porter's analysis of eighteenth-century society in general and medical consumerism in particular. Stanley Jackson's historical study of melancholy has also been tremendously important, not least because the relatively consistent 2,500-year symptomatology of melancholia places the activity of eighteenth-century medical classifiers in context. It is difficult to subscribe to an exclusively "social construction of madness" when confronted with consistent evidence that serious derangement existed and was recognized for centuries. Further, restricted attention to the perspective and motives of medical men puts the deranged "subjects" in a peculiar and ultimately untenable position: imbuing them with "inner wisdom" (which is lost the minute they *capitulate* to the language of Reason), losing sight of them completely, or, most grievous of all, ignoring the very real torment brought on by horrific visions and delusional beliefs.

Rejecting the Foucauldian critical perspective does not betoken a conviction that madness had some true, *essential* characteristic, triumphantly discovered by enlightened clinicians able to "read nature in the mind of the mad." There is certainly much to scrutinize in the fateful transition from religio-astrologic conceptions of madness to scientific-organic perspectives, and one needs to look carefully at the role of professional devices and desires in proffering an exclusively medical conception of madness. After having examined the testimony of lay jurors, medical witnesses, and prisoners, however, I was struck with the richness of courtroom dialogue, particularly the images that flowed between the alleged insane and their classifiers, and between the lay witness and the medical expert. One needn't adopt an either-or position: medical categorization as *imposition* or medical classification as "discovery." The keepers and the kept were very much part of their culture, and the images and metaphors employed by *all* parties to make sense of severe mental torment needs to be placed in the context of contemporary concerns and anxieties. One can hardly ignore the role of a physician's subscription to a particular school of medical psychology, since his courtroom language is likely to be freighted with the imagery of a specific scientific tradition. It is scientific tradition, however, not "professional colonization of the witness box," that one hears in this courtroom testimony. Assertions to professional expertise, when they do appear, seem to have been born in the designs of ambitious attorneys, endeavoring to secure an acquittal, rather than in the professional aims of soi-disant usurpers of the courtroom. Claims to professional skill surface in the process of cross-examination: they are rarely used to legitimize testimony at the outset. When they do surface, however, they illuminate an important step in medicine's assertion of cognitive expertise in "the mad business."

What follows, then, is a survey of the assertion and negotiation of extreme mental states in insanity trials heard in London's central criminal court between the years 1760 and 1843. The criminal trial was a particularly compelling forum for the display of extravagant derangement and the assertion of a specialist's opinion regarding its existence and consequence. Although civil proceedings in which the decision to commit individuals to asylum or to relieve them of their right to manage their affairs necessarily addressed basic cultural as well as legal notions about self-management and responsibility, the conjoining of crime and madness produced something rather more combustible than the sum of its two volatile parts. With two hundred or so offenses for which an English citizen could be put to death, criminal prosecution was serious business in the late 1700s. That a felon could be executed for the theft of buttons or other mundane items exceeding the trifling amount of thirty shillings provides ample evidence that Londoners—at least those in a position to shape legal policy—looked to the courts as the guarantor of private property and unimpeded commerce. One should therefore not be surprised to find the great majority of the insanity pleas in the eighteenth century raised in seemingly mundane (though *capital*) theft. Stealing assumed Olympic proportions in eighteenth-century London and could be the ticket to the gallows if the price was right. There was therefore every reason to raise the possibility of an exculpatory defense when one faced such high stakes. That a felon caught red-handed should escape the full force of law and receive an outright acquittal (before 1800) or a "special verdict" (after 1800) not only invoked standard concerns about criminal responsibility and blameworthiness but kindled fears about coddling a criminal class, particularly in view of the sevenfold increase in indicted offenders for the years 1805–1842.

The insanity trials discussed in this book did not therefore take place against a backdrop either of expansively humane attitudes regarding crime and punishment or of a drop in the incidence of crime. It hardly seems surprising that there were seriously deranged prisoners who availed themselves of an "insanity defense" when conditions warranted. That a new sort of insanity plea was created and accepted, one that could hardly have been envisioned at the dawn of forensic-psychiatric testimony and that coincided with a dramatic increase in criminal activity, is quite a different matter. The evolving role of the medical witness coincided with a fundamental reconceptualization of the relation between criminal responsibility and madness. Insanity "became" something very different by the mid-nineteenth century, but the role contributed by any one courtroom participant in this critical transformation is bound up with the changing dynamics of the criminal trial itself and ultimately with larger cultural questions concerning human agency. Lawyers and jurors, prisoners and prosecutors complemented, contradicted, and contextualized the testimony of medical experts on a trial-by-trial basis.

Between 1760 and 1843, the English courtroom faced not only famous insanity trials but the crimes of more than three hundred decidedly mundane offenders that became the occasion for the display and negotiation of mental derangement. An army of ordinary people—neighbors, lovers, coworkers, and relatives—trooped into the Old Bailey to comment about the prisoner's "bouncing out of the room in a mad freak," "rolling his head around in a kennel," and the "want of connection between his ideas." In more than half the trials, prisoners themselves addressed the court and offered jury and spectators a glimpse of madness from the "inside." Mad-doctors also appeared in increasing numbers. Although their testimony must be considered within the context of a criminal trial fairly teeming with "community experts," it is the imagery of this new *expert* witness that captured most graphically the emerging Victorian conception of insane criminality: a will out of control. The world of the morally insane was imparted to the jury by the new specialist in mental medicine in words and images that rendered the determination of responsibility increasingly problematic for generations to come.

SOURCE OF HISTORICAL MATERIALS AND SAMPLE

Contemporary historians and social scientists have exploited a range of documents to investigate the universe of eighteenth-century criminality and the prosecution of apprehended felons. Because no national crime statistics are available until 1805, surviving official records, including indictments, trial rosters, recognizances, and depositions, constitute the best opportunity for reconstructing criminal prosecution in the 1700s. The most frequently employed record has been the indictment: the formal charge laid against the prisoner by the grand jury. Analyses of indictments have permitted researchers to track the types of crime the grand and petit jury saw most often, the yearly fluctuations and regional variation in crime frequency, and the social and relational characteristics between victim and offender.[2] This record of formal charges can then be supplemented with fragmentary assize records and jail delivery lists to examine the charges and outcomes that followed the grand jury's decision to indict. Charges and outcomes, however, provide only the bare outline of a dynamic process that created one of the liveliest and most fateful forums in eighteenth-century London culture: the criminal trial. Although plays, newspapers, and novels tried to capture the drama of trial and punishment, standard literary devices are fragmentary and selective and rarely do justice to the vernacular of the age and the clash of personalities witnessed in court.

Fortunately we have a curious publication known as the *Old Bailey Sessions Papers* (hereafter, *OBSP*). Beginning in 1674 these pamphlets report the trial outcomes of every prosecution at the Old Bailey, the London trial court that adjudicated felonies committed in the City and in the contiguous county of Middlesex.[3] The reports of the Old Bailey's sittings (the "sessions") were written for nonlawyers and sold to the general public within days of the trials. In 1775, the Common Council for the City of London ordered the publication of these papers, thereby institutionalizing a practice already undertaken by "enterprising commercial printers" who had dispatched shorthand writers to the Old Bailey to record the proceedings.[4]

That this publication was intended for a lay readership both increases and limits its utility for contemporary historical research. The *OBSP* capture the language of ordinary London citizens through direct quotation of courtroom testimony and offer an array of interactions available in no other source: direct examination and cross-examination of witnesses, occasional instances of instructions to the jury, questions asked of witnesses by the jury, and a record of the prisoner's defense. But rich and illustrative as these verbatim narratives are, they were not meant to serve as legal documents, which means that much law-related detail is doubtless missing. We do not know what was said in many trials that were hopelessly compressed. In these instances, one cannot be sure if what survives were virtual summary hearings or the shorthand writer's exercise of editorial judgment to omit part of the proceedings. Maddening as these deletions are, it is clear that the *OBSP* constitute the best source we have to glimpse the trial-to-trial workings of the Old Bailey in the eighteenth century.[5] As John Langbein explains, "they emphasize the factual detail of witnesses and defendants' statements, especially in sensational cases," which reinforces their usefulness when one is researching the atypical prosecution, whether in terms of the type of crime or the introduction of unusual testimony.

This book was constructed by extending Walker's survey of the *OBSP* to identify cases in which mental derangement was mentioned by one of the court participants as a possible exculpatory defense. Walker surveyed approximately half of the years covered here; his work is reasonably comprehensive for the years 1760 to 1815, deleting three periods: the 1770s and two five-year segments in the 1780s and 1790s. After surveying these years myself, I extended his study to include trials heard between 1816 and 1843. All prosecutions between these years had to be examined because merely counting "insanity verdicts" would fail to give a reading of all trials in which a defense was forwarded but rejected.

A particular advantage of using the *OBSP* to chart historical change is the opportunity to glimpse the evolution of the "insanity trial" itself. Or rather, the insanity *trials* themselves because criminal prosecutions that saw the introduction of "the mental element" into courtroom testimony took a variety of forms in the late eighteenth and early nineteenth centuries. Certainly juries at the Old Bailey witnessed prosecutions that the twentieth-century observer would find very familiar: the intention to plead insanity is made at the outset of the proceeding, medical witnesses appear in court to attest to the bizarre mental world of the prisoner, and the jury returns an acquittal "on the grounds of insanity." This rather straightforward presentation of a defense "case," however, was by far the exception.[6] In most instances, jurors learned that mental derangement would play a part in their deliberations after the trial was well under way. The typical eighteenth-century trial began with the victim reporting the sequence of events surrounding the theft or assault and was followed by witnesses who corroborated the story. In some trials, the victim might happen to mention the distracted state of the accused, or a medical man—called to the scene of the crime to assist the victim—might note in passing that the offender appeared in an agitated state. Following such offhand remarks, the content of courtroom inquiry changed radically. It was no longer the details of the theft or physical attack that were at issue but the prisoner's mental state.

Another variant of the "insanity trial" proceeded as a straightforward investigation only to conclude—as most trials concluded—with the prisoner's defense. Rather than contest the prosecutor's story, however, a prisoner might simply say "I was senseless" or "I was out of my wits." Such statements could range from straightforward, unadorned assertions—"I have a cut in my head and am subject to fits"—to more elaborate, textured renderings of mental assault and confusion—"As I sat by the fire something came over me, I could give no account of it; I could get no command of myself." Not all prisoners were so articulate or so coherent; a number of "ranters" easily conformed to theatrical images of a raving lunatic. In all, some 331 trials between the years 1760 and 1843 (ranging yearly from between 4 to 8 per 1,000 trials) included some form of "insanity trial." The purported madmen—and madwomen—their crimes and defenses, and the witnesses who appeared on their behalf constitute my focus.

It may surprise the reader to learn of allegedly insane prisoners taking an active role in their defense or making any statement at the trial in hopes of mitigating punishment. It would be the rare contemporary insanity trial in which the defendant took the stand, but today's court is structured by a lawyer-dominated adversarial process that was almost totally absent in the late eighteenth and early nineteenth centuries. Lawyers were certainly present at trials, but their role was circumscribed by rules that prevented them from making opening and closing statements, summing up the "case," and addressing the jury.[7] Not until the Prisoner's Counsel Act of 1836 could lawyers assume the role of advocate associated today with an activist defense. Before then they were restricted to examining and cross-examining witnesses.

The reason for the curb on counsel was a long-standing principle of English jurisprudence: no one could better speak about the facts than the prisoner. Since the court was in essence a fact-finding exercise, direct confrontation between the aggrieved party and the accused—typically a medieval view of the trial—was thought to elicit all that a jury need consider. As late as 1721, one finds enduring traces of this sentiment: "[E]very one of Common Understanding may as properly speak to a Matter of Fact, as if he were the best Lawyer . . . it requires no manner of Skill to make a plain and honest Defense."[8] This is not to imply that lawyers were absent from the *OBSP,* only that their participation was in theory confined to questioning witnesses, a role that could be very considerable indeed. In fact, the *OBSP* reveals that lawyers were nowhere as constrained as legal precept supposedly mandated. Throughout the eighteenth century there are definite signs of a softening of the stricture regarding the advocacy role of defense counsel, as seen, for example, in a trial in 1786 that begins with "Counsel for the Defense" informing the court that "the defense is insanity."[9]

The increasing presence of lawyers acting on behalf of the defense has generated intriguing speculation regarding the sequence of events that might have led to an aggressive advocacy for the accused. We learn from John Langbein, for example, that until the 1730s, attorneys seldom appeared for the prosecutor (the victim) and never for the defense. Yet toward the end of the century, London associations are well documented as privately sponsoring victims to prosecute alleged offenders. The London Society for Prosecuting Felons was clearly responding to the perceptions that defense counsel was become alarmingly effective and that victims had an obvious need to avail themselves of legal representation. One begins to suspect a classic "chicken or egg" riddle here: prosecuting societies employing lawyers to challenge defense counsel, who were themselves employed by prisoners to counter the prosecutors' use of legal help earlier in the century. Regardless of how the process of active advocacy began, there is no ambiguity regarding the effects of lawyer-dominated trials, which were in clear evidence by the mid-nineteenth century. Questions surrounding the admissibility of evidence and the attendant diminution in the role of the judge, the decreasing frequency in which prisoners addressed the court, and the demise of the speedy trial all arise once the attorney moves to center stage. At the beginning of the period under review, however, the attorney played as marginal a role in the prosecutions of the allegedly insane as with ordinary offenders.

In sum, the early stirring of what is now referred to as an "insanity trial" is hard to discern as a unique event in the history of English criminal justice. Bystanders and even participants at the Old Bailey could hardly have distinguished the eighteenth-century insanity trial from day-to-day criminal prosecutions, except for the added element of derangement in the spoken prisoner's defense or the direction courtroom inquiry took once a witness mentioned the accused's distraction immediately following the crime. Character witnesses—ubiquitous throughout the century— also appeared in the infrequent proceeding that considered the prisoner's bizarre behavior. But here, too, the character witness was in the business of establishing the ordinary lawfulness of the prisoner, and how "out of character," how *unexplainable* the alleged behavior was, given the accused's habitual functioning. Other witnesses—neighbors, lovers, co-workers—appeared to retell accounts of odd conversation and histrionics. Of course, it was also the prisoner's character that was on trial in insanity cases. That a normally law-abiding person could commit such an horrendous deed *had* to reveal a momentary frenzy.

The realization that these trials constituted a separate species of prosecution was further forestalled by the unexceptional nature of the prisoner's defense. A putatively insane offender put forward "senselessness" or "insensibility" with much the same (lack of) emphasis as another prisoner who stated: "[I]t was distress that led me to it." Not until the 1780s, when the *OBSP* detailed instructions of the jury by the bench, did contemporary readers of the *OBSP* and courtroom bystanders begin to sense that the standard elements of eighteenth-century criminal justice—the appearance of prosecutor, on-scene witness, character witness, and occasional prisoner's defense—were taking on a different focus and cast of characters. By the late 1700s, the question was no longer "[D]id he do it and does he deserve to hang?" but was the prisoner, in the words of a judge instructing a jury, "a mere instrument in the hands of Providence?"

Crime, Punishment, and the Jury in Eighteenth-Century England

*I*F A CITIZEN OF LONDON IN THE LATE TWENTIETH CEN-tury were to be magically transported to a courtroom in the late eighteenth century, one wonders which of the many seemingly bizarre elements would be most startling. Would he or she, for example, even notice the virtual absence of lawyers in a prosecution dominated by a judge who examined, then summarily dismissed, witnesses with an approving comment or a sarcastic aside? Might our time traveler marvel at the speed of the prosecutions, with thirty to forty trials convened in a day, heard by the same jury members, who huddled in the open courtroom and announced their verdict within minutes of the last witness? Or would our visitor find most remarkable the obvious and blatant perjury on the part of the jury, as it returned verdict after verdict that conspicuously misrepresented the value of the stolen goods? To further bewilder our court bystander, the jury's creative fact-finding elicits not a disapproving glare from the judge but a conspiratorial wink.

In fact, the past twenty years of historical scholarship have yielded several noted "time travelers," whose work has illuminated the constraints and pressures that animated the eighteenth-century judicial system. To twentieth-century eyes, the speedy trials, garrulous and chatty judges, and juries willfully and routinely returning verdicts that stopped curiously short of the letter of the law seem at best strange and at worst decidedly lawless. Historians have therefore sought out an array of features—the scope and type of criminal activity, the economic and social relationship of victim and offender, the social composition of the jury and its likely effects on fact-finding—to explain the motivation and principles that animated the dispensing of justice two hundred years ago.[1] These studies reveal the care that was taken to select *qualified* juries, to frame precise and lawful indictments, and to ensure a proper forum to consider the accused's alleged wrongdoing before the state could exact punishment. Yet eighteenth-century jurisprudence was also characterized by several features that leave one wondering about, for example, the justification for denying the accused the right to full legal representation, the virtual paucity of rules of evidence to test the probity of testimony, and the propriety of unlimited and uncensored editorializing by the judge following the appearance of a witness.[2] Historians and sociologists have therefore sought to illuminate the legal culture of eighteenth-century England: how courtroom participants attempted to make sense of their role in the administration of justice.

The one inescapable reality hanging over the eighteenth-century trial like a sword—or actually a noose—was the Bloody Code: the two hundred or so crimes punishable by death. Actually, capital punishment did not attend two hundred separate types of crimes but rather several hundred "particular offenses," most involving some form of theft.[3] Lacking a general definition of larceny or embezzlement, the criminal law in early modern England listed the theft of buttons separately from the theft of sheep, the theft of bricks from London Bridge distinct from the theft of bricks from one's employer. Such precise articulation and the mandating of death for less than monumental losses—grand larceny was set at thirty shillings—speak volumes about the social anxiety and insecurity of the propertied classes in eighteenth-century England. Between the Restoration and Robert Peel's reforms in the 1820s, capital crimes grew from 50 to somewhere between 200 and 220. The standard reasons given for the seemingly heartless and unwieldy code—in addition to the fears of victimization of those capable of enjoining Parliament to pass yet another act—were the absence of punishments short of death (deprivation of liberty had yet to present itself as a sanction) and the lack of a metropolitan police. Lacking professional crime fighters, London had to rely on private prosecutors, justices of the peace, and constables to seek out malefactors and procure evidence. Though constables were doubtless committed to bringing wrongdoers to justice, it was commonly feared that many offenders eluded detection. Parliament thus placed most of its confidence in the deterrent effect of capital statutes that exhaustively enumerated any and all material items one could possibly contemplate stealing.

For punishments to deter, however, the imposition of sanctions had to be immediate and certain.[4] Though trials in England were certainly conducted in a timely manner, the imposition of the sanctions of the Bloody Code was nowhere as certain as its architects had envisioned. That so many felons convicted of capital statutes escaped the gallows—finding themselves convicted of a theft clearly undervalued by the jury—suggests that the eighteenth-century trial operated as a sentencing tribunal, in which evidence of criminality took second place to evidence of good character.[5] When the trial began, there was little doubt that the accused had stolen the goods: the thief had most likely been caught red-handed. Within weeks, or often days, the criminal trial began, starting with the victim's fresh memory and the likely corroboration of on-scene witnesses and perhaps a constable. Following the testimony of the victim/prosecutor and assorted witnesses, the accused was given an opportunity to contest the facts presented to the court. Before the prisoner's defense, however, eighteenth-century trials have a curious added dimension that suggests that guilt or innocence was not the only, or indeed pivotal, question facing the jury.

Throughout the 1700s, one finds the prominent participation of character witnesses who attest to the accused's solid respectability and hard-working nature. Certainly character witnesses are not unheard-of in contemporary criminal justice, but one notes their appearance at sentencing hearings rather than at the guilt-fastening tribunal itself. Two hundred years ago, these two moments in decision-making—guilt or innocence, life or death—were melded into a single determination. When facts were in dispute, the accused's likelihood of having performed, or even contemplated, such a crime was set against the context of lifelong respectability, steadfast adherence to principles of hard work and thrift, and a respected position in the community. Since many prisoners had been caught with the goods still in their possession, character witnesses were often their only hope of being spared the ultimate sanction. The interposing of character witnesses in the guilt-fastening phase of adjudication clearly signaled that something beyond the immediate crime was under deliberation, in large part because a guilty verdict carried such dire consequences.

Or rather, such dire *probable* consequences. Throughout the eighteenth century, the imposition of a death sentence was regularly and frequently circumvented by a number of contrivances at various stages of the trial. For instance, a judicial recommendation for mercy could animate a Royal Pardon.[6] On occasion, such petitions carried the jury's endorsement, thereby adding a measure of "community support" to bolster the trial judge's petition to the Crown. In addition a felon could also escape the gallows by pleading "benefit of clergy" following a first conviction.[7] Pursuant to legislation in 1717, the English court substituted transportation in place of execution for prisoners convicted of a felony or serious misdemeanor.[8] Although this provision ostensibly meant that convicts claiming benefit of clergy were to be transported to the British Colonies in America for seven years of indentured servitude, not all crimes were clergyable; grand larceny was conspicuously excluded.

The jury therefore played the most conspicuous and influential role in the mitigation of the draconian Bloody Code. Time and again juries returned "partial verdicts," findings of guilt that held felons responsible for only a part of the value of the stolen goods—in effect downgrading the theft to a clergyable offense. The resort to partial verdicts does not seem to be a political attempt by ideologically motivated jurors to assault the power structure and inhumanity of the English criminal law.[9] Although transportation was certainly a reprieve compared with agonizing public death, it still meant involuntary servitude and forced repatriation to a far-off and dangerous land.[10] Still, jurors' reluctance to bring the full weight of the law to bear has challenged historians and criminologists to search for the principles and procedures that animated such decision-making.

Jurors were not the only courtroom participants who could limit Parliament's excesses. Judges could affect case outcome by insisting on a standard of proof that required the jury's virtual certainty of the offender's guilt. When such proof was lacking, the jury was free to return a partial verdict of a lesser felony—petit larceny, for example—which resulted in transportation. Further, the bench actively encouraged the undervaluing of goods, again resulting in a conviction for a less-than-capital crime.[11] Confronted with the profusion of eighteenth-century offenders found guilty of theft of goods valued at twenty-nine shillings, one must either assume a remarkably unified pricing policy or a remarkably unified social sentiment in which nullification of the letter of the law was encouraged by actors throughout the criminal justice enterprise.

This does not, of course, explain how twelve "good men and true" selected from among several options to render what was in effect a sentencing deposition. Empirical analyses of those who received partial verdicts suggests a set of considerations that predictably guided discretionary decision-making. Prisoners most likely to receive a partial verdict were female, young, supporting a family, or stealing in times of high food prices.[12] But could one also refer to these verdicts as *principled* decisions: Was there a rationale behind the jury's finding? Leaving aside the extension of (benevolent) paternalism to female offenders, is it only "compassion" or "sympathy" that inspired the decision to downvalue the stolen goods of the young, or those with pressing familial responsibilities, or those squeezed in times of economic hardship? That these variables are seen to operate at the guilt-fastening rather than sentencing stage begs a further question: How did jurors conceive of culpable behavior? What made an alleged felon's act *understandable* and consequently less censurable?

Thomas A. Green has drawn attention to decision-making in the early modern English courtroom by inquiring into how the jury pondered the "constraints" under which the offender acted.[13] Green is particularly interested in the jury's re-creation of the circumstances surrounding the crime. Did the felon act as a free agent, and thus deserve the full force of the law's retributive justice, or was he or she a mere "product of the environment"—the effect of some antecedent cause "out there" in the universe, be it youth (developmental immaturity) or the pressure of economic distress? Juries then as now provided no clue to their thought processes—except, of course, for the verdict. In the case of verdicts that purposefully mitigated the severity of the common law, Green's inference is both plausible and persuasive. Prisoners who fit into the categories most likely to receive partial verdicts could have been convicted capitally or acquitted outright but were not. Instead, juries returned predictable partial verdicts that conveyed a finding of guilt but with a nod to an intervening consideration that made the felon less than fully responsible in the jurors' eyes. Such constraints never became part of the courtroom dialogue because they were not needed: the near absolute standard of proof provided a handy justification for a partial verdict.

Green wonders if juries concealed their thought processes from themselves, using the exacting standard of "certainty of guilt" to preclude a more thoroughgoing consideration of the prisoner's capacity to exercise will. Although this question is impossible to answer, it behooves the historian of jury behavior to inquire how these social actors understood their participation in court. Jurors were, after all, operating in a highly structured social setting, with an array of options and consequences to select among and an array of prisoner "types" to consider. The young offender, for example, has historically occupied a privileged place in English jurisprudence owing to behavioral immaturity.[14] Central to this youthful "condition" is an inability to conform behavior to the requirements of conventional society. Youthful offenders have not learned to control their nature: "immature" urges and desires leave them at the mercy of emotional forces they do not quite understand. One might say that they have been "constrained" by youth. Legal theory accordingly sought a protected place for juvenile offenders until such age that responsibility was thought to obtain. In similar fashion, destitution and distress leave one prey to forces that one could normally resist in times of emotional and financial security. Was it sympathy (alone) that animated partial verdicts when juries confronted youthful offenders and desperate family providers, especially in times of rising food prices?[15] Was it solidarity with the plight of the poor or a recognition that hunger, fear, and desperation sap one's ordinary resolve and remove societal constraints on law-abiding behavior?

Peter King has persuasively demonstrated the influence of destitution and youth in the trial judge's decision to request a pardon following a capital conviction.[16] Judges summed up their views regarding the effect of "necessity" in familiar ways: "[I]n a moment of distress and want [he] fell into the commission of a crime," or "[I]t appeared to have been done from the press of great distress." What is novel is that such "widely agreed criteria" were being used to assess culpability, not only "just desserts." The odyssey of *pardoning* factors from the sentencing to the conviction stage may seem nonproblematic because of the apparently widespread social support, but in fact something very profound in terms of Western jurisprudence was in evidence. Jurors who chose to "sentence by conviction" were ushering in a host of considerations regarding human will at a much earlier stage in criminal prosecution.[17] Green's thesis regarding the jurors' growing interest in constraints and social determinism therefore also finds expression in judicial efforts to mitigate the harsh and unwieldy code of offenses that mandated death.

Evidence of a dramatic change in popular beliefs regarding constraints on human agency can also be found in the profusion of non compos mentis findings returned by coroner's juries following a suicide. What in the seventeenth and early eighteenth centuries was an anomolous verdict grew to the incredible level of 97 percent by the late 1700s. As with the preceding instances of jury decision-making, the harshness of punishment following a verdict of felo-de-se (self-murder) doubtless contributed mightily to the jurors' eventual avoidance of the finding of willful action and criminal intent. Still, the draconian sanctions—mutilation of the corpse and confiscation of property—had been standard throughout the early modern era. What was different in the late eighteenth century appears to have been a growing conviction that suicide was an understandable calamity, rooted not in temptation by the devil but in secular trauma, such as disappointed love or financial ruin. In the late 1700s suicides brought on by such interpersonal distress were themselves seen as the action of a demented person; the suicide was *evidence* of insanity. Human agency, the capacity to retain reason and self-control, was apparently constrained by the force of social calamity and bitter personal disappointment.[18]

Naturally one undertakes such a speculative reconstruction of an eighteenth-century juror's mental and hence decision-making process with extreme caution. Yet any effort to understand how courtroom participants in the 1700s understood their place in the dispensing of justice must consider the factors likely to have informed their decisions. One constraint that the late eighteenth-century jury was beginning to consider in fundamentally new ways may have been the prisoner's capacity to form intent: the resolve to commit a criminal act. Where the jury usually faced a prisoner whose character witnesses alluded to distress or youthful immaturity, the eighteenth-century *insanity* jury was about to be introduced to a host of ideas implying constraint in qualitatively new ways. Although historical scholarship bearing on madness and the law has traditionally considered insanity trials as sui generis prosecutions somehow beyond the day-to-day functioning of the court, they were in fact spectacularly ordinary, at least at the level of offense, offender, and type of witnesses who appeared. Seen in this way, insanity initially emerged as a further—not necessarily a novel—"constraint" for the jury to consider.

CRIMINALITY AND INSANITY

Whether they stole, burgled, embezzled, pilfered, purloined, thieved, shoplifted, or picked pockets (at a public hanging, no less), eighteenth-century Londoners were legendary for their light fingers. Most crime was opportunistic and petty: there is little evidence that a criminal class targeted the propertied in any systematic way. As Robert Peel concluded on the eve of his efforts to rationalize the scale of punishments, "[S]ix out of seven were charged with theft, most for petty crimes."[19] Historical studies put the proportion closer to one-half to three-quarters, but it is clear from studies of eighteenth-century indictments and nineteenth-century official crime reports that the main caseload at the Old Bailey was petty theft (though sometimes "grand," as in larceny): stealing from pubs or inns, "borrowing" household or workshop items, shoplifting items from the doorway of a shop. Personal crimes—assaults, murders, rapes—rarely amounted to one-tenth of the criminal prosecution throughout the 1700s and through the mid-nineteenth century. By the end of the 1800s, personal offenses had risen only to 15 percent. Then as now personal crimes usually centered on family relations, targeting minors and children as the victims. And like contemporary domestic crime, violence and alcohol were often linked.[20]

At least through the late 1700s, the crimes of the purportedly deranged offer an almost identical picture: property crime was by far the most frequent offense. Beginning with the 1760s, property crimes comprise between two-thirds and three-quarters of crimes committed by the putative insane. Most offenses were listed simply as "theft" in the *OBSP*, but notation is also made of breaking and entering, stealing, embezzling, and forgery. Among the insane, however, personal crimes make up three to four times their proportion in the general caseload at the Old Bailey, averaging about 30 percent throughout the years 1760–1843 (fig. 1.1).

Although one might associate the evolution of the jurisprudence of

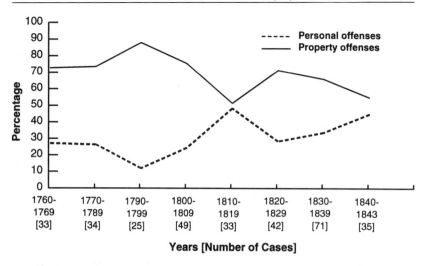

Figure 1.1 Type of offense as a percentage of total cases alleging insanity

Note: Personal crimes = murder, assault, and kidnapping. Property offenses = stealing/theft, burglary, embezzlement, forgery, counterfeiting, and breaking and entering. Nine offenses that defied the "personal/property" classification are not considered, including bigamy, "inciting to mutiny," treason, "being at large" (returning to England before a term of transportation had elapsed), and rioting. There were 3 such offenses in the periods 1770–89, 1790–99, and 1820–29. The Ns of these periods are 34, 25, and 42, respectively.

insanity with lurid personal attacks or attempted regicide (since the most famous cases in the late eighteenth and early nineteenth centuries concerned attempted or completed murder), the great majority of crimes in which prisoners (and others) raised mental derangement as a possible exculpatory defense were almost tediously normal.[21] The "ordinariness" of such crimes, however, does not appear to have affected judges' readiness to instruct juries regarding the law's position on insanity. Elaborate instructions were just as likely to be issued in forgery and "intent to defraud" cases as in a murder trial. The prisoner's defense also took little cognizance of the crime at issue; expressions of senselessness, being out of one's wits, and knowing "nothing about the affair" were uttered by prisoners who stole, shoplifted, or embezzled as well as by those who attacked loved ones for no apparent reason.

One noticeable trend, however, is the increasing proportion of insanity trials in which a personal attack is present (see fig. 1.1). Indeed, by the 1840s, the proportion of property to personal crimes had almost reached parity. It may well be that, beginning in 1823, the removal of capital sanctions from most property offenses made the prospect of a limited jail term more attractive (compared with an indeterminate confinement to a madhouse) to prisoners contemplating a defense strategy.[22] Although personal crimes had climbed noticeably, the majority of insanity pleas were still heard in property-related prosecutions, in which the items stolen and the social relationship between victim and offender (shoplifter to shopowner, "opportunistic" petty thievery) left little to distinguish between the "insane thief" and a non-deranged partner-in-crime.

Prisoners who raised a plea of mental derangement also failed to distinguish themselves in terms of gender: indeed, the "sane" and "insane" populations were remarkably similar. About 80 percent of offenders indicted by the eighteenth-century grand jury were men.[23] This proportion is identical to the universe of allegedly deranged offenders: insane women are neither underrepresented nor overrepresented relative to their non-distressed sisters. In terms of offenses, purportedly insane women show no greater propensity to personal attacks than sane women; approximately one-quarter of each group were tried for homicides or assault, and fully 75 percent were involved in petty theft or the occasional forgery. As George Rudé found in his survey of crimes tried at the Old Bailey during the first half of the nineteenth century, 72.3 percent of all female offenders were prosecuted for some form of larceny, almost exactly the proportion in women's "insanity" trials.[24] In terms of personal assault, one offense did indeed distinguish putatively insane male and female prisoners. Infanticide was unique to women prisoners and introduced conceptions of organic disturbance following childbirth that made its gender-association obvious. Trials for child murder also distinguished sane female from male offenders—the issues attendant on the prosecution of this crime centered more often on gender than sanity. In sum, there is little difference in offender or offense characteristics to alert the attentive court participant or historical researcher that something new was in the works.

Would the daily reader of the *OBSP* notice a difference in the jury's likelihood to acquit in cases that featured an insanity defense? Certainly juries and judges were not unfamiliar with the concept of "mitigating factors" in the selection of punishment, or even in determining the degree of guilt (as suggested by evidence of "principled" partial verdicts).[25] In trials where the prisoner alleged mental debility, however, mitigation meant something rather more: it addressed the fundamental issue of blamelessness. The jury's decision was not a partial verdict but an outright acquittal (before 1800). How did acquittal rates in insanity trials compare with late eighteenth- and early nineteenth-century rates in general?

The acquittal rate is certainly central to any examination of how juries considered the credibility of the trial participants and the fit of legal tenets to what they had seen and heard. The reasons for any one verdict vary, however: a jury's finding is likely to be affected by a host of factors not all of which are immediately apparent to the historical researcher. One jury might vote to acquit because the prosecution appeared to have been motivated by spitefulness or excessive retribution. Another might conclude that the property ownership of the disputed item was sufficiently obscure to preclude distinguishing between victim and "appropriator."[26] The oft-cited rigorous standard of proof, especially in light of incredibly harsh sanctions, may also have worked very much in the accused's favor, with unclear and difficult-to-resolve issues of ownership falling against the prosecutor. This would certainly not be the first time in the history of criminal justice when "fixed" sentences generated leniency.

Perhaps because of the variety of factors that could affect the jury's disposition to acquit, recent efforts to quantify eighteenth-century jury verdicts in and around London have produced a range of findings. Surveying the Essex courts, Peter King found that fewer than half of those indicted for major property crimes in southeast England were convicted as charged. Approximately one-third were acquitted on "true bills," and 12 percent received partial verdicts.[27] J. M. Beattie's study of property crime in Surrey in mid-century found approximately one-third of the defendants guilty of a capital charge, one-third acquitted, and one-third guilty of a lesser, partial charge—that is, petty larceny or simple (non-capital) grand larceny.[28] The outright acquittal rate from these two studies therefore rests at approximately one-third, suggesting that in a fair proportion of cases jurors were willing to entertain the possibility that the accused was wrongly indicted, the evidence was insufficiently presented, or the prosecutor's action was motivated by spite.

Were jurors also willing to entertain the possibility that the offender was insane? It is difficult to specify with precision if insanity was the telling consideration in instances of acquittal because the special finding of "not guilty by reason of insanity" does not appear before 1800. After passage of the Criminal Lunatics Act, the *OBSP* make a concerted effort to explain the grounds for the verdict."[29] After 1800, the *OBSP* reveal the effect of Parliament's intervention: of the 131 defendants who escaped conviction, 60 percent were acquitted "by reason of insanity," and 10 percent were found unfit to plead. About one-fourth of those who escaped conviction, then, were acquitted outright, at least as far as the recorded verdicts indicate.

The practical significance of outright acquittal in contrast to the "not guilty by reason of insanity" (NGRI) verdict is clear and compelling: by law the second group faced detention "awaiting the King's pleasure," whereas felons acquitted outright were free to walk out of court. Why did juries refrain from uttering a "special verdict" in trials that so obviously concerned deranged offenders? Perhaps the evidence did not warrant conviction. Alternatively, the jury may have considered the prisoner to be deranged but harmless, and therefore not in need of confinement. Often family members appeared in court to announce their willingness to house their unfortunate relative, so the need for supervision could be met informally. The simple notation "not guilty" was likely to be misleading for these trials because the entire scope of the defense rested on the allegation of insanity, not a challenge to the prosecutor's version of the facts. These prisoners freely admitted wrongdoing, relying on the assertion of a debilitating mental condition to escape conviction. In computing the acquittal rate for this sample, I have added outright acquittals to the NGRI verdicts in those cases where the prisoner's mental state was the subject of the defense. Also included are those who were found "unfit to plead," because the jury's conviction that the individual was too deranged to come to trial would likely have been manifest at trial and highly unlikely that a conviction would have been forthcoming. When these seemingly different verdicts are taken into account, the overall acquittal rate between 1760 and 1843 fluctuated between 37 percent in the 1790s and 63 percent during the 1840s, with an overall rate of 51 percent. In fact, the rate hovers quite narrowly around 50 percent for every decade except for the two anomalous time periods already mentioned.

In an earlier publication I drew attention to the need to separate property and personal offenses because the perceived stability in the overall acquittal rate after a trial as potentially significant as James Hadfield's called for further study.[30] Hadfield's case, which prompted the Criminal Lunatics Act, introduced the concept of delusion into the jurisprudence of insanity. Although the significance of this case will be discussed in the following chapter, it is important at this point to emphasize the departure initiated with this variant of partial insanity. An act could be "coolly" and "rationally" planned, yet still be the work of an insane person. If delusion precluded an appreciation of the moral wrongfulness of criminal actions, the prisoner could not be said to be the culpable author of an act: the accused had not (legally) intended the crime. When personal and property crimes are separated, it is clear that acquittal rates diverge demonstrably after 1800 (fig. 1.2).

The type of offense that animated the insanity trial appears to have made little difference in acquittal rates before 1800: rates fell for both personal and property crimes from a peak of approximately 50 percent in the 1760s to a low of about 35 percent in the 1790s. The impact of

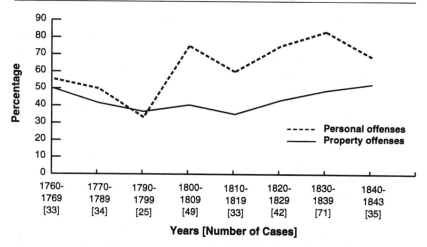

Figure 1.2 Acquittal rates in insanity trials, by type of offense

Note: This figure updates Eigen, *Intentionality and Insanity,* fig. 2.2. Differences include: changes in acquittal rate to low 50% range from mid-40% (correction of computational errors); addition of several cases in 1770s; inclusion of 3 forgery cases in the 1790s (formerly excluded from category of shoplifting and other petty crimes). The general range of the acquittal rates remains substantively the same.

the Hadfield trial—and passage of the Safe Custody Act—in 1800 appears to be negligible for those accused in property offense: decade-by-decade fluctuations are modest, returning to almost the precise percentage for the years 1830–43. In personal crimes, however, the acquittal rate rises sharply at the beginning of the nineteenth century and climbs to a remarkable 83 percent in the 1830s before falling to 68 percent in 1840–43. In comparison with the late eighteenth century, acquittal rates in personal crimes are nearly double.

Again, caveats are in order. Given the documented proclivity of juries to mitigate the harsh provision of eighteenth-century criminal law, verdicts acquire a range of meanings, not least the sentencing prerogative. Were juries more likely to acquit after 1800 simply because they could be assured of safe custody of a dangerous person? If so, why shouldn't this apply to property offenders as well as those committing personal assault? If juries were really interested in making "dispositional" decisions with their verdicts, why not simply convict the felon and ensure the criminal's prompt removal from society? One might argue that a sophisticated, experienced juror considered an indeterminate sentence preferable to a six-month confinement in Bridewell, increasingly the sentence property offenders received by the second quarter of the nineteenth century.[31] Is this too "modern" a sensibility to attribute to juries 150 years ago: better the asylum than the prison because the former incarceration is likely to last longer? As intriguing as it is to speculate on juror psychology, we might better inquire into other features about the trials that might have influenced the jurors to acquit so generously in personal crimes.

One place to look would be to the vitality and resourcefulness of the accused's legal defense. Although attorneys were officially limited in their defense role, the deft questioning revealed in the *OBSP* suggests that there was more than one way to address a jury.[32] Any speculation regarding fluctuations in the acquittal rate therefore cannot overlook the influence of an evolving advocacy bar, skillful in eliciting testimony and framing questions to the prisoner's advantage. Of course, the prosecutor could also obtain legal representation, so the increasing presence of advocates could have worked the other way as well, and in property crime, perhaps, the two may have checked each other's influence. Character witnesses were also vital to insanity trials because the neighbor or coworker who could supply graphic illustration of derangement and long-standing lunacy lent vital support to the prisoner's plea. Among trial witnesses no individual was questioned more closely or examined with greater skepticism and precision than the medical man. Alone among witnesses, the medical witness was permitted to venture an opinion regarding the sanity of the prisoner. The influence his opinion carried and the authority his words conveyed have therefore been the subject of much historical speculation.

Influence and authority are of course subjective assessments not readily discernible in jury verdicts. One can begin to speculate about the impact of medical testimony, however, by examining the changing frequency with which medical witnesses appeared over time. An analysis of the *OBSP* reveals that between 1760 and 1843, medical participation in insanity trials grew from approximately one trial in ten throughout the late 1700s to one in two by the 1840s (fig. 1.3). With the exception of the 1820s this growth appears to be linear overall, reaching its high point by mid-century. Although it would appear that by the 1840s, at least, the psychiatric medical witness, in a form immediately recognizable to the modern eye, had most certainly "arrived," his participation was uneven regarding the type of crime in which he appeared.

Medical witnesses clearly were far more likely to appear in an insanity trial animated by a personal crime than one invoked by a property offense. The reasons were likely to include the reform of criminal sanctions—a growing restriction of capital sanctions to violent personal

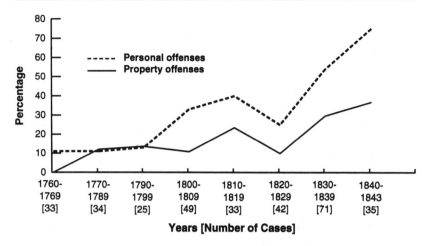

Figure 1.3 Comparison of medical participation rates by type of crime

Note: The unit of analysis is the trial, not the number of medical witnesses who appeared in each trial. The most appropriate measure to use in gauging the growing participation of a new type of witness is the proportion of cases that feature these witnesses relative to all other cases, not the number of medical men who might happen to appear in any one trial.

offenses—and the installing of medical men in prisons and jails. Many medical witnesses first encountered the prisoner on their visiting rounds in the jail, having been sent by the court to interview the defendant because of the likelihood of an insanity plea. Judicial authorities probably reasoned that personal crimes were "more worth the effort" (because of the severe sanctions) and therefore concentrated their medical personnel on the more serious crimes. A greater proportion of "personal" offenders may also have had a history of medical treatment and therefore greater access to physicians, surgeons, and apothecaries who could be subpoenaed to supply a "medical history." Finally, it is possible that medical witnesses sought out personal crimes—especially famous ones—because they were sure to attract attention and were a highly visible forum in which to assert professional expertise. In the McNaughtan trial, for example, two medical witnesses testified who had not even examined the prisoner but felt compelled to offer their services to the court (and perhaps to increase the sale of their books). In the trial of Edward Oxford, the number of medical witnesses and the ambitious scope of their testimony suggests that the high drama and possible dire consequences of personal crimes played a role in the preference medical men showed for these types of wrongdoing. Whatever the reason or reasons, by the 1840s, medical witnesses were appearing in four out of five insanity trials animated by a personal offense.

The availability of acquittal rates and medical participation rates naturally invites inquiry into any apparent correspondence between the two (fig. 1.4). Of course, such a comparison could be meaningful only if the sole variable in the trials were the appearance of medical witnesses, which was hardly the case. The content of the prisoner's defense, the role of the attorney, and cultural attitudes about madness and criminal responsibility, however, were unlikely to remain constant. Acting separately or in concert, these elements could easily alter the jury's acceptance of a plea of derangement. Still, the introduction of medical testimony ushered new considerations into the insanity trial—the opinion of an expert versus the (mere) observations of the neighbor, the cultural authority of scientific medicine over the social familiarity of folk wisdom—inviting speculation on the influence this one innovation might have carried.

Again, it is important to stress that had there been a direct correspondence between the two rates across the nine periods there would still have been the need for cautious interpretation because other features of the trials were not held constant and the jury's decision-making could hardly have been limited to medical testimony.[33] Further, the full influence of medical testimony probably cannot be measured in the aggregate because the impact any one medical witness was likely to have on courtroom dialogue was not necessarily felt in the immediate case but may have influenced the minds and the opinions of those who heard him in court and read his words in the *OBSP*. The importance of medical evidence is better measured by the texture of narrative testimony, the cultural and legal issues brought directly into a criminal prosecution, and the legitimacy medical witnesses claimed from years of experience in asylum management. The debate they sharpened and the "constraints" they illuminated were likely to ripple through court sessions they did not even attend. Jurors after all sat on thirty to forty trials at a time; medical witnesses need not appear at a particular trial to have their images and speech be part of a juror's deliberation. In this context, it is intriguing to speculate about the rise in acquittal rates by 1843. Were jurors becoming accustomed to medical testimony; was it often an *expected* part of an insanity trial?

As compelling as such questions are, the cultural influence and enduring effect of medical testimony cannot be measured in terms of percentages and proportions. Indeed, the very construction of graphs and tables risks a dangerously reductive conversion of dense qualitative narratives into quantitative data. Certainly some readings can be taken with

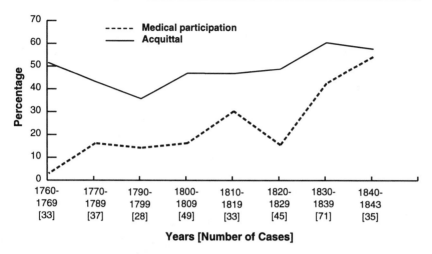

Figure 1.4 Comparison of rates of acquittal and medical participation

Note: Includes 9 offenses excluded from earlier figures because they did not fit the "person/property" classification. The Ns for periods 1770–89, 1790–99, and 1820–29 are therefore 37, 28, and 45, respectively.

relatively little distortion: type of crime, items stolen, the *fact* of a medical appearance. Verdicts, however, cannot be reported as though they were self-evident. In addition to the myriad elements that could influence the jury, even the notation "not guilty" could be ambiguous in the context of an insanity plea. Within the parameters I have set up, however, I am reasonably certain that an acquittal following a trial that so clearly turned on the prisoner's mental state—one in which the prosecutor's "facts" were not in dispute—can with confidence be grouped with expressed findings of "not guilty by reason of insanity." Regrettably, not all trials are reported in exhaustive detail, and some suffer lamentable compression. Quantitative measurements are therefore kept to a minimum in the chapters that follow, introduced only where qualitative material can be expressed helpfully in numerical display.

A further problem underlying the presentation of rates—even where their construction is relatively straightforward—is that the *fact* of the percentage may obscure a far more interesting inquiry. For example, the observation that medical men became increasingly active in insanity trials begs the questions why were they in court at all. How did they arrive there? At whose instigation were they testifying? The real mystery in these historical documents is not the relation between acquittal rates and med-

ical participation but the evolving cultural dynamic that produced so
many medical witnesses in the 1830s and 1840s in the first place. Prisoners and their attorneys could certainly have drawn from an available
pool of medical men since at least the beginning of the nineteenth century. Forensic-psychiatric witnesses need not have been qualified in
"mental medicine" to testify; indeed, mental medicine was the most in-
choate of specialties in the early 1800s. Any physician—or surgeon or
apothecary for that matter—was equally likely to have treated a patient
with an ailment that featured mental distress, and there certainly was no
bias in the courtroom against the "general physician" testifying. Yet the
medical man in the insanity trial was an exceptional feature, at least until
the second quarter of the nineteenth century. Most often a neighbor or
a co-worker or even the victim supplied the court with tales of the accused's derangement. The majority of defendants in the years 1760–1843
were acquitted without the services of a medical witness (see fig. 1.2); the
overall acquittal rate fluctuated around 50 percent, well above the rate
of participation of medical witnesses for most of this time. The medical
witness was therefore entering a forum characterized by a host of issues
and a cast of characters that had already put forward its own, decidedly
nonprofessional conceptions regarding madness. Although at first glance
this might seem to present a major obstacle to the assertion of unique
insight and special knowledge, the cultural acceptance of mental debility
in general and "insane criminality" in particular provided the medical
witness with a propitious forum: a courtroom already growing accustomed to the idea of human limitation.

INSANITY AND EIGHTEENTH-CENTURY "CONSTRAINTS"

Every insanity trial ultimately focuses on the jury's consideration of the
prisoner's intention, yet the expression of the jury's determination is limited to the moment it announces the verdict. How jurors perceived the
medical witness (or increasingly medical witness*es*), and what weight they
gave his testimony can be addressed only indirectly because juries left no
notes. Perhaps one way to recreate the jury's decision-making process is
to consider insanity acquittals in the context of eighteenth-century partial
verdicts: efforts taken to mitigate the severity of punishment by considering various constraints on human choice. Insanity verdicts would therefore serve as further evidence that juries in the late eighteenth and early
nineteenth centuries were beginning to contemplate (and expand) the
influence of social determinism on human action.

The ambiguity of human behavior—whether the individual was the author of his or her actions or whether actions were the mere product of a force independent of will—found full expression in the early nineteenth century with the advent of positivism. Free will versus determinism was, of course, hardly a nineteenth-century concern; its roots lie deep in Western thought. But notions of social determinism found an especially articulate voice in the late 1700s, as death penalty reformers increasingly drew a picture of criminals as the mere products of their backgrounds.[34] No doubt the ever-looming code of capital sanctions added urgency to the philosophic debate. It would not be hard to imagine that jurors brought into the Old Bailey the cultural debate about human agency, and one other element, too: experience. The characteristics and circumstance of any one offense (and offender) were set against the context of dozens of other prisoners and other offenses, resulting, one suspects, in a perspective that regarded the appropriateness of various forms of punishment and their fit to various types of people. The result of this repeated experience of assessing character, presence of intent, and punishment was an increasing conviction of the degree to which constraint functioned— in whatever social determinist form. Jurors perceived some "sane" offenders as meriting ultimate sanction and others as operating under distinct constraints—whether of poverty, immaturity, or dire family circumstance. Early in the nineteenth century jurors were asked to consider a further "constraint" when testimony by medical witnesses brought intent and free moral agency to the center of the debate.

We have noted that little in offender and offense characteristics distinguished insanity trials for special attention. Further, the parade of character witnesses drove home how much any particular trial resembled the one just before and the one soon to take place. Where insanity trials differed, of course, was in the particular way the prisoner denied responsibility and in the increasing appearance of medical witnesses to support the claim of distracted mental state. The task for juries in both kinds of trials, however, was more similar than one might suspect. When they returned partial verdicts in the *sane* trials, juries were in effect drawn into the accused's circumstances, reaching a verdict that reflected their understanding of how social actors in that condition could be expected to act.[35] In spite of supposed differences between the prisoner in an insanity trial and the juror just described, one wonders if a similar dynamic was not in fact under way in these specialized trials as well.

For all the cultural associations that attended insanity, the course of the years 1760–1843 made the allegedly mad prisoner not more alien but rather more familiar, more knowable, more *understandable*. The thrust of courtroom testimony, from neighbors, relatives, and particularly the medical witness, was to sketch out not a "sympathetic" and "pitiable" creature but a person whose functioning, while obviously disturbed, was nonetheless surprisingly intelligible. In particular, courtroom testimony permitted jurors to glimpse the world through the distorted lens of the prisoner and to contemplate the criminal act as the product of *constraints* that operated independently of will.

Though atypical in its frequency and in its cast of characters, the insanity trial of the late eighteenth and early nineteenth centuries may well have been shaped by the penchant for mitigating the Bloody Code that had initiated the juror's interest in constraints. Seen in this light, the criminal law reforms of the 1820s and 1830s drastically narrowing the scope of the Bloody Code did not relieve the jury of its mitigating role but rather changed the terms of the debate from social to physical and psychological constraints—terms that would be framed *expertly* by the emerging forensic-psychiatrist.

Insanity
THE LEGAL CONTEXT

> Gentlemen, we are none of us exempt from the effects of disease
> or accident; judge of me as you would of a friend or a brother, or
> as you would wish to be judged yourselves, under the same
> circumstances in point of fact, and under the same misfortune in
> point of reason.
> —Francis Paar, *Old Bailey Sessions Papers,* 1787,
> case 158, 1st sess., 222

*I*NDICTED FOR *"PERSONATING"* AND *"ENDEAVORING TO*
receive interest" on securities belonging to Isaac Hart, Francis Paar concluded his prisoner's defense by appealing to jury members to imagine
themselves "under the same misfortune in point of reason." Paar's misfortune originated in a frightful head injury that left him "totally ignorant" of his actions during sudden mood shifts and feelings of rage. Now,
in 1787, he found himself (inexplicably) at the Old Bailey. On the day of
the forgery, the jury learned, the prisoner had been spotted lurking about
the bank, watching "for an opportunity to commit this offense . . . [then]
. . . at half 2:00, the time when they are most hurried at the transfer of-
fice," he asked to receive his money, giving his name as Isaac Hart and
signing the receipt as such. The purposeful manner in which he executed
the forgery was doubtless underscored by the judge when he advised the
jury to consider the "artful means" and the "deliberate plan" that would
appear to "overturn the possibility of a defense of the kind set up by the
prisoner." Paar's "kind" of defense was insanity. The manner in which
he advanced his plea, and the way the judge instructed the jury in considering events surrounding the perpetration of the crime, recreate the
legal context that framed the early years of the insanity plea.

England's rich history in the jurisprudence of mental derangement and
criminal intent can be gleaned from an array of sources—formal treatises,

fragmentary case decisions and contemporary commentary, verdicts in celebrated trials.[1] But these historic sources also carry inherent limitations for historical reconstruction, regardless of the authority they would appear to convey for subsequent texts and verdicts. One must wonder how closely the legal scribe's views reflect the thinking of the period in which he wrote or how representative a particular verdict might be, especially since it was the celebrated trial that usually made its way into the historical record. Were the trials of the notorious and the proclivities of their respective juries also reflected in the prosecution of the decidedly ordinary? Although it is critical to ground eighteenth-century verdicts and the issues that surrounded them in the history of English legal thought, it is no less vital to inquire how historical tenets of jurisprudence were actually practiced day-to-day. To that end, this chapter sets out the legal strictures regarding the insanity plea, focusing specifically on its justification in common law and how late eighteenth- and early nineteenth-century judges instructed juries to consider evidence presented at the trials in light of the historic legal principles that allowed for acquittal. Especially prominent among the legal concerns of this period is the court's willingness to entertain the possibility of a range of mentally distracted states—specifically, the status of "partial insanity" as sufficiently debilitating to merit a finding of blamelessness.

Francis Paar's defense, for example, did not rest on "partial" insanity. The accident that damaged his reason and "intellects" left him in such a state that he had no knowledge of the events recounted at his trial—in fact, no recollection at all of the events at the bank. As ship steward aboard the *Lady Jane,* Paar had sustained horrendous head injuries when he fell overboard, smashing his temples against the side of the ship. As the ship's cook testified, the prisoner "did not recover the whole voyage . . . [He was] quite altered; he had no understanding after the accident." An array of character witnesses echoed the cook's statement: "Before the accident he was a steady, sober and assiduous man; and a man of sense." After the near drowning, he was subject to inexplicable mood shifts and fits of rage. A neighbor recounted, "All of a sudden he jumped up and took the poker out of the fire, and said, he would knock his wife down . . . he would not mind killing her any more than he would kill the bird in the cage." Acknowledging this episode, the prisoner reported other occasions on which, "I am informed I have since my last voyage, twice attempted her life, without provocation, when but a moment before I was behaving with the greatest fondness; of those facts I was so totally ignorant, that I would not have believed them, but upon the solemn assurances of persons who would not deceive me."

Paar's defense therefore rested on a state of mind occasioned by head injuries that left him ignorant of certain episodes of his behavior—so ignorant that he was clearly "absent" at his own crime. As he explained in his defense, "My character in every part of my life has been without reproach; is it to be supposed that I would turn villain in an instant, and for nothing?" After Paar's former shipmates and neighbors corroborated his claims to an excellent character, contrasting it with the bizarre behavior brought on by his derangement, the judge began his instructions relative to insanity in the following way:

> It is my duty to tell you before I observe on the evidence, what in point of law that defense ought to amount to; . . . a man who is so far disordered in his mind, as to be utterly incapable of distinguishing between right and wrong, good and evil, and the necessary tendency of his own actions, is not responsible for those actions; he is in truth not a moral agent, and he is not answerable personally, because his actions want that which is the essence of any crime, which is felonious and criminal intention; but it is not every degree of mental disorder, it is not every derangement of mind, arising from distress or circumstances, or from temporary causes that will amount to that kind of justification.[2]

The judge did not, however, inform the jury *which* derangement or *what* degree of mental disorder would suffice. Instead, he instructed the jurors to consider whether they judged Paar capable of discerning good from evil and capable of knowing the consequences of what he did at the time of the forgery. It was their duty, he informed them, to decide the degree to which the sea injury had altered him, although, the judge was quick to add, "The evidence does not prove that [he] was at all time utterly incapable of knowing what he did; on the contrary, he has gone about conducting his own affairs, though he has shown strong symptoms of a disordered mind."

The judge left little doubt about his own belief regarding the significance of the prisoner's "disordered mind" in relation to the crime. Advising the jury "you ought to acquit him" if convinced the prisoner had acted under a disordered mind, the judge then drew the jury's attention to the artfulness employed in the act:

> Now the nature of personating another man, does in itself bespeak a kind of deliberation, and a kind of wicked discretion, which rendered it of all other the most unlikely to admit of the defense of insanity; and if in this case it should appear that the prisoner had made use of artful means to get at the knowledge of that stock possessed by Mr. Hart; if he had laid a deliberate plan for the commission of this fact; if he had made himself like him in dress or voice, or made any particular de-

scription of him, that would have gone a great way indeed to overturn the possibility of a defense of the kind set up by the prisoner.[3]

Should the jury conclude the impersonation to be not a "premeditated artful design" but an impulse that arose "of the moment" owing to a disordered mind, without "having knowledge enough at the time to form a criminal intention," such findings, the judge allowed, would go a great way to acquit the prisoner. Paar, however, was not on trial for an impulse that precipitated a sudden and totally unprovoked attack on a wife but for a forgery that evinced planning, preparation, and pinpoint timing. How a disordered man might gain knowledge of the victim's accounts and the exact sum due and then write the name of that person on the cheque was left for the jurors to ponder. But not for long, and not to the prisoner's benefit. Following his conviction and the subsequent pronouncement of the sentence of death, Francis Paar heard the judge accede to the jury's request to recommend mercy of the king. But the judge also added, "I would not wish this unfortunate man to flatter himself, with hoping too much is to be expected from it."

Aside from the judge's "observations" with reference to the events surrounding Paar's forgery, several features in this trial were fundamental to the law's concern with insanity. First, the judge reminded the jurors that moral agency rested on "felonious and criminal intention."[4] An actor who could not discern good from evil could hardly be said to be a free agent and was consequently not answerable for an act. The judge prefaced this point by saying that such a determination was not only a "point of law" but a point of "justice, humanity, and reason." But, he continued, it was not "every degree of mental disorder, every derangement of mind" that would amount to a justification for the defense. Whatever mental disorder the jurors might "discover," their task was to determine the vital connection between the mental state and the prisoner's capacity to appreciate the wrongfulness of his actions.

Although other judges in the late 1700s gave juries explicit instructions concerning the law's insistence on total—as opposed to partial—derangement, the judge's instructions in the Paar trial exemplify the critical element for assigning culpability: the prisoner's intent. The presence of derangement, physical accident, or mental impairment doubtless affected the prisoner's intellect, but the jurors learned that this did not absolve them of the need to determine exactly what it was the offender *meant to do*. Only one who understood the consequences of criminal actions and chose to do evil could be said to have acted intentionally. Judges therefore instructed jurors to look beyond manifest signs of distraction to consider the prisoner's capacity to understand the nature and consequences of the criminal act. Did he or she retain sufficient mental capacity to comprehend the difference between right and wrong and, understanding this, choose to do evil?

THE LEGAL CONTEXT

If guilt arose only in the commission of an act, the effort to reconstruct the mental state of the offender at the time of the crime would matter little. Such a system of *absolute liability* characterized Anglo-Saxon law until at least the time of the Norman Conquest. One of the legacies of the Norman kings' centralization of regionally specific legal codes into a common law applicable to all subjects of the realm was their incorporation of the canon law position on moral guilt. For the Church, questions of criminal responsibility were not limited to whether an individual had indeed committed an offense. In the eyes of ecclesiastics—who for the most part made up the Norman judiciary—moral guilt was a necessary element for the attribution of culpability.[5] In time, the sinfulness of the wrongdoer came to be described as evil intent, or *mens rea.* In his monumental work *On the Laws and Customs of England,* the thirteenth-century scribe Henri de Bracton grounded this mental element in the principle *voluntas nocendi:* the will to harm. Attention to human will was of course not unique to Bracton in Western legal thinking; one finds the declaration "madmen have no will" as early as A.D. 533 in Justinian's Digest. Bracton, however, was the first English lawyer (he was also chancellor of Exeter Cathedral *and* chief justiciary of the highest court in the realm) to incorporate the mental element into legal writing: "For a crime is not committed unless the will to harm be present . . . In misdeeds we look to the will and not the outcome."[6] In essence, the law conceived of people as capable of free choice, a free exercise of will. Choosing to do evil revealed a wicked will and an evil intent. For criminal culpability to be imputed, the act must be accompanied by intent.

Assuming that most human behavior is willful, under what conditions (or mental states) can a person be said to have acted without choice? Bracton again drew on Justinian to describe the blameless as "not much different from brutes which lack reasoning." Bracton's focus was clearly on reason, the particular faculty that clerics and philosophers have historically isolated in distinguishing humans from other species.[7] Four centuries later Lord Coke incorporated Bracton's conception of the "will to harm" in his reasoning in Beverly's Case (1603): "The punishment of a man who is deprived of reason and understanding cannot be an example to others. No felony or murder can be committed without a felonious intent and purpose."[8]

Deranged offenders were not the only class of wrongdoers to challenge the court's ability to impute moral guilt. The capacity to form a will to harm was also germane to another type of offender whose ability to appreciate the nature of an action—its wrongfulness and consequences—was open to dispute. Although the minimum age of criminal responsibility was seven, children between the ages of seven and fourteen could be convicted of a felony if the court believed they were able to tell good from evil. When Coke compares the madman to the child of fourteen rather than the infant under seven, it is clear that the incapacity to form intent, like the defense of infancy (naïveté, innocence) is meant to be a *finding* by the court.⁹ A child might be below the age of discretion (fourteen) yet be fully culpable for a felony if a jury deemed him or her capable of distinguishing between right and wrong. Though young, the youth was clearly not "young enough." In a similar vein—as we saw in Paar's trial—a deranged offender, though impaired, might be not "deranged enough."¹⁰ And therein lay the problem that has bedeviled insanity trials from the early modern period to the present day. Children who were too young to understand the consequences of what they were doing and adults who were too demented to understand the nature of their actions could easily fall outside the realm of culpability. Neither could be said to have understood the nature of the harm they were committing. Neither could be said to have acted with a *will to harm,* the law's conception of intention. The jury's difficulty clearly rested with the deranged (and the young) who, while doubtless "less" coherent (or mature) than the average adult, yet retained sufficient mental capability to know that their actions were wrong.

In 1736 Matthew Hale's *History of the Pleas of the Crown* made its first printed appearance, containing the most expansive treatment to date regarding the existence of degrees of impairment and their necessary legal significance. Hale's work initially echoes Bracton and Coke: "If totally deprived of the use of their reason, [the demented] cannot be guilty ordinarily of capital offenses, for they have not the use of their understanding, and act not as reasonable creatures, but their actions are in effect the condition of brutes." By Hale's time, reason, understanding, "and brutish condition" had become part of an omnibus conception of insanity. It was the deprivation of reason that precluded the forming of intent. Individuals who could not reason were incapable of understanding the nature of their actions; they were unable to choose to do evil. Hale, however, does not rest with the criterion of a "total deprivation of reason" but proceeds to consider the potentially explosive concept of partial insanity:

There is partial insanity of mind; and a total insanity. Partial insanity is either in respect to things . . . Some persons, that have a competent use of reason in respect of some subjects, are yet under a particular *dementia* in respect of some particular discourses, subjects or applications; or else it is partial in respect of degrees; and this is the condition of very many, especially melancholy persons, who for the most part discover their defect in excessive fears and griefs, and yet are not wholly destitute of the use of their reason; and this partial insanity seems not to excuse them in the committing of any offense for its matter capital; for doubtless most persons, that are felons of themselves, and others are under a degree of partial insanity, when they commit these offenses; it is very difficult to define the indivisible line that divides perfect and partial insanity, but it must rest upon circumstances duly to be weighed and considered both by judge and jury . . . the best measure I can think of is this; such a person as laboring under melancholy distempers hath yet ordinarily as great understanding, as ordinarily a child of 14 years hath, is such a person as may be guilty of treason or felony.[11]

The conventional interpretation of this famous passage associates partial insanity with melancholy: "deranged by degrees." Hale's other type of partial insanity concerned fluctuating states of distraction punctuated with intervals of lucidity. Lunacy, the term commonly employed to describe such a state, was well recognized and often linked to phases of the moon by no less an authority than Hale. But by definition lunacy was a transitory condition. Few medical specialists in early modern England would venture an opinion regarding the length of time a "lucid interval" might last. Such imprecision rendered lunacy a troublesome "diagnosis" since one could not be sure if the lunatic's crime had been committed during a period of distraction or in a lucid interval. Although lunatics were thought to exhibit only a partial insanity, Hale did not exclude them automatically from exculpatory consideration: "In the heights of their distemper . . . the person that is absolutely mad for a day, killing a man in that distemper, is equally not guilty, as if he were mad without intermission." Crimes committed during a lucid interval, in contrast, were "subject to the same punishment, as if they had no such deficiency."[12]

The legal significance of the term "partial," therefore, depends very much on how one reads this section from Hale's famous treatise. He clearly rejected that form of partial insanity commonly known as melancholia: insane by degrees. These persons retain sufficient reason, "as great an understanding as ordinarily a child of 14 years hath," to leave them answerable for their actions. In the first sentence of the passage cited above, however, it is unclear if those suffering from the other type of partial insanity—partial in respect of some subjects—should be con-

sidered as one would the melancholic or the lunatic in the manic phase
of derangement. When deranged, Hale writes, the lunatic is "equally not
guilty, as if he were mad without intermission." Construed in this way,
the individual whose madness is manifest only in episodes would seem
to qualify for exemption. Hale pointedly entrusts the decision to the jury,
who must "weigh and consider" the particular circumstances surrounding any one case.

One cannot help but empathize with the jury's task when faced with
categories as indistinct as "total" and "partial" insanity. Short of raving
delirium—a condition that hardly permitted much criminality—what did
"total deprivation of memory and understanding" mean? A "perfectly"
deranged person could hardly be capable of much deliberate harm. When
a formerly sane person suffered a grievous head injury and periodically
"went off"—later claiming to know nothing of the violent assault (or
bank forgery)—were terms like "partial" or "total" really very useful?
Although such criteria as possessing a "will to harm" or a capacity to
"tell right from wrong" were eminently logical and justifiable bases for
excluding the insane from criminal responsibility, there were simply no
clear, accessible definitions of derangement judges could include in their
instructions to a jury that might indicate what "threshold level" might
preclude criminal responsibility.

Although Hale's categories were invoked in late eighteenth-century
instructions to the jury, an analysis of the evidence presented at the Old
Bailey reveals that most prisoners were neither idiots nor melancholics,
neither totally insane nor "partially" deranged—if partial is defined in
terms of derangement by degrees. They suffered *periodic* violent frenzies,
bouts of delirium, *paroxysms* of mania, as well as general states of "insensibility" and "fits." In short, they suffered periods when they were
"not themselves." That prisoners later regained mental coherence, described the state they had been in to the court, and were subsequently
acquitted suggests the jurors' acceptance of the notion of a "partial"
insanity, revealed in moments of episodic madness usually brought on by
outrageous beliefs or haunting fears. Hale himself considers the possible
exculpatory significance of a "temporary phrenzy" in a 1668 trial of a
married woman who murdered her child.[13] Confessing her crime freely,
the prisoner recounted that "after some sleep, she [had] recovered her
understanding, but marveled how and why she came thither [to the jail]."
The jury was charged with determining if she "had any use of her reason
when she did it," and if so, they were to find her guilty. If, however, they
"found her under a phrenzy, thereby reason of her late delivery and want
of sleep, they should acquit her."

The prisoner unquestionably suffered a period of deep distraction, but how was the jury to deduce if she yet retained "any use of reason" when she murdered her child? Hale suggests that one way to answer this question was to look for a rational reason to kill the child. A woman could *reasonably* kill a child to hide her shame, for example, or to stem a husband's jealousy if she feared he might conclude that the child was not his. Given a "rational" incentive, the *phrenzy* could appear counterfeit. Hale's reasoning was endorsed by judges in the late eighteenth century who reminded the jury of the possibility of an all-too-sane motive animating the particular crime. The jury may not be able to visualize the actual paroxysm of mania the defendant was said to have endured, but when the judge asked a neighbor, "Did you know that his wife had a little money of her own, independent of [the prisoner]," there seemed to be more than a little method to his madness.

Hale's case of temporary frenzy is therefore instructive for a number of reasons, not least for the observation that a "total insanity" need not be permanent. This unfortunate woman, for example, recovered her understanding and remained rational throughout the trial. Further, the inference regarding the prisoner's capacity to discern right from wrong was to be drawn from any sign of prevarication: in this case, any attempt to hide the infant or an effort to flee would reveal not only that the woman knew the nature of her act but, more important, that she knew it to be wrong. Although there was usually little direct evidence of the accused's intention or "will to harm," the prisoner's knowledge that an act was morally transgressive could sometimes be inferred from steps taken to elude detection. The ready prompting by a judge to search for a rational motive for a "frenzied act," signs of dissimulation when confronted with the deed, or attempts to elude detection could be critical elements for the jury's reconstruction of exactly what the prisoner understood he or she was doing. If the accused was totally confused and befuddled, it was hard to conclude that he or she was capable of choosing to do evil. If, however, efforts had been taken to avoid detection, or if a rational reason for the crime could be discerned, it was much easier to infer basic understanding and, by implication, the requisite ingredient for making a choice. The jury's ultimate task was thus to determine whether the events surrounding the action revealed intentionally chosen behavior—a will to harm—or the tragic effects of insanity.

THE WILD BEAST OF EIGHTEENTH-CENTURY JURISPRUDENCE

Two trials have earned a secure niche in the history of criminal insanity because they provide early evidence of the court's thinking regarding the degree of derangement required for a finding of nonculpability. At the trial of Edward Arnold in 1723, Mr. Justice Tracy reminded the jury that "guilt arises from the mind, and the wicked will and intention of the man. If a man be deprived of his reason, and consequently of his intention, he cannot be guilty." But, continued Tracy, "it is not every frantic and idle humour that will exempt him from justice . . . it must be a man that is totally deprived of his understanding and memory and doth not know what he is doing, no more than an infant, than a brute or a wild beast." In the evolution of the insanity defense, the judge's construction has come to be known as the Wild Beast Test.[14] Tracy's words remind the twentieth-century reader that the key element in culpability was intent: not motive, not desire, not purpose. Did the actor retain the capacity to foresee the consequences of criminal actions, to understand the nature of what he or she was doing? Only someone who retained the capacity to comprehend the "tendency" of his behavior could be said to have chosen a certain action: to exercise will. To this end, the judge in this case asked the jury to consider Edward Arnold's (seemingly coherent) purchase of powder and shot in contemplation of his attack on Lord Onslow. Was it likely that someone who did not know what he was "about" could procure the implements of a crime? Do "wild beasts" negotiate commercial transactions?

One way to address the "right from wrong" criterion was to compel jurors to consider the events surrounding the crime from the offender's perspective. In Arnold's case, was it possible for him to execute a plan yet fail to understand the nature and quality of his acts? It is worth remembering that eighteenth-century notions of mental functioning did not entertain a "suspension of moral consciousness" in the midst of active pursuit of a plan. One hundred years later, just such a state of "contrivance without consciousness" would be claimed as an understandable and recognizable phenomenon by a new generation of asylum physicians who would enter the court with innovative conceptions of mental derangement. Arnold was convicted—suggesting that in his day at least, when jurors were confronted with "rational" action on the day of the crime, they inferred the presence of intentional behavior.

Lawrence Shirley, earl Ferrers, was certainly less of a "wild beast" than Edward Arnold, but his trial for an intemperate assault on his servant centered on much the same issue: the degree of impairment necessary for acquittal.[15] Specifically, Ferrers's prosecution in the House of Lords chronicles the fate of an untried species of derangement to support an insanity defense and the reaction of England's solicitor general to such a construction. "The defense I mean is occasional insanity of the mind, and I am convinced from recollecting within myself, that at the time of this action I could not know what I was about." With this as his defense strategy, Ferrers called upon no less a medical figure than John Monro, physician superintendent to Bethlem Hospital, whose familiarity with the prisoner was limited to treating the earl's late uncle. When asked by the earl to name the usual symptoms of lunacy, the medical witness responded: "Uncommon fury, jealousy, or suspicion without cause or grounds." The obviously equivocal nature of these "symptoms" of insanity was the subject of the solicitor general's remarks to the jury. Did these symptoms reveal insanity or simply a vicious character? The criterion in considering culpability, after all, was the want of reason—not the signs of a malicious heart. The solicitor general's remarks to the jury reveal the two constant elements of the jurisprudence of insanity: sufficient impairment to render the actor oblivious to actions and the inability to distinguish between good and evil:

> If there be a total permanent want of reason, it will acquit the prisoner. If there be a total temporary want of it, where the offence was committed, it will acquit the prisoner: but if there be only a partial degree of insanity; mixed with a partial degree of reason; not a full and complete use of reason but (as Lord Hale carefully and emphatically expresses himself) a competent use of it, sufficient to have restrained those passions, which produced the crime . . . if there be thought and design; a faculty to distinguish the nature of actions; to discern the differences between moral good and evil, then upon the fact of the offence proved, the judgment of the law must take place.[16]

Ferrers's failure to employ "occasional insanity" in his defense should not necessarily be read as a rejection of partial insanity. Monro's testimony was less than compelling, and Ferrers's examination of the medical witness was singularly inept[17] and his demeanor so unpleasant and obnoxious that his own legal adviser voted against him. The prisoner's characterization of his occasional insanity would probably not likely have been accepted in any event. His fury was not insanity at all, and it would not take a huge interpretive leap for members of the House of Lords to see an analogy between the prisoner's vituperative bouts of anger and the melancholic's "derangement by degrees." Although one cannot be sure what the Lords were actually rejecting in Ferrers's defense, his trial remains a hallmark of English jurisprudence because of both the clear articulation that total insanity (however defined) remained the sole *expressed* criterion for an acquittal and the first appearance of a medical witness to address the symptoms and features of insanity as a disease.

Arnold and the earl certainly deserve prominence in the historical reconstruction of the law's disposition regarding criminal insanity, yet one wonders whether the sentiments expressed by the bench and the solicitor general were shared by later judges. Were judges likely to be similarly engaged in the jurisprudence of insanity when the defense was brought forward by ordinary prisoners tried for the theft of buttons or the murder of the non-elite? Of perhaps more immediate importance to the historian of forensic medicine was whether the publisher of the *OBSP* was "similarly engaged" in the jurisprudence of insanity to *record* these instructions. As mentioned earlier, the *OBSP* were intended for lay readers: sensational testimony took precedence over the details of judicial and prosecutorial procedure because the sensational sold more papers. Fortunately, fifteen examples of judicial instructions survive in the *OBSP* between the years 1784 and 1816. There is no way of knowing if the sentiments held by these judges were shared by their brethren on the bench, or indeed if entirely different sets of instructions were given in other trials, although this seems unlikely. Criminal trials featuring testimony about mental derangement were infrequent events—often the occasion for fantastic tales, both comical and horrifying—and were reported in such graphic detail that there is little reason to believe that the judge's observations, when offered, would be deleted.

When judges instructed the jury on the principles of the law, few could forebear taking the occasion to inform the jurors of their *personal* views regarding the prisoner's claims to insanity, often providing jurors with a veiled (or not-so-veiled) suggestion regarding how they should find the defendant. In 1784, for example, a judge at the Old Bailey summed up his view of the prisoner's defense this way:

> And it seems to me, as far as I can judge from the result of the evidence, to have happened under the effect of some disorder that had seized the man, and affected his spirits, and deprived him to a certain degree of reason, and that particularly rendered him suspicious, among other people, of his wife . . . [A]nd nothing alarms a man who has any symptoms of insanity about him, so much as the idea of being taken care of as an insane man; there is nothing that impresses them with so much terror, and there being no medical man present that I know of, I take upon me to say so, it having fallen within my own knowledge, nothing alarms them so much, nothing irritates them so much, as the idea of being treated of as insane.[18]

No juror could have missed the judge's ready acceptance of the prisoner's distressed state of mind, the manifestation of "symptoms of insanity about him," and his taking it upon himself to venture an opinion, "there being no medical man present." This last comment is particularly intriguing because medical men were *rarely* present throughout the late 1700s, and the remark appears to signal the willingness of at least this judge to entertain the opinions of medicine regarding insanity. The instructions also remind us that the court was not necessarily contemptuous of a plea of derangement or eager to expose gaps in the logic of a prisoner's story. This jury's task was doubtless simplified when the judge explicitly endorsed the prisoner's claims of sufficient derangement and consequent blamelessness and supplemented the defense with observations of his own.

That the bench could also offer observations against the defendant is clear from the Paar trial, described at the beginning of this chapter, in which the judge, employing such loaded terms as "deliberation" and "wicked discretion" challenged the jurors to conclude that such dissembling did *not* betoken willful, chosen behavior. Reading such instructions several centuries later, one is struck by the latitude judges enjoyed in "instructing" jurors on the criterion for an insanity acquittal. These observations could include brief comments—"such a clear case of lunacy, I think we may with perfect confidence rely upon it"—to elaborate summaries of evidence, legal precepts, and fully developed arguments for and against the prisoner's plea.[19] Although few judges went so far as to follow a witness's testimony with the instruction "Then you will acquit to be sure, Gentlemen," the bench was adept at articulating the law's concern with intent and at suggesting ways to sift through the evidence to determine whether the prisoner knew the "tendency" of his or her actions.[20]

One wonders, of course, how juries received such direction and how useful legal strictures were when jurors confronted criminal acts that appeared to be both purposeful *and* deranged. Was mental derangement one more "constraint" for the jury to consider against the backdrop of their willingness to weigh the press of external circumstances on the exercise of human will? How were evolving conceptions of the will working their way into Victorian notions of criminality and human agency? Three cases, selected to illustrate moments from the thirty years in which judicial instructions appeared at the Old Bailey (1784–1816), follow. Included in this selection are extracts of judicial instruction that address the question of human agency, the enduring insistence on "total insanity," and judicial attempts to delineate (and dismiss) various "species" of mental impairment.

A Mere Machine

On 5 March 1784, William Walker stabbed his wife, Ann, with a "clasp knife," mortally wounding her with one thrust to her chest. At his trial, Walker could produce no character witnesses, nor indeed any persons who could give an account of his history of derangement, except for a neighbor who described the prisoner as "like a man not fit for me to be with . . . [he would] run on talking a heap of stuff." This was apparently sufficient evidence for the judge, who advised the jury, "That is speaking more satisfactorily to you, Gentlemen, than if he had said he was mad." The prisoner's only defense, uttered at the conclusion of the trial, was: "I am not sensible as I did kill my wife, and please you my Lord." The judge's opening remarks to the jury focused on a single point: whether this man was "in his right mind or no, whether he did it from motives of wickedness and malice towards her, or whether he did it under the impression of some distemper of mind which had deprived him of the use of his reason." If the jury determined that distemper had in fact prevailed, "though his hand committed the offense, in the consideration of law as well as upon the plain principles of reason and justice, no crime can be imputed to him in doing it."

Freely conceding that there could be no doubt that Walker committed the assault, the court then addressed the issue of human agency:

> [I]f you should see any reason to collect from the evidence . . . that he was not in possession of his right senses, and of his right mind, but that it was done under the pressure of some disorder of mind, occasioned by something that you and I cannot get to the bottom of, that will make him nothing more than a mere instrument in the hands of Providence, and he is not at all answerable to the laws of God or man for what he has done, any more than the simple knife could be answerable that gave the fatal blow.[21]

Following these comments, the judge examined those elements in the case that appeared to speak "against the man": the prisoner initially endeavored to justify the act, "accusing [the victim] of behaving ill to him, [a circumstance that] seems to denote that he was in possession of himself, that he knew what he was doing, that he meant to do it, and that he did it on motives of malice urging him to revenge." The judge's comments did not end here, however, for he reminded the jury of a report of a conversation in which the prisoner's talk "was that of a man whose brain was touched . . . he talked of his wife's fetching him away in a cart." Walker's trial had in fact been the occasion for the judicial comments regarding the prisoner's suspicion of his wife: "Nothing alarms a man, who has any symptoms of insanity about him, so much as the idea of being taken care of as an insane man."

The judge's concluding remarks centered on Walker's "rage . . . the effect of distemper" for which the prisoner was not answerable:

> [I]t appears to me, that this was the unhappy effect of rage against this woman, conceived in consequence of distemper of mind, brought on

by disease, and that under that impression the violence was committed. The man's afterwards coming to his senses will not alter the nature of the case, if it was committed under the impression of insanity, and the mind disturbed and deprived of its powers of governing the man: he is not answerable, and you must find your verdict, Not Guilty.[22]

Underscoring this last point, the judge added: "Indeed he is either guilty of the crime of willful murder, or he is a mere machine." After the jury returned a verdict of "not guilty" the judge advised that the prisoner "must not be discharged" but rather "confined, and taken proper care of." Although it may have taken Parliament sixteen years from the date of Walker's trial to pass the Criminal Lunatics Act—prescribing confinement for prisoners acquitted on the grounds of insanity—there are indications in post-verdict comments by the court that a de facto policy of detention was instituted by some judges at the Old Bailey.

The case of William Walker was one of a cohort of five trials heard between the years 1784 and 1789 that offers the most comprehensive instructions to the jury in the late eighteenth century. In Walker's trial, one hears clear and compelling language regarding how the jury was to discern intention. What did this actor *mean* to do; was he capable of choosing *not* to do it? When the judge asked the jury to consider a mind "deprived of its powers of governing the man," the clear implication was that some other power was governing him, just as he had governed the knife. Judicial instructions therefore combined "disease," the misfortune of being "in the hands of Providence," and the (consequent) utter lack of "answerability." The jurors were therefore instructed to acquit the prisoner if they deemed him a "mere machine," no more culpable than the "simple knife" that he wielded.

The question of "non-thinking" action—by implication, action without intention—was addressed a year before the trial of Francis Paar by a judge who instructed the jury, "though mechanically it is the act of the body . . . yet it is not the act of the mind, [and] all moral agency and accountability must be taken away."[23] The forces that might be responsible for the removal of human agency were variously described by judges as "the visitation of God (or Heaven)," "a nervous fever that seized his spirits," or "occasioned by something you and I cannot get to the bottom of."[24] One should quickly add that the "spirits" that seized the brain could not be in bottled form. A jury in 1787 was advised that, regarding a prisoner who "voluntarily inflames his blood by drunkenness, [and] draws out that madness which before was lurking in it, the law does not excuse him." To be guiltless, then, the prisoner clearly had to have no role in bringing on the derangement.[25]

Although the image of man as a machine, animated by some force independent of will, may seem to carry a certain intrinsic intelligibility, the jury still had to decide whether the prisoner was capable of "knowing what he was about"—that is, was the prisoner's action *intentional?* How was the jury to define the state of the prisoner's intellects at the time of the crime? One possible way—remarked by almost every judge—was to search for evidence that the prisoner could distinguish right from wrong. When there was clear evidence of evasion or an attempt to flee, this was relatively easy. For most juries, however, the task of discovering such an abstract concept as "possessing a will to harm" and "knowing right from wrong" doubtless proved daunting. One wonders how (and whether!) these criteria structured the jury's deliberation. Did "knowing right from wrong" help jurors to assign culpability or confound their task by the need to conjoin a metaphysical will to a "visitation from Heaven"?

Although questions regarding the prisoner's capacity to distinguish right from wrong may historically have justified a "principled" exculpation in common law, a review of judicial instructions in the late eighteenth century suggests that this query may have served another, perhaps more instrumental, purpose. It appears that asking this question was actually part of an effort to gauge the *extent* of prisoners' distraction—their capacity to know their "tendency." In 1786 jurors in two trials heard the following instructions: "[A] person not in his senses, or so disordered as to take away the faculty of distinguishing right from wrong, and of knowing the tendency of the act which he does at the time [performs only a 'mechanical' event: it is not] the act of the mind,"[26] and "[Y]ou must be satisfied at the time this fact was committed, his mind was in such a state of distraction, that he could no longer be sensible of the internal distinction between right and wrong, more especially this distinction between the affection that was due an affectionate wife, in the savage outrage he committed upon her."[27] When William Walker eagerly invited the neighbors into the house to view his freshly slain wife, he revealed either unparalleled brazenness and perversion or complete obliviousness to the reprehensible nature of his deed. One suspects that his mental derangement was *revealed* by his inability to recognize what was so horrible about his deed. In an intriguing way, the legal criterion could serve as the jury's diagnostic tool. Perhaps "knowing right from wrong" and retaining a capacity to understand the nature of one's acts served as a critical window into a distorted mind. Although it is traditionally alleged that the law has been materially and profoundly shaped by the expanding "medicalization" of deviance, the relations between medicine and law may in fact be much more nearly reciprocal. The legal setting itself—its exigencies for acquittal—may well have shaped cultural understandings about the nature of madness. Further, jurors may have found it absolutely essential to convert the criterion of "right versus wrong" into a tool for gauging the extent of mental derangement because late eighteenth-century judges offered them few guidelines for defining sufficient capacity to comprehend wrongdoing.

A Case of Suicidal Forgery

On 17 July 1786, Samuel Burt signed two fateful documents. The first was a counterfeit bank draft to which he affixed his employer's name, the second a letter to his employer confessing the deed. At his trial, Burt's attorney endeavored to construct an insanity defense based on the prisoner's unambiguous intent "to destroy his own existence." Defense counsel deftly constructed the image of a young man both despondent and depressed, who saw conviction and execution as the only way to escape his miserable condition. Following the appearance of witnesses who confirmed the prisoner's sorry history of sadness and melancholy, the judge instructed the jury:

> [T]he defence of insanity or disorder of mind where it is carried to a sufficient degree, is a defence for all crimes whatever, from the highest to the lowest, because in order to constitute criminality . . . it must be knowingly and voluntarily done . . . [T]he essence of forgery is the intent to defraud, and if therefore the party is incapable of knowing what he does, he can have no such intention, for he can as a moral agent have no intention at all: but you observe, that I have stated to you that it must be a *total derangement* of the mind; and it will be, therefore for you to consider, whether there is any evidence in this case that can go any thing near that length; for unless it goes that length, it is my duty to tell you, however it may approach to that degree of disorder . . . [U]nless it goes that length, it does not amount to a justification.[28]

Summing up the evidence and articulating this stricture, the judge reminded the jury that the prisoner's letter to his employer clearly revealed that he knew the act to be wrong; the reason behind it, "a criminal purpose of destroying his own life," could hardly be taken as sufficient distraction to reveal total derangement of mind. "I cannot, therefore, consistent with my duty, tell you that in point of law, all the facts put together, this defence does amount to a justification; but you are at liberty to form a very different opinion."[29]

Samuel Burt's ordeal did not end with a conviction and a sentence of death because the jury returned to the court to recommend mercy, believing that he "laboured under some degree of mental disorder." The quality of mercy, however, was indeed strained because it purposely thwarted the prisoner's elaborately planned demise. Burt implored the jury to reconsider: "[I]t is death that I wish for, it is death I seek; for nothing but death can extricate me out of the troubles which my follies have brought upon me." This was apparently too much for the judge, who admonished the prisoner, "To come uncalled into the presence of your Creator is highly criminal of itself; he who made you best knows when you shall have fulfilled those purposes for which you were created [and] it is therefore the highest degree of presumption in you, to take the secret judgment to yourself . . . [as for the punishment which your crimes have merited] it is your duty to submit to, but not to desire."[30]

Judges were capable of employing unequivocal language regarding total derangement: "[U]nless it goes that length . . . however much it approach[es] that degree of disorder . . . it does not amount to a justification." *What* length, however, was unclear. This defendant was doubtless under great pressures, although he hardly qualified even as "partially" insane, let alone totally deranged. But what if Burt's carefully wrought plan for execution concerned a religious or a political end? Suppose that to Burt's delusory mind, his mortal end was actually a beginning: the Second Coming. What would it take to turn the same degree of planning and foresight regarding the likely consequences of his act into prima facie evidence of insanity sufficient to merit an acquittal? Would not the recognition of such a state of mind and its consequent action fundamentally blur the notion of "insane by degrees"?

Fifteen years after Burt's intricately planned suicide, the trial of another would-be felo de se tested the boundary between total and partial insanity by introducing the first successful form of "partial insanity" into English jurisprudence. Although James Hadfield's acquittal for the attempted assassination of George III has been attributed to a number of factors—the gross disfigurement of his head caused by war wounds, the benefit he received by being permitted assistance of counsel—the fact remains that the prisoner clearly knew the probable consequences of his deed. In fact, his own execution was central to his purpose; his delusion mandated his death at the hands of the state. Why did Burt's capacity to appreciate the wrongfulness of his act and the consequences that would certainly accrue not also condemn James Hadfield—who was no less "clear" about his actions—to the hideous death accorded treasonous assassins?

The anomalous features of Hadfield's trial make it difficult to isolate any one factor or set of factors as *the* critical element in his successful insanity plea. The availability of legal counsel is certainly one element. Attempted regicide elevated the assault to high treason, warranting full legal assistance because of the fatal consequences that followed conviction. Some commentators attribute Hadfield's acquittal to this fact alone, because it gave him access to perhaps the most brilliant legal mind of the day, Thomas Erskine. Together with other participants at the trial, Erskine listened attentively as the attorney general repeated the familiar words regarding mental derangement and criminal responsibility: "[I]f a man is completely deranged, so that he knows not what he does, if a man is so lost to all sense, in consequence of the infirmity of disease, that he is incapable of distinguishing between good and evil—that he is incapable of forming a judgement upon the consequences of the act which he is about to do, that then the mercy of our law says, he cannot be guilty of a crime."[31] In fact, the attorney general managed to include not only direct references to Coke and Hale but also the reasoning that animated the Arnold and Ferrers cases ("the ability to form a steady and resolute design") and the standard question: At the moment of the crime, was the prisoner capable of forming criminal intent? The prosecutor's description of insanity was tendentiously rendered: Hadfield had procured a firearm and positioned himself at the Drury Lane Theatre to get the best possible shot at the king—in short, he had exhibited such a "steady and resolute design" that his first words on being wrestled to the ground clearly revealed his intended target. Far from being a madman in a frenzy, the prisoner exhibited his capacity to formulate a plan fully mindful of the consequences. He understood that his life would be forfeited.

Rather than question the attorney general's construction of Hadfield's ability to formulate a plan and distinguish right from wrong, Erskine chose to confront directly the criterion of "total deprivation of memory and understanding." He asked rhetorically whether such a person could even be capable of committing an act, criminal or otherwise. Some memory, some understanding must be retained by the insane, and Erskine proceeded to interpret Coke and Hale's principle of "total insanity" in such a manner that an individual could be aware of his or her actions without being conscious of their moral wrongfulness. To this end, the defense attorney introduced the concept of delusion, which "unaccompanied by frenzy or raving madness [was] the true character of insanity." Manifestly avoiding any "wild beast" imagery to denominate the insane, Erskine drew instead on a Lockean conception of madness: "if the 'premises from which they reason' are uniformly false and cannot be shaken with clearest of evidence, then he's suffering from the disease of insanity." Mindful of frequently voiced judicial sentiments regarding the proper criterion of mental distress—"it is not every mental disorder or every derangement of mind [that will exculpate]"—Erskine stipulated that the crime had to be the "immediate, unqualified offspring of [his] disease."[32]

Hadfield's delusion stemmed from millenarian beliefs that his death (at the hands of the state) was required to effect the Second Coming. He had apparently come under the sway of another True Believer, Bannister Truelock, who told him that he was the true descendant of God and that Hadfield "might be a very great man . . . by becoming [His] son." Erskine did not rest with his construction of intellectual delusion but reportedly drew the jury's attention to Hadfield's war injuries: eight saber scars to the head that Hadfield had received during the Napoleonic wars. Immediately following this injury, the jury learned, Hadfield had "constant intercourse" with the Almighty, who told him that the world would end soon unless, like Christ, he would sacrifice his life for others. Two medical witnesses testified that Hadfield's head wounds were sufficient to cause damage to the brain and that these wounds were probably the cause of his insanity. One witness, a Dr. Creighton, added that Hadfield spoke rationally on all matters unrelated to the subject of his lunacy.[33] As Richard Moran reports, the jury never left the box but responded to the judge's comment that "this prisoner, for his own sake and for the sake of society at large, must not be discharged" by returning a finding of "not guilty," being under the influence of insanity at the time he committed the act.

The significance of Hadfield's acquittal in the history of legal thought regarding partial insanity has been a matter of debate because there is no way of knowing what the jury found most persuasive: the logic of Erskine's defense, the gross disfigurement manifest in Hadfield's war wounds, or a combination of the two. A portion of the prisoner's skull had reportedly been "sliced off by the sword of a Frenchman." It may well be that a mixture of patriotic sentiment (it was, after all, a *Frenchman's* sword), horrific scarring, and the deft introduction of delusion together produced the acquittal.[34] Although Hadfield's trial produced no legal standard along the lines of the McNaughtan "right versus wrong" defense, or even the "wild beast" test, Erskine successfully introduced into English jurisprudence the notion that a cool and calculated act could still be the act of a mad person. Neither the attorney general nor the judge challenged Erskine's "delusion" defense. Further, Hadfield's ordinary activities on the day of the atrocious act were not recounted to the jury as evidence that Hadfield knew very well what he was "about." When a medical witness commented on the prisoner's ability to speak rationally on all matters unrelated to his lunacy, one sees the close fit of delusion to Hale's variant of partial insanity "in respect of things, [though they] have a competent use of reason in respect of some subjects, [they] are yet under a particular *dementia* in respect of some particular discourses, subjects or applications."[35]

Erskine's achievement in the Hadfield trial was to give sustained scrutiny to the law's traditional criterion of "total insanity." What did this standard amount to? Specifically, Erskine asked jurors to expand their search beyond signs of histrionic, beastly antics to include a consideration of the prisoner's *ideas*. James Hadfield was afflicted with profound misunderstandings of what he was "about" and of the delusory consequences of his act—not the king's death, but the Second Coming—that, though he appeared sufficiently calm as not to arouse bystanders, he possessed a madness sufficiently "total" to exempt him from culpability. Most important, Hadfield saw the world though a lens so profoundly distorted by his ruling delusion that for him the act was not a moral wrong. Here was a profound challenge to centuries of the jurisprudence of intent: the divergence of moral from legal transgression. As long as behavioral or conversational signs revealed madness, the inference of knowing right from wrong or the tendency of one's action could follow conventional assumptions about derangement: only someone who was insane would talk or act in such a manner. In a court of law, the confusion revealed in the inability to distinguish "between the affection due an affectionate wife and [the] savage outrage [the prisoner] committed against her" became translated into the inability to tell "right from wrong." But Hadfield's confusion was an insanity of a different—though no less debilitating—sort. His action bore the outward appearance of purpose and planning, yet he retained no capacity to appreciate the actual—that is, legal—consequences of his behavior. By the law's notion of intent, Hadfield had not chosen to shoot the king. What was generally conceded to be an unambiguous *legal* wrong was to him no *moral* wrongdoing. Indeed, it had become a moral and behavioral *imperative*.

Although delusion was fast becoming a standard category in early nineteenth-century medical texts on the true nature of insanity, the Hadfield acquittal did not inaugurate delusion's "career" as a regular feature of the insanity defense.[36] It was another twelve years before delusion was introduced into testimony at the Old Bailey by a medical witness, and eighteen more before it became the most frequently invoked term to justify a diagnosis of insanity. At most, Erskine's efforts revealed a major fault line in the law's traditional reliance on "total insanity" for a finding of irresponsibility. He located something else as well: a way into the juror's imagination most likely lacking in such global abstractions as "knowing right from wrong" and "knowing the tendency of his actions." The skillful attorney had in fact challenged jurors to enter the world of James Hadfield, to see the world as he saw it, and still to find him culpable. Not all attorneys, however, were so clever with images, not all prisoners were so lucky as to disport grotesque head wounds received in battle, and not all judges were so willing to permit a frontal assault on the law's traditional criteria for acquittal, as our final case reveals.

Tears from the Bench

> Gentlemen of the jury, you are now to try an indictment which charges the prisoner at the bar with the willful murder (here the learned judge was so hurt by his feelings, that he could not proceed for several seconds) of Mr. Spencer Perceval, (in a faint voice) who was murdered with a pistol loaded with a bullet . . . (here again his lordship was sincerely affected, and burst into tears, in which he was joined by the greatest portion of the persons in court) a man so dear, so revered as that of Mr. Spencer Perceval, I find it difficult to suppress my feelings. As, however, to say anything of the distinguished talents and virtues of that excellent man, might tend to excite improper emotions in the minds of the jury, but [I] would with-hold these feelings which pressed for utterance from my heart, and leave you, gentlemen, to form your judgment upon the evidence which has been adduced in support of the case, undressed by any unfair indignation which you might feel against his murderer, by any description, however faint, of the excellent qualities of the deceased.[37]

At his trial in 1812 for the murder of Prime Minister Spencer Perceval, James Bellingham told the court the tale of his horrific imprisonment in Russia: "banded from prison to prison, and from dungeon to dungeon, fed on bread and water, treated with the utmost cruelty." All his efforts to entreat the British minister in Russia to intercede on his behalf came to naught, and though he was eventually released, he was "plunged into ruin" and debt. On returning to England, Bellingham was recommended "backward and forwards" from one government minister to another, from a marquis to the Privy Council, from the Privy Council to the Treasury. Finally, receiving no satisfaction from Spencer Perceval himself, Bellingham entered the lobby of the House of Commons, and when the prime minister appeared, shot him fatally in the chest. When asked "what could have induced him to do such a thing," he replied, "want of redress of grievance, and refusal by government." At the trial, the prisoner amplified this brief explanation: "I had no premeditated or personal malice towards that gentleman; the unfortunate lot had fallen upon him as the leading member of that administration which had repeatedly refused me any reparation for the unparalleled injuries I had sustained in Russia for eight years with the cognizance and sanction of the minister of the country at the court of St. Petersburg."[38]

Bellingham's preoccupation with his cruel treatment in Russia had unquestionably grown into what we would now call an obsession that culminated in the murder of the man who symbolized his political victimization. A character witness at the trial commented on Bellingham's "derangement" concerning his captivity in Russia: "[I]t is known to myself and Mr. Bellingham's friends that he has been in a state of perfect derangement with respect to this business he has been pursuing." The witness then recounted an episode involving a member of government that revealed "a strong mark of insanity."[39] The intriguing difference between this case and Hadfield's is the difference between a delusion and what the Bellingham judge called a fancy. Had Bellingham merely *believed* he had been incarcerated in a Russian prison and then held the prime minister responsible, the case might have been made that this "error" betokened a mind sufficiently deranged as not to carry responsibility for wrongful actions. Instead, Bellingham's memory of his very real imprisonment had apparently festered—then exploded—in a resentment so great that his rage required a target, even if that target bore no particular resentment or malice toward the prisoner.

In Lord Chief Justice Mansfield's eyes, however, this was not insanity (a defense raised not by Bellingham but by his friends on his behalf). After reminding the jurors that a man who could not distinguish between right and wrong, who was so "destitute of all power of judgment, could have no intention at all," he delineated various "species of insanity":

> Some human creatures are void of all power of reasoning from their birth, such could not be guilty of any crime. There is another species of madness in which persons were subject to temporary paroxysms, in which they were guilty of acts of extravagance, this was called lunacy, if these persons committed a crime when they were not affected with the malady, they were to all intents and purposes amenable to justice: so long as they can distinguish good from evil, so long are they answerable for their conduct. There is a third species of insanity, in which the patient fancied the existence of injury, and sought an opportunity of gratifying revenge, by some hostile act; if such a person were capable, in other respects, of distinguishing right from wrong, there is no excuse for any act of atrocity which he might commit under this description of derangement.[40]

The justice then enumerated all the "rational" acts Bellingham was capable of performing on the day he shot Perceval. Not only was the prisoner under no restraint or the care of a medical man, but he had come to London by himself, "was perfectly regular in all his habits, in short there was no proof adduced to shew that his understanding was so deranged, as not to enable him to know that murder was a crime."[41] Of course, Hadfield had also come to London on his own and was "regular [enough] in his habits" to escape attention when he waited in the Drury Lane Theatre for the king to arrive: in short, there was no proof to show that *his* understanding was so deranged that he could not know that murder was a crime. One difference between the two shootings was of course that one was fatal and one was not. (One might add that Bellingham's target was a more sympathetic victim, but that would be hard to prove.) But there was a major difference between the two impairments. Hadfield's perceptual confusion was termed a delusion, and when it was explained to the jury, the idea successfully introduced the notion that a legal wrong might not be perceived as such by an actor whose perceptual vision was profoundly distorted by a delusive lens. No such imagery attended Bellingham's "species of insanity." As described by Chief Justice Mansfield, the prisoner's error was a "fancy" and his consequent behavior "an opportunity to gratify revenge." Clearly, Bellingham's grievance did not involve religious visions or manipulation by a powerful co-conspirator. Still, one wonders what an Erskine might have made out of Bellingham's "derangement with respect to this business he has been pursuing," or how a different judge might have characterized Bellingham's "species of insanity." Indeed, the "species" Mansfield described with such authority had little or no resonance in the medical literature of the early nineteenth century. As described by the judge, such resentment would hardly qualify as a form of "derangement"; rather, it more resembled intemperance or an unresisted impulse.

Whatever Bellingham's actual mental distress, Mansfield's instructions demonstrate the power of the court to shape and set testimony in context, as well as to alert jurors to various points on which the law was "very clear." Evidence from the *OBSP* reveals that some judges at least took this part of their role very seriously and did not necessarily "lean against the prisoner." When they did, as in the Bellingham case and in others in which they pointedly drew jurors' attention to any "concealment," their bias and influence were evident. Regardless of whether they personally believed the prisoner to be mad or sane, when judges expressed a clear opinion on the matter, it appears that they expected the jury to ratify it rather than deliberate. After a lengthy summation, a judge in 1786 thought he was bringing matters to a close when he instructed, "I think that public justice will be satisfied, if after this long enquiry, on the ground of a temporary insanity, which this man had laboured under for four or five days before this fact, you think that this man is not guilty of the crime imputed to him in this indictment."[42] Far from assenting, the jury announced, "My Lord, we wish to go out," to which the judge testily replied, "Oh, if you wish to go out, I must state the evidence to you; because if you do not feel it at once in the way in which I have stated it, it is fit I should state the whole evidence to you." To no one's surprise, least of all today's reader of the *OBSP,* the jury "conferred a short time" before reaching the verdict "not guilty."

A PERFECT INSANITY?

But for the insistence under canon law that criminal responsibility must rest on both legal *and* moral guilt, a great deal of soul-searching might have been avoided in the English courtroom. By the standard of absolute liability, the insane, the young, and the fatally clumsy were equally culpable once it was established that they had committed the physical act. The act was the measure of harm done. Beginning with Henri de Bracton in the thirteenth century, and continuing to the early modern era, the conjoining of moral and legal guilt fashioned the idea of felonious intent, which came to sit at the heart of criminal responsibility. That the insane should be excused from the imputation of moral (and legal) guilt was clearly acknowledged. The *reason* they should escape censure was equally well established. What remained problematic, and increasingly so by the early 1700s, was the articulation of a level of impairment sufficient to warrant the excuse. There simply were no clearly defined, culturally recognized "species" of madness which, by their presence, constituted "legal" insanity. One person's delusion could well be another's fancy.

Although the medical historian is tempted to seize on the significance of an acquittal (or a conviction, for that matter) as a benchmark in the evolving jurisprudence of insanity, scrutiny of the *OBSP* leaves one wondering how any particular case might have fared with a different cast of characters and a somewhat differently disposed judge. This means not that a coherent legal disposition can never be adduced from a historical study of courtroom verdicts but rather that any inference regarding "the law's position on insanity" must be tempered with an awareness that however standard some instructions may appear, it took a jury of lay citizens to apply the principles and a judge who sometimes "interpreted" the evidence as he imparted these principles to produce a verdict. Any inference one hopes to draw from these verdicts must therefore begin with judicial instructions, which translated legal precepts into daily courtroom understanding.

What does a review of judicial instructions tell us? First, judges do not appear to have had a visceral reaction regarding the idea of insanity as a criminal defense: instructions from the bench both supported and rejected arguments regarding mental derangement. In most cases, jurors were advised on both sides of the issue and what they were to look for in the event they decided to convict or acquit. Although "evenhanded" instructions were given, it is not hard to discern a measure of bias on the part of a particular trial judge, from tendentious definitions of various "species" of derangement to such comments as "This is not the behavior of a madman, gentlemen, he rather overacts his part."[43] Second, judges most frequently invoked notions of "knowing the tendency of his behavior" and "knowing right from wrong" as the criteria juries should use in "finding" the requisite level of insanity. Both of these cognitive capacities flow directly from the law's concern with intentionality, but their practical use for a jury's deliberation can be only a matter of speculation. Short of manifest prevarication and obvious concealment, it is difficult to imagine how juries discerned either of these "signs" in rendering a determination regarding a prisoner's sanity. Direct evidence of being "regular in his habits" on the day of the crime seemed to suggest an awareness of what one was "about," and yet once delusion and other states of impaired consciousness entered the picture, it is doubtful if supposedly "purposeful" acts surrounding the crime actually revealed an actor aware of his or her "tendency."

"Knowing right from wrong" was trickier still. The judge in Samuel Burt's trial deftly employed this criterion to argue that the forger's painstaking effort to inform his victim of his crime might have revealed a man in distress, but a man who nonetheless knew that what he was doing was wrong—regardless of motivation.[44] But few judges had such compelling evidence of obvious design; most had to content themselves with instructions that stressed general notions of "state of mind," "being in one's senses," and the various conditions—natural and supernatural—that rendered a person "unknowing of what he does." Although a few judges cited Hale's stricture of "total derangement," no definitive clues for detecting such a threshold were given. Most juries were left to consider a range of mental states in their deliberations of what exactly the prisoner had intended. That the prisoner later "recovered" did not preclude the possibility of an earlier state of utter derangement. That the act was premeditated did not necessarily mean that the prisoner knew what he or she was "about." Instead, jurors were asked to consider the mental world of James Bellingham, William Walker, and Francis Paar from the vantage point of evidence adduced in each particular case and against the backdrop of historic legal tenets of knowing what one was "about" and "knowing right from wrong" as invoked by the judge. These defendants were in no way atypical of the period. Most prisoners occupied positions on a continuum of derangement well within the extremes of braying wild beasts at one end and brooding, Byronic melancholics at the other. That approximately half the prisoners who raised mental derangement as a defense in the late 1700s and early 1800s met with success suggests that however legal opinion might insist on the criterion of "total derangement" a good many prisoners well short of complete insanity were routinely acquitted by the courts. Judicial instructions regarding "tendency" and "knowing right from wrong" were apparently interpreted by juries to accommodate states of partial insanity as well. Why were juries willing to acquit defendants whose derangement fell noticeably short of the law's constant criterion of total insanity?

One suspects that London's citizens were applying widespread cultural understandings regarding madness the law had failed to recognize. Bracton's original conception of a "will to harm" rested on the conviction that man had control of his will. The only possible explanation for criminality was either total insanity (owing to some exceptional condition) or malicious intent. That the will could serve any master but its human possessor was not recognized or at least not acknowledged by the law. Cultural understandings about madness, in contrast, appeared to accept the notion of alternative possession—of a will that could be subverted by powerful passions or lead one into conscious though totally abhorrent action. The weakness in the law's strictures regarding insanity was that they rested on the firm conviction that someone could not be insane and still retain an awareness of what he or she was doing. Whatever such a state was called, the frequency of acquittals indicates that jurors were less convinced than Bracton and Hale that perfect insanity alone could account for unintended criminality.[45] These acquittals support T. A. Green's belief in a growing cultural recognition of constraints on human behavior and a reluctance to censure a prisoner for inhabiting a world that may have led him or her unwillingly into criminality. Were people witnessing an increasingly intelligible universe of madness that, though frightening, was also frighteningly *familiar?* It was after all to a universe shared by prisoner and juror that Frances Paar referred when he entreated the jury, "Gentlemen, we are none of us exempt from disease or accident; judge of me . . . as you would wish to be judged yourselves."

Insanity and Medical Psychology

*E*VEN IF JUDGES IN THE LATE 1700S AND EARLY 1800S HAD tried to supply juries with explicit criteria for "finding" insanity, they could hardly have looked to the contemporary medical literature for consistent definitions and universally accepted "symptoms." Although medical writers increasingly argued that madness was both understandable and even curable, the defining characteristics of mental derangement remained elusive. Was madness mere intellectual incoherence or defective control of impulses? Were the "perfectly" insane capable of committing a crime? What possible insight could the fledgling specialty of mental medicine provide into legal questions concerning criminal responsibility and the "will to harm"? For the medical historian, a final question presents itself: To what extent did medical opinion inform conventional beliefs about madness, and to what extent did it merely reflect them?

Roy Porter has persuasively argued that psychiatry was very much "shaped from below."[1] Mental disturbance had been an everyday fact of life since at least the Middle Ages; beliefs about mental derangement were deeply rooted in common culture, and it did not require a medical specialist to bring the cause and course of madness to light. Notions about physiognomy and character, for example, may have found articulation in Franz Joseph Gall and Johann Gaspar Spurzheim's medical tracts, but the "science of character" these phrenologists advanced was more a refinement and a systematization of folk beliefs than a bold hypothesis. The early nineteenth-century vogue for speaking about one's passions may similarly have found elaborate expression in the medical perspectives of Philippe Pinel and James Cowles Prichard, but the power of unruly feelings to unsettle the mind were standard lore among common folk. Further, those eighteenth-century Londoners who appropriated William Cullen's *nervous* terminology to describe the state of their nerves were in fact employing a medical vocabulary that was itself drenched in cultural metaphor, one that used the language of nerves for the purpose of social differentiation.[2] The man who was therefore anxious about his nerves or his wife's *passions,* or convinced that his clerk's head shape and facial features revealed character, was not set upon by medical theories imposed from above. If he read the medical texts at all, he would probably have nodded in agreement.

The growing corpus of medical texts was, however, something more than mere inventories of current folk beliefs about madness. Authors took elaborate care to situate mental derangement in a new mechanistic universe, attentive to scientific detail and, when possible, based in clinical experience. Still, the knowledge-base of psychiatry was informed by widely held convictions about the humors, religious demons, and skull fractures, as well as the popular belief that madness was a legible entity. Indeed, it is sometimes difficult to characterize as expert beliefs that so often resemble common sense; yet they were clearly fashioned to substantiate a specialist's way of knowing. Whoever constituted their intended audience, and whatever their professional or academic pedigrees, these medical authors provide a bridge to common cultural understandings about the many faces of derangement and afford a vital resource for speculating about how the English juror heard courtroom evidence and considered a judge's instructions. For our more immediate purposes, the medical literature of this period offers a key for understanding the significance of images and metaphors to be found in medical (and, not surprisingly, lay) testimony in insanity trials. Although only a few medical authors were actually named, conceptions of the mind associated with various schools of medical psychology are evident in the specialists' courtroom use of such terms as "moral insanity," "lesion of the will," and "monomania," as well as lay witnesses testifying to "a faulty connection between ideas," "violent passions," and a belief that "he was bidden to do it."

Just as there was no shortage of lay images and common understandings surrounding madness in eighteenth-century England, so literary, philosophical, and scientific writings about insanity abounded. Although courtroom images and metaphors must be situated in the medical lore and literature of the day, a comprehensive survey of medico-scientific ideas relative to insanity could easily fill several volumes. Thoughts about madness recapitulate fundamental themes in Western intellectual inquiry: the problematic relation between mind and body, the curious odyssey of the soul from religious to secular moorings after the Restoration, and repeated efforts to delineate the physiological and spiritual anatomy of melancholy, mania, and delirium. In this chapter I highlight four approaches to medical psychology that appear to have vied for scientific and popular acceptance in the years 1760–1843.[3]

First, a number of madhouse keepers and medical attendants expressed the nature of insanity in terms of intellectual delirium: faulty reasoning, loose connections between ideas, the ruling sway of a "predominant idea." Broadly termed *associationism,* this school addressed principles of thought common to all persons. A second school aimed to explain the opposite: the particularity of character that distinguished one person from another. The explanation for such idiosyncratic behavior was sought in pronounced physical alteration of specific organs of the brain. Among the behaviors of most interest to phrenologists were instances of derangement limited to a particular sentiment or idea and linked directly to extraordinary, seemingly inexplicable episodes of criminal behavior. A third school of medical psychology, which grew out of French asylum supervision, broke with the associationist tenet that madness was necessarily a matter of intellectual delirium and asserted instead the existence of a type of insanity that was unaccompanied by mental confusion. Finally, borrowing from both associationism and the French clinicians, a fourth approach posited a fully formed moral insanity, in which the afflicted person's moral sensibilities, not ideas per se, were altered. This insanity was revealed in the very absence of a motive for the outrageous act.

Each school carried particular significance for the discussion of criminal responsibility because each touched, in one way or another, the issue of partial insanity. The totally deranged, intellectually incoherent babbler was difficult neither to spot nor to explain in the eighteenth century. Their neighbor's eye and ear perceived unambiguous clues. From 1760 to 1843, however, the signs of madness in medical texts grew increasingly mysterious. The "partial" insanity associated most often with Hale's melancholic, insane "by degrees," was increasingly replaced by the circumscribed insanity of the felon deluded on just one subject, pathologically aroused by an irritation in only one brain organ, monomaniacally consumed by a singular idée fixe, or insane only in terms of the moral sentiments. Because these individuals exhibited sane functioning in all other concerns and thought, the temptation to refer to such a state as a partial insanity was very real but also very misleading, at least in terms of medical thought. When in the throes of the particular subject or idea, such a person was "mad as a hatter." The schools of thought are therefore important not only for the record they provide of the transition in medical psychological opinion regarding the possibility of a derangement limited to a particular area but also for the implications such opinion carried for the legal concern with human agency. Speculation regarding what the eighteenth-century prisoner *understood* about the nature of his or her actions squarely addressed the contemporary legal conception of human choice and responsibility: intent was inferred from the felon's probable knowledge of the circumstances surrounding the wrongful act and its likely consequences. "Control" of behavior was determined at the level of cognition: what the felon *knew* at the time of the crime.

When intellectual insanity receded as the exclusive species of derangement and an insanity of perverted sentiments and passions assumed an increasingly prominent place in medical writing, one could no longer infer intent from the offender's "knowledge" of the circumstances alone. Knowledge and (self) control could operate more or less independently. Embedded in efforts to account for the more recondite character of insanity, therefore, were direct implications for the assignment of individual criminal responsibility.

MADNESS AND PHYSICALISM

It has become commonplace to speak of the "protean face of madness" in histories of mental derangement, for the best of reasons: insanity has assumed a maddeningly expansive array of appearances, adroitly eluding attempts to discern its "true nature."[4] In one age, the melancholic, the manic, and the frenetic comprise the universe of derangement. In another, the religiously possessed, the delusional, and the suicidal capture the imagination of medico-scientific theorists. In still another, the monomaniac, the demonomaniac, and the tristemaniac come under the specialists' gaze. Whether associated with blood-flow, understimulation or overstimulation of the nerves, or a rich diet, madness has retained a link to physical distempers since antiquity. Although its effects might appear to be centered in the mind (or soul), for centuries lay and medical personnel placed the origin of the problem in some form—and location—of bodily malfunction. The earliest and certainly most enduring placement was advanced by the second-century Greek physician Galen, who maintained that all disease was traceable to a disturbance in the balance of the body's four humors—fluids that mediated communication between mind and body.[5] Each humor was correlated with a temperament, so that, for example, an excess of black bile was thought to be responsible for melancholia. The historic association of melancholy with darkness and gloom, fears and shadows, is traceable to its early and enduring association with the humor that gave it the name. Humoralism's influence was still felt seventeen centuries after Galen; contemporary references to persons as phlegmatic, choleric, sanguine, or melancholic provide ample evidence of the Western proclivity to associate temperament with bodily functioning and further evidence of the close correspondence between lay and specialist beliefs.[6]

Although humoralism has had a tenacious hold on Western thinking, by the end of the 1700s psychological contemplation about human beings was defined mostly in terms of anatomy and physiology, centering primarily on the nerves and their role in relaying external sensations to the brain.[7] The relation between such physiologically based psychology and philosophy's contemplation of the nature of madness highlights the intriguing connection between a generation of *nervous* scientists and the empirical rationalist John Locke.[8] This late seventeenth-century theorist conceived of the mind as a tabula rasa, housing no innate ideas and therefore dependent on the senses for "raw data" from the outside world. "Knowledge" was composed of sensory inputs that internal, mental operations eventually conjoined into ideas, conceptions, and associated thought chains. In Locke's opinion, madness was inherent not in the overthrow of reason but in the reasoning process itself: "[H]aving joined together some ideas very wrongly . . . [the mad] mistake them for Truths . . . as though incoherent ideas have been cemented together so powerfully as to remain united."[9] For eighteenth-century psychologists, the operation of "right reason" therefore required the orderly and uninterrupted flow of physical stimulation to the senses, which in turn relayed to the brain the appropriate mental images (ideas) for proper consideration.

Although Locke's schema and the derivative school of associationism found general acceptance in the marketplace of medico-psychological ideas in the late eighteenth and early nineteenth centuries, one of his images remained especially influential: the marked discrepancy between the insane person's conception of the world and external reality. Whether they called it "deluded imagination," "notional insanity," or "an erroneous association of ideas on particular subjects," late eighteenth-century medical writers (and some medical witnesses) invoked a Lockean conception of the insane as those who "reasoned from false premises."[10] Certainly there were forms of derangement more global in scope than an error in perception and belief; raving lunatics were clearly afflicted with more than (mere) deluded belief.[11] Ranters and lunatics, after all, were ubiquitous in folklore. Locke's faulty reasoners, however, suggested another, potentially more challenging mystery to decode: the possibility of derangement limited in scope, which rendered the afflicted totally insane only when the subject of the error was touched on. At that moment—and only so long as their mind was turned to the error—the deluded were "much out of [their] mind as any person that was in Bedlam."[12]

The increasingly recognized form of distraction known as derangement particular to one subject was not "partial" in terms of degree of derangement—that is, classic melancholia—or in terms of its effects. When in its throes, the sufferer was totally mad. Yet it is clear from judicial instructions in the late 1700s that the term *partial* referred to any variant of mental impairment short of classic raving mania. These judicial instructions became increasingly unhelpful as such culturally familiar terms as *mania* and *melancholia* were scrutinized by a new generation of medical practitioners whose professional experiences with the insane through asylum superintendency differed qualitatively from the infrequent encounters with the deranged of most general physicians, surgeons, and apothecaries. The opportunities these new professional experiences offered for sustained observation and comparison of different "species" of insanity (in Mansfield's terms) translated into a host of new terms and explanations about the causes and "natural history" of madness. In some cases, echoes of Locke come through loud and clear. In others, radically new forms of materialism and mentalism are evident. Common to all, however, was a growing interest in discarding traditional notions of partial insanity in favor of concepts thought to reflect more accurately the communication between mind and body. Specifically, the new classifications reveal a growing interest in the complex relation between thought and volition. Fundamental to centuries of Western legal theorizing about the attribution of criminal responsibility, the autonomy of the will was increasingly scrutinized as the natural hierarchy of the mind over the passions began to erode.

ASSOCIATIONISM AND FORMS
OF PARTIAL INSANITY

In the eighteenth century, medical writers most often employed the term *delirium* to signify the disordered behavior and verbal pandemonium associated with madness. Of Latin origin, *delirium* (*de lira*) literally means "out of the furrow." The delirious had strayed off the (mental) track, much as a plow animal might stray out of the furrow. The term also conveyed the similarity between madness and the mental distraction of a person in the throes of a high fever. In fact, "delirium without fever" was a common description of madness.[13] By the 1700s, delirium had come to be associated with fears and preoccupations derived from prolonged and unequal stimulation of the nerves that relayed sensory stimuli to the brain. As a result of aberrant *nervous* excitation, mental images became distorted, the memory could no longer recollect the orderly association of ideas, and the sufferer was left in delirious confusion.

In 1749 David Hartley drew together scientific opinion regarding the centrality of nerves to nervous disease, speculation about the gross anatomy of the nervous system, and Newton's doctrine of vibration to describe the relation between neural activity and mental processing.[14] The implications for insanity were direct and immediate: as the rational mind depends on an accurate "reading" of external reality through the proper excitation of nervous fibers that transport the stimulation to the senses, so insanity must result from defective stimulation—excessive and prolonged—which materially alters the vibration of the nerves. The incredibly rapid succession of ideas precludes sober reflection and deliberation. The brain is bombarded with thoughts, and confusion ensues as the afflicted person either misconstrues the motives of others or delusively constructs an imminent threat to his or her life. Such fundamental errors in perception were also highlighted by William Battie, physician to St. Luke's Hospital, who described derangement as "deluded imagination": "[T]hat man and that man alone is properly mad, who is fully and unalterably persuaded of the Existence or of the appearance of any thing, which either does not exist or does not actually appear to him, and who behaves according to such erroneous persuasion." The afflicted person's "erroneous persuasion" was directly traceable to the constitution of the nervous substance. "Before an external object can create any sensation whatever, it must produce several intermediate effects: motion, impulse, and pressure." The insane person's delusive construction of events was therefore sought in physiological malfunction: the mechanisms of sensation. "Something must be impressing itself on the particles of the medullary substance."[15]

It is vital to remember the materialist underpinnings of Battie's well-known formulation, "deluded imagination," to refer to the disorder of the nervous substance responsible for the erroneous perception by the senses and the resulting misassociation with a mental idea. Battie's use of *delusion* more closely resembles the eighteenth-century conception of delirium—distorted perception and errors in cognition—than that of later writers, who increasingly restricted delusion to circumscribed intellectual error. Thomas Arnold, another madhouse physician, speculated on forms of insanity, anticipating the use of *delusion* to signify derangement limited to a particular topic. In an effort to delineate various "species" of insanity, Arnold stressed Locke's contention that sensation *and* reflection constituted the sources of human knowledge.[16] The human mind was either "employed" with objects of sensation—represented in the mind as ideas or images of sensory products—or "occupied" with the objects of reflection, which Arnold called "notions." The term refers to whatever the mind perceives or discovers, or *thinks* it perceives or discovers. Disturbances in either source of knowledge constitute separate forms of insanity. "Ideal insanity" closely resembled Battie's formulation: a state of mind in which the individual imagines that he or she sees, hears, or otherwise perceives things that do not exist. This form of insanity seems to come closest to the contemporary use of the term *hallucination.* Ideal insanity was therefore primarily a sensory disturbance, resulting in unnatural and bizarre associations about misperceived sensory products.

"Notional insanity," in contrast, owed its existence to the reflective power of the mind. A person so afflicted perceived external objects that actually exist in the universe, but "conceives such notions of the powers, properties and designs of things and persons as appear obviously and often grossly erroneous to the common sense of the sober and judicious part of mankind." Where the person in the grip of ideal insanity knows no more of his or her physical surroundings than a person in the delirium of a fever, one who is notionally insane "properly perceives, and distinguishes [external] objects, knows where he is and who are about him." Arnold places "delusive insanity" here because of its uniquely reflective features, "without the smallest distinguishable trace of ideal delirium . . . [and] . . . with the sound and unimpaired use, in every other respect, of the rational faculties . . . the patient, in relation to some particular subject or subjects, is under the influence of the most palpable and extraordinary delusion."[17]

The use of the word "patient" is worth noting here. Arnold's professional gaze, like Battie's, was informed by his experience as a madhouse keeper. Although medical philosophers since antiquity had commented on a form of madness that could exist alongside the afflicted person's sane understanding in all other matters, Arnold's use of "delusion" to signify errors in judgment limited to a particular subject was grounded in the newly emerging specialist's unique experience. Certainly *delusion* was not a new term, although its meaning could range from a misperception of sensory input (illusions or hallucinations) to a misconstruing of an event or a notion to a preoccupation with a haunting fear or a threatening idea. The historic association of delusion with fear dates at least to the Greek conception of melancholia: a state of mind consumed with the prophecy of doom and catastrophe. The conjoining of delusive fear with melancholia—often concerning abandonment by God—continued into the Middle Ages and beyond. In the seventeenth century, Robert Burton grouped religious delusions, idiosyncratic religious beliefs, and obsessive religious anxieties under the category "religious melancholia."[18]

Although Arnold was interested in delineating separate states of derangement, for him the ancients' employment of such terms as *delirium, mania,* and *melancholy* reflected a lamentably imprecise diction: "I cannot in this place forbear taking notice of the latitude which the ancients often allowed themselves in the use of words: in which, indeed, too many of the moderns, partly from the poverty of language . . . have followed their example."[19] His introduction of ideal and notional insanity sought to ground clinically based observations in a Lockean framework of how the mind functioned: through sensation and reflection. Where ideal insanity clearly resonated with historic images of raving delirium, notional insanity was given a home (if not a particularly convincing explanation regarding its supposed circumscribed properties) in the dominant discourse of sensation and associated abnormal ideas.

Other contemporary medical writers focused on distinguishing forms of madness other than generalized delirium. Birmingham physician John Johnstone isolated the critical presence of a "predominant idea." In madness, "external objects make nearly the same impression as when the mind is whole, till the hallucination (the predominant idea) interferes and deranges all the trains of thought with which it is intermixed." In delirium, there was no one predominant idea, only "a wild and incoherent jumble of ideas."[20] The power of a ruling idea was also the focus of George Edward Male, a founder of English medical jurisprudence. Insanity, he wrote in 1818, "may be called a delusion, or an erroneous association of ideas on particular subjects."[21] Sometimes referred to as the essence of insanity, sometimes used to delineate a species apart from generalized delirium, *delusion* appeared with greater frequency in medical texts at the dawn of the nineteenth century, clearly betokening the conviction of a number of well-published medical authors that limited forms of insanity, particularly an insanity limited to particular beliefs, existed.[22]

Medical opinion, however, was far from unanimous on the possibility of a circumscribed derangement. One of the period's most voluble maddoctors, John Haslam, apothecary of Bethlem, pointedly rejected the notion. The insane, Haslam wrote, were equally deranged on a wide variety of subjects. The apparent "display of rationality" was but a lucid interval. Let the conversation be extended, let the discourse drift to "the favorite subject . . . afloat in the mad man's brain, and [the observer] will be convinced of the hastiness of his decision." Haslam argued that "intensity of idea" did not distinguish mania from melancholia; "equal derangement" reigned in both types of madness; "partial insanity" was indeed a mistaken "sensory perception" on the part of the *observer*. If medical writers believed that partial insanity could co-exist with "apparent rationality" on all other subjects, such diagnoses revealed the superficiality of their interaction with the distracted. Yet Haslam did acknowledge the existence of gradations in impairment. There were times, for example, when the mad could "conduct themselves with propriety, and in a short conversation will appear sensible and coherent." Such episodes, which Haslam was willing to call "lucid intervals," did not, however, signify a return to sanity. When the trained observer persisted in the interview, it soon became apparent that "the smallest rivulet flows into the great stream of derangement." In contrast to the sufferer who knew no cessation in his torment, such persons might be described as "partially insane," but there was no doubt that for Haslam, the operative term in the diagnosis of partial insanity was *insanity*.[23]

For other medical writers, partial insanity consisted not of alternating states of delirium and lucidity but of derangement confined to a predominant idea, or "notional" insanity confined to a certain subject. But a materialist grounding for this particularity in thought disturbance was not forthcoming. Given Hartley's initial physiological model, which drew together nerve endings, vibrations in the nervous fluid, the senses, the brain, and associated mental images, it was not at all clear how the mind could be deranged on only one subject. Even at the level of "proper associations" and unproblematic "combination of ideas," considerable difficulties remained. How did ideas form, and where did they lodge? In part, the problem could be traced to Hartley's less-than-explicit nexus between physiological sensation and associated mental ideation. These sensations, he wrote, "leave certain vestiges . . . or images of themselves, which may be called, Simple Ideas of Sensation."[24] But how did sensations "leave" ideas behind, and where were these ideas stored, to be recalled later by other, associated ideas? Without a conception of the brain that allowed for the storage of discrete ideas—any of which was capable of independent distortion—partial insanity, either delusive or notional, was difficult to square with the associationist model.

Associationist tenets also failed to address two important issues with legal implications. Did the will play a role in the construction of a "train of thought," or did ideas "cement" themselves independent of individual volition? James Mill saw a role for the will in calling up an idea independent of association or in compelling one idea to elicit another.[25] Associationist psychology, however, did not accommodate a vital, conscious will, mediating between thought and action. The second limitation concerned the "generalist" scope of associationism. Associationism was at best a schema with which to comprehend general theories of perception and cognition. How could the model address the singular thought and behavior characteristic of the more exaggerated forms of insanity—for example, as seen in outrageous and *uncharacteristic* criminal behavior? This shortcoming was the starting point for the next school of medical psychology.

PHRENOLOGY AND THE SEARCH
FOR INDIVIDUAL DIFFERENCE

The very strength of associationism—that it offered an explanation of thought processes common to all humans—was a severe limitation when the issue of individual variation was posed, an issue fundamental to the legal assessment of the criminal lunatic's capacity for thought and choice. In contrast, a second school of medical psychology used individual variation as its starting premise. Identifying no fewer than twenty-seven faculties of the mind, each with a corresponding organ in the brain, noted neuroanatomist Franz Joseph Gall proposed a model that sought to account for specificity of character and behavior. Although he was not the first physician to assert that the brain was the organ of the mind, Gall was unique in arguing the mind's dependence on the brain in such detail.[26] Human intellectual and moral propensities, he believed, were situated in the physical organization of the brain. Individual variation in talent, intellectual acumen, and emotional control were directly traceable to the peculiar physical development of the cerebral organs that housed each faculty. The explanation for human functioning therefore shifted from a focus on the process of human thought to a consideration of internal instincts and propensities.

According to Gall and the phrenologists who followed him, Locke's view of madness—disordered reason and erroneous judgment—referred only to persons suffering a general aberration or a complete insanity. To account for more localized, restricted forms of derangement, one had to seek the particularity of character in the dominance of one or more of the twenty-seven determinate organ-faculties. Because these organs functioned independently, any one psychological faculty could be separately deranged.[27] A criminal act committed by an otherwise kind and gentle person could be attributed to a pathological "organ of self preservation," an organ of "sexual gratification," or an organ of "cunning." Some physical alteration in the organ—overdevelopment or underdevelopment—was discoverable either by cranial inspection or by autopsy. The explanation, then, could not be more straightforward: the associated psychological faculty had (of course) been distorted because its sensory messages had been refracted through a damaged organ.

Although individual eccentricities and prodigious talents (or *appetites*) were obviously grist for the phrenologists' mill, criminality afforded immediate and intelligible examples of seemingly inexplicable behavior. Phrenological texts in the second and third decade of the nineteenth century fairly brimmed with instances of the killing of beloved infants and cherished lovers or the stealing of unwanted items.[28] Such "uncharacteristic" acts were readily explainable by a conception of a mind governed by autonomous proclivities. Indeed, the notion of insanity limited in scope to a particular idea or set of notions could not have found a more accommodating home than in the fledgling school of phrenology, which frequently invoked seemingly inexplicable criminal acts committed by reasonable people as evidence of the independence of cerebral organization. Further, the phrenologists' attention to two specific elements directly implicated legal conceptions of culpability: an incapacity to distinguish the presence of diseased functions of the mind and the "irresistibility of action." According to asylum keeper David Uwins, one's inability to recognize an error in thinking—commonly termed *delusion*—was the "pivot upon which insanity turns." Without delusion "we may be many things"—melancholic or criminal, perhaps—but "we are not mad."[29]

Gall's fellow phrenologist J. G. Spurzheim stressed the second element, irresistibility, in addition to intellectual error. He alluded particularly to this characteristic in recounting the tale of a man who pleaded with his intimates to restrain him, "[his] propensity to murder was quite involuntary."[30] This derangement, however, was limited to the will: no alienation of memory, imagination, or judgment was present. Although Spurzheim usually defined insanity in both cognitive and volitional terms, it was apparent that sometimes the "knowing" insane could be "carried away" to perform acts for no rational purpose. It was the precise nature of being "carried away" that sat at the heart of phrenology's peculiar relation to criminal responsibility. In a phrenological tract of 1838, George and Andrew Combe—representing medicine and law—commented on convicted murderer Richard Dean's cerebral organs and the effect of variations in size on Dean's functioning:

> [T]he different mental faculties are here seen acting like so many limbs of an automaton, when their different organs happen to be excited by external objects, those which are largest taking the lead. Thus Amativeness, and apparently Adhesiveness, excite Destructiveness, and Dean first resolved to kill Sarah Longman. Impelled . . . by the diseased energy of his large Destructiveness, he could not refrain from murder . . . After giving scope to Destructiveness, his moral organs came into action, and he was overwhelmed with remorse, and gave himself up to the police. His subsequent conduct shews the continued diseased action of his various organs. He prayed fervently,—a manifestation of his large Veneration; he lamented [his putative lover's] exposure to a wicked world,—a manifestation of his Benevolence and Adhesiveness, he spoke of Voltaire and Tom Paine as in hell,—a manifestation of Destructiveness . . . In short, his whole conduct is marked by the strongest

indications of insanity, and I do not envy either the state of intellectual illumination or the feelings of judge and jury who sent him to the scaffold as a criminal, rather than to an asylum as a lunatic. After a knowledge of Phrenology has reached the public mind, such an exhibition as this will be impossible.[31]

It is impossible to miss the unqualified materialist determinism in the Combes' language: "Impelled . . . by the diseased energy [of a cerebral organ]," "limbs of an automaton" "could not refrain." The clear implication of such a rendering of the mind was that the individual was powerless to resist the action of the diseased organ. Yet Gall had been explicit at the outset that it was not the organ that induces murderous acts but rather a "weakened capacity to withstand the impulsion." Nature, after all, was the source of our propensities, faculties, and sentiments. Moral evil and aggressive propensities were inherent in human nature and were not necessarily brought into play by the organ of destructiveness.[32] Yet such statements begged the question of what the organ's role was in generating the nefarious deed. To claim that the size of the organ corresponds to the dominance of its associated faculty in the organization of character inescapably suggests that size equates with influence. Further, if we all share innate destructive urges, how does the organ of destructiveness contribute to (dictate?) the course of behavior? Gall called the cerebral organ "the material condition which renders the manifestation of a faculty possible," yet he was less clear regarding the nature of the relation between faculty and organ. The founder of phrenology may have tried to preclude accusations of (godless) materialism by his vow "not [to] investigate the nature of soul and body," yet traces of just such a connection are evident in phrenological tracts in the late 1830s.[33] One finds not "innate faculty" or "natural propensity" in these works but an array of socially undesirable organs—"propensity to conceal," "propensity to hoard"—and their associated faculties, which bide their time, poised to strike. Although humans are not responsible for having propensities, phrenologists such as Gall, Spurzheim, and George Combe maintained that they *are* capable of comparing and choosing among motives, hence the crucial importance of proper socialization.[34] Where the capacity to select among ideas and decide to act was impaired, the individual was insane, although Gall for one was never very specific regarding how much alteration necessarily restricted criminal responsibility.

No such reticence afflicted phrenology's eager proselytizers, however. Writing in 1832, Forbes Winslow avers that "the slightest departure from a healthy condition of the brain giving rise to deranged mental manifestation, in my opinion, ought to be looked upon as insanity."[35] The problem, of course, was that no one knew what a "healthy condition" of the brain *felt* like; phrenologists simply asserted that the cranium *appeared* to be augmented over the relative location of the organ "responsible" for the act. A depression on the skull could also explain the foul deed because it betokened *under*development in, perhaps, the "organ of amativeness." For still other crimes, the direction in the variation of organ size seemed to contradict the expected relation, but an explanation could always be found. A woman who killed her child was found to have an enlarged "organ of parental love," quickly explained as a "too intense" love for the child. Abnormal size was clearly the key: alterations in either direction promised a ready explanation.

The popularity of phrenology is easily understood. The promise of a "science of character" has always intrigued, whether the clues are found in the lines in one's palms or the position of one's stars.[36] For Gall and his followers, "personhood" devolved into an assortment of determinate faculties and a comprehensible map of cerebral organs. Armed with a chart of the cranium and appropriately labeled organs, one could read the vagaries of human character "like a book." Indeed, the fit of "specialist" knowledge with enduring cultural beliefs was never closer. Physiognomy has long been held to contain the secrets of inner states: the utter transparency of blushing, for example, or the bulging eye (bovinus occulus), which revealed mania it its most legible form.[37] The considerable popularity of phrenology in the second quarter of the nineteenth century did not, however, extend to everyone. Gall's credentials as a neuroanatomist could carry this "science of behavior" only so far—the simple truth remained that he could not demonstrate the existence of "determinate organs." In addition, his psychology of innate faculties had the same shortcoming as previous explanations of mental functioning that relied on inborn, inductive mental capacities: circularity. Such accounts confused classification with explanation. Still, Spurzheim's public lectures and publications eventually reached a wide audience, offering an intriguing conception of a modular mind that could house the proclivity for sweeping derangement while the afflicted person appeared sane in all other faculties.

"Partial alienation" to Gall was not a matter of lucid intervals: it was not the ebb and flow of derangement that happened to leave the individual in a lucid condition in particular moments. Partial insanity was, rather, the sweep of mental disorder once a particular idea sparked the corresponding intellectual or diseased organ of the brain.[38] Moments of calm were not resting periods between deranged outbursts but sanity itself. This derangement was partial only in its geography of the mind: at times discovered, at others circumnavigated. Such insane persons could neither recognize it for what it was nor resist its terrible power. The idea of a partial insanity, however, defied clear and continuous definition—just as madness and its associated states (delirium, mania, lunacy) were rarely defined with precision or consistency. The delineation between total and partial insanity appears to have originated in the distinction between mania and melancholy, and yet here, too, the differences seem more apparent than real. True maniacs—those historically distinguished from melancholics by the violence of their affect—were not climbing the walls or drooling on their keepers twenty-four hours a day. They had spells of quiet repose in which conversation was possible and social intercourse not unheard of. Phrenology's contribution to this conception of an insanity limited to a particular subject was the proffering of a modular mind, capable of housing isolated, raving delirium that nonetheless left the afflicted person sane in all other subjects.

Gall's equivocation regarding the nature of the impelling force of a diseased faculty or organ and the individual's capacity to resist it meant that phrenology had an ambiguous relation to criminal responsibility. In lectures on "illusive liberty" and free agency, Gall's failure to articulate a persuasive argument for exempting from accountability a person with a diminutive "organ of philoprogenitiveness" begged the question of phrenology's true significance for legal culpability. Still, although Gall's characterization of circumscribed derangement may have been too formulaically drawn (the twenty-seven determinate organs seem to have existed more in Gall's *mind* than in people's *brains*), his model of separate and discrete psychological functions kept current the debate concerning partial alienation: the possibility that madness resided only in one area or idea.

MÉDECINE MENTALE ET DÉLIRE PARTIEL

Where Gall evinced a certain diffidence, a circle of physicians in France showed no such reluctance to formulate a conception of insanity in which derangement of will and feeling existed *independent* of mental impairment. This assertion in fact appeared to bolster phrenological attempts to depict an insanity in which deranged individuals were horrified by what they were doing yet were powerless to stop. In such a state, however, some form of mental incoherence—usually delusion—was routinely thought to have been present. In stark contrast, Philippe Pinel coined the term *manie sans délire* to denote a condition in which the individual was under the dominance of an abstract fury yet suffered no accompanying "lesion of understanding." In putting forward an exclusively *affective* insanity, Pinel and his two principal followers, Jean-Etienne-Dominique Esquirol and Etienne-Jean Georget, challenged not only the centrality of reason to human functioning but, by implication, the requisite mental element that comprised felonious intention. Pinel expressly based his innovative rendering of a nonintellectualist insanity on sustained and repeated conversations with asylum inmates; he concluded that understanding could remain unaffected while the sufferer was carried away by a force (the will?) beyond reason's power to restrain.[39] Although he did not fully draw out the implications of his theory for forensic law, manie sans délire made it much harder to discern the actor's intent. Since mental coherence could remain intact while the afflicted person was swept away by emotions, how could one gauge the presence of purposeful resolve from mere observation of behavior or casual conversation? How does an autonomous will reveal itself to the onlooker?

The diagnosis that best symbolized the innovative departure of the new French school was *monomanie*. Pinel's student Esquirol coined this term in 1817 in an effort to refine the centuries-old standard name for partial insanity, melancholia. Partly because of its equally long association with black bile—an increasingly *unscientific* connection, given the rapid decline in the popularity of humoral theory—and partly because of its traditional association with a gloomy and sorrowful demeanor, Esquirol chose to drop the term altogether. The diagnosis of monomania retained the former melancholic preoccupation with a particular subject but combined the state of *monomaniacal* absorption with an excitable, indeed expansive, disposition.[40] Had Esquirol stopped here, it would be hard to see *monomanie* as a significant departure from Cullen's "partial insanity" and Arnold's "notional insanity," since all three seemed to share a common defect of understanding. (Pinel's original metaphor—a "lesion of understanding"—drew on fashionable developments in medical theory concerning the specificity of diseases.) But intellectual error was only one form of monomania. There were also *monomanie instinctive* and *monomanie affective*. Independent of the intellect, the emotions and the will could suffer "lesions," rendering the afflicted helpless to "reason" his or her way out of derangement. The intellect was not suspended but *overridden*. Esquirol described persons in this state who "perform acts and hold odd, strange and absurd conversations, which they regard as such, and for which they censure themselves."[41]

Unlike Gall and other phrenologists who addressed only indirectly the implications of their schema of mind and body for questions of free will and criminal responsibility, Esquirol—and especially his student, Georget—contemplated the full legal implications of an "impaired volitional faculty." The interests of law were perhaps most directly challenged by

Georget's neologism *monomanie homicide,* which propelled its victims into murder and its proponents into turbulent border wars not only with the legal community but within medical circles as well. On grounds of logic alone, homicidal monomania was a problematic concept. If faculty psychology had long been criticized for its circular reasoning, homicidal monomania had to appear suspect as an "explanation" for murder. It also looked ludicrous and dangerous. "The need to murder to satisfy passions or perhaps a system is not illness or insanity. The doctrine of monomania tries to excuse crime by crime itself."[42] Monomania was thus forcefully denounced by the lawyer Hannequin and by representatives of the medical community who questioned the existence of this separate category of insanity. Homicidal monomania appeared to some medical writers as so much "murderous fury," not as an insane state that should preclude responsibility. "There is crime on the part of a madman when the means of carrying out the act have been weighed and carried out in order to satisfy a desire that is contrary to the eternal moral law."[43] Urbain Coste, a medical contemporary of Georget, was especially anxious about the effect homicidal monomania would have on the definition of criminal responsibility, and eventually broadened his critique of the concept to a questioning of alienists' "special capacity" to enlighten the court about matters of mental medicine: "The truth is that any honest man would be as competent in the matter as Mr. Pinel or Mr. Esquirol, and would have the advantage of being free from scientific prejudice . . . [these doctors] substitute for the light of natural reason the ambitious ignorance of the schools."[44] Lawyers and jurists were particularly dismissive of this "species" of insanity, not only because evidence of monomania could hardly be forthcoming except in the criminal act itself but also owing to the bedrock legal conviction that insanity was a matter of intellectual delirium. A man was not insane unless he "has lost either the consciousness of his own being or way of being, or of his social condition, or the relations of outside objects to himself and to each other."

The legal response to monomanie homicide was generated in large part by Georget's formulation: "lesion of the will." The notion that the will could be diseased was beyond the pale for the judiciary: it seemed to dismiss the very question of self-control and moral management. First articulated in 1825, when Georget distinguished affective and ideational components of monomania, lesion of the will became the subject of a number of publications later in the decade and a recurrent theme for asylum superintendents who claimed that their professional experience afforded them the opportunity to distinguish the existence of nondelirious insanity.[45] To bolster their claims, medical writers quoted patients who expressed an utter helplessness in the face of a will out of control:

"Je ne puis m'empêcher; c'est plus fort que moi! (I couldn't help myself; it is stronger than me!).''[46]

The often vitriolic tenor of the debate surrounding lesion of the will and monomanie homicide was animated by a host of concerns. There was the obvious logical difficulty of trying to explain a crime (and the consequent legal difficulty of absolving a putatively insane malefactor) by positing an autonomous disease or lesion. One has only to think of parallel crime-driven pathologies: a rape *impulse,* a forgery *lesion,* a pickpocket *paroxysm.* Further, the only evidence of the "disease" was the crime, suggesting the sort of circularity that dogged faculty psychology. Then there was the collateral concern of blurring the line between insanity and criminality, with the obvious implication that *all* criminal actions could be eventually declared the result of some mental affliction. Ultimately, one must confront the inescapable problem of an (exclusively) emotional insanity, a phenomenon that left consciousness intact. Lawyers as well as general physicians found a truly emotional insanity dangerously wrong. Histrionic displays had always been traceable, at least theoretically, to intellectual delirium. Indeed, Esquirol himself had initially been reluctant to accept the notion of a monomania devoid of intellectual delirium.[47] Jan Goldstein sees a professionally driven motive in Esquirol's change of heart: the need to close ranks around Georget and his embattled concept and to formulate a nosology particular to alienists that would legitimate their claims to unique knowledge.[48]

The concept of monomanie homicide certainly brought forensic psychiatrists and the law into sharp disagreement, encouraging *médecins aliénistes* to form a united front against the harsh criticism of the legal community. But one suspects that the concept was not difficult for alienists to defend. Monomanie homicide stemmed from the role Pinel attributed to the passions and the imagination in fashioning behavior. An individual in the throes of manie sans délire was swept into a furious state by a pathological turn of the passions or perhaps by a "diseased" imagination. This formulation reveals a major "disaggregation" of the mind's elements: as insanity became "de-intellectualized," reason separated from will, and emotions separated from reason.[49] Pinel's appointments at the Parisian hospitals Bicêtre and the Salpêtrière provided the first clinical setting for sustained interaction between medical observers and the insane, an opportunity for a comparison of like and dissimilar cases. These experiences, one suspects, led to a reconsideration of prevailing notions of will, intellect, and emotion, eventually producing a set of new mental states: manie sans délire and monomanie affective, instinctive, intellectuelle, and, eventually, homicide.[50]

That a novel milieu was the setting for professional claims to cognitive insight does not mean Pinel and his circle merely "read nature" in the minds of the mad. Nor should the intellectual context in which new forms of insanity were envisioned and denominated suggest that Pinel and his circle were disinterested clinicians with no stake in the eventual classification of insanity. Any efforts to gauge the influence of socially driven interests purportedly revealed in a nondelirious insanity, however, must be at least as attentive to the opportunity for unprecedented sustained interaction between asylum physicians and patients—the ability to compare like and dissimilar cases—as it is to self-interested ambition of the classifiers. Whatever professionally driven exigency operated to "find" monomania (and other variants of a nondelirious insanity), the clinicians' *mania* for diagnosis had to accommodate the verbal and behavioral expressions exhibited in a hitherto unavailable population of inmate-patients. One suspects, therefore, that professional ambition is only part of the story. The historian of medicine who seeks to reconstruct the creation of novel "ways of seeing" (and classifying) must also consider the resource of human "material" found in asylums and the possibilities this population afforded a generation of keepers eager to transcend a mere custodial function.[51]

The critics of monomania eventually succeeded in diminishing medical enthusiasm for this neologism: by the 1850s, asylum registers reveal a sharp drop-off in asylum admittees with this diagnosis.[52] Still, monomania in all its variations signified the first break in the tradition of insanity as necessarily an intellectual disturbance. The new medical conceptualization carried both direct and *expressed* implications for the problematic attribution of criminal responsibility. Monomania was of course a version of the partial insanity concept, except that the individual while in its throes suffered a full-blown derangement. It would no longer be sufficient to report that an individual was aware of the nature and consequences of his or her behavior because intent—that is, choice—could not be inferred from cognition alone.

THE DISEASED WILL AND MORAL INSANITY

Although Georget's conception of a lesion of the will may have fallen on hostile ears in France, several medical writers in England found common cause with the attention paid to the passions and defective impulse control. James Cowles Prichard, an English physician trained in Edinburgh, enlarged the focus of the debate regarding the nature of insanity by declaring the emotions (or passions) to be "another class of mental phenomena distinct in their nature from ideas."[53] Although he freely conceded that some forms of madness were confined to disordered intellectual faculties, Prichard contended that pathology could exist in "a morbid perversion of the feelings, affections, and active powers, without any illusion or erroneous conviction impressed upon the understanding: it sometimes co-exists with an apparently unimpaired state of the intellectual faculties."[54] The moral character and morbid feelings themselves were (separately) deranged. By moral insanity, Prichard meant

> The loss of voluntary power over the succession of ideas [which] is so great in a certain period of dementia, that the individual affected is incapable by an effort of mind of carrying on the series of thoughts to the end of a sentence or proposition. He hears a question, apprehends sometimes its meaning, and attempts to answer; but before he has uttered the half of his reply, his mind becomes confused and bewildered, some accidental suggestion turns aside the current of his ideas, which are too loosely associated to remain, even in a short train, coherent: his expressions become consequently absurd and irrelevant.[55]

Prichard rejected the materialism inherent in the early associationism of Hartley, substituting ideas borrowed from the Scottish school of "common sense" philosophy. For Prichard, this meant a return to a conception of the mind as constituted by innate, inductive faculties.[56] Inherent faculties of attention, memory, and comparison actively sorted, arranged, and stored the ideas that were the basis for knowledge. Another faculty, imagination, was particularly vulnerable to excitement by the passions and the emotions, resulting in a mind disturbed in its capacity to compare (among ideas, between reality and fantasy) and to judge. When reason is thus "dethroned," the will is no longer restrained by judgment, and the sufferer is *driven* mad by his or her passions.

John Conolly, physician to Hanwell Asylum, also used tenets of faculty psychology in his medical writing. He specifically isolated the faculty of comparison (among such other faculties as attention, memory, and imagination) in his treatise on insanity of 1830: "the madman concludes that what is only illusion is reality." When the faculty of comparison cannot be exerted, when the sufferer cannot examine and revise his "morbid association, respecting the motives of friends or relatives," the mind is no longer sane. The culprits, according to Conolly, were the passions and the emotions, which so excited the imagination that the victim's mind was distracted by "a direct impairment of the composing power, and consequently, the judgment."[57]

The passions clearly had autonomous power to produce madness. In the state of "instinctive madness" the sufferer did not fail to understand that actions were wrong because he or she was "confused" or "deluded."

Indeed, Prichard explicitly and repeatedly disparaged the courts' increasing reliance on delusion as the "sign" of insanity. In his opinion, the intellect was in a far different state: the "moral" in moral insanity referred to a perversion of the natural feelings and sentiments, not an error in perceiving the moral wrongfulness of the act. Emphasis on emotional derangement did not necessarily mean that the afflicted person was clearheaded: when the passions possessed the mind, there was a "disordered exercise of the intellectual faculties."[58] Still, whatever intellectual delirium existed, moral insanity was primarily an alienation of feelings, of natural sentiments, of how one ought to *feel* in social life.[59] The questions such a characterization of the mind left unanswered were themselves *maddening*. How does one account for an awareness of one's actions without a corresponding exercise of comprehension and understanding? How did the morally insane suffer a suspension of the mind's faculties but not an absence of consciousness?[60] Prichard's image of the morally insane is somewhat akin to being a bystander at one's own crime: not unmindful that you are carrying out some horrific deed, but oblivious to the thoughts and actions that link you to the role of perpetrator.

The notion of an autonomous will in moral insanity offered an explanation for the inexplicable: killing a beloved infant, stealing unwanted items, firing a loaded pistol at the queen for no possible reason. Indeed, the very want of a motive suggested a blind force that "neither reason nor sentiment determine." Whatever intellectual level accompanied blind passion, moral insanity spoke to the impulsive nature of the will, which drove the afflicted person into motiveless, revolting activity. The precise nature of the will, however, was problematic. Before Prichard, common sense philosophers limited their speculation about the power of the will to that of controlling (mental) associations. Indeed, one of the reasons sleep and dreaming intrigued medical theorists was precisely because all voluntary operations, such as reasoning and recollection, were suspended in these states. In sleep, subjects "present themselves" to the mind without active effort; people retain no active power to compare them with ideas stored in the memory. Individuals thus enjoy no power of reason in this suspended state; they cannot intrude on this process *at will*. In similar fashion, the insane cannot regulate their train of thought in madness, particularly if an idea engrosses the attention, crowding out every other subject. Prichard's use of will, however, extends beyond the mental association to control one's actions once the force of passion disorders intellectual powers and propels one into criminality, much like monomanie homicide. But he is not explicit regarding the precise nature of will, at times depicting it as a demonic force, at others seeing it as an adjunct to the intellect, overridden once passions have their way.

Prichard recognized two distinct roots to the concept of moral insanity. There was the obvious connection to monomania and similar forms of pathology restricted to volition; the French school had forcefully advanced a form of insanity in which individuals retained consciousness even as they were carried away by impulses not of their choosing. Of equal importance, however, was the meshing of a purely instinctual insanity with the growing preoccupation with defects of impulse control in Victorian England. In a study of nineteenth-century criminal and social policy, Martin Wiener draws attention to a fundamental Victorian anxiety—the will out of control. Surveying social documents from popular literature to tracts in social and population theory and publications of "social statistics," Wiener presents a compelling picture of the Victorians' deep-seated apprehensions about the maintenance of public order once individuals were freed from tradition, community, and social hierarchy. What force would counter instinctual passions and *appetites*?[61] Such sustained attention to unruly passions makes the formation of a concept like moral insanity perfectly understandable (if not inevitable). As Wiener points out, Victorian alienists and "utilitarian social reformers shared the same cultural objective": fostering self-governing, responsible citizens who were capable of exercising inner behavioral control. Although one would be hard pressed to pronounce whether monomanie or cultural anxiety about unchecked desires contributed most to the conceptual birth of moral insanity, it is very clear that insanity was fast becoming a matter of defective impulse control and unrestrained will rather than defective reasoning or fatal confusion.[62]

REWRITING THE JURORS' JOB DESCRIPTION

The conviction that insanity consisted of an inability to separate fact from fantasy was hardly unique to the medical psychology of Prichard and Conolly. "Notional" insanity, enlarged organs of parental love, and monomania all suggested a mind preoccupied with one idea impervious to corrective thoughts. Common sense philosophers were unique in the prominence they accorded the will in maintaining an orderly thought process. The will, according to Victorian sensibilities, was engaged in a perennial restraining of the passions, endeavoring to moderate their claims on judgment.[63] In a crisis violent passions overcome the will, generating error in the sensory impression of external things. The ravages of moral insanity thus extended beyond an inability to distinguish right from wrong: the will itself was impaired. The law's fundamental criterion for assigning culpability—willfully chosen behavior—was about to encounter a conception of insanity that spoke directly to the issue of volition without addressing what prisoners necessarily *knew* about their acts. Jurisprudence from Bracton and Hale to the instructions of eighteenth- and early nineteenth-century judges had centered on the critical question of will: Was the prisoner capable of exercising a choice? And this question had traditionally been framed at the cognitive level. Assuming that the accused understood the nature of the act and the difference between right and wrong, evidence of intent was inferred from the act itself. Conversely, one who was fatally confused regarding the consequences of wrongful action and was unable to appreciate the difference between right and wrong could not be said to have acted willfully. He or she had not *chosen* to do evil.[64]

The years 1760–1843 were a period of evolution in medico-philosophical theorizing, which approached the question of willfully chosen behavior in a qualitatively different way. The notion that the passions and will were under the control of reason was increasingly questioned; at first indirectly by Hartley's rendering of ideas cementing themselves (with no apparent role for the conscious, sovereign will) and by the phrenologists' depiction of character as under the dominion of discrete organs of the brain. Although the founder of phrenology equivocated on the issue of materialism and human choice, such physiological psychology carried broad implications for the issue of moral action. Médecine mentale and moral insanity engaged the issues of moral choice and criminal culpability directly. The popularizers of moral insanity and lesion of the will implicated diseased volition at the center of insanity: "the loss of voluntary power," "incapable . . . of carrying on the series of thought," impelled the afflicted into motiveless and revolting activity. Prichard's notion of moral insanity confronted the law's insistence on a will to harm.

The progression of medico-psychological conceptions of madness takes on added meaning when one considers the change in the "job description" of the juror from the midpoint of the eighteenth century. His assignment had initially been twofold: to "find" insanity and to determine if the insanity was the right sort. It was not enough to discover significant mental derangement: the juror had to discern a necessary debility in the prisoner's capacity to understand the moral wrongfulness of his or her actions. Jurors could not look to the medical psychology of the day for assistance in drawing this all-important inference. Insanity in the late 1700s was a matter of intellectual incoherence, faulty reasoning, mistaken impressions on the organs of sense. Questions of will were not central to medical theorizing and did not play a prominent role in the ruminations of a Battie, an Arnold, or even a Haslam.

All of this would change profoundly in the early 1830s and 1840s. Thinking about insanity now *began* with the will, and understandably so.

The Victorian imagination envisioned the will as the agent responsible for coordinating all living functions, particularly the balance between mind and body. Given a conception of madness tailor-made to the law's fundamental concern with intent, will, and self-control, the nineteenth-century juror found his assignment simplified. When he found moral insanity, lesion of the will, or "that black spot on his mind by which I mean delusion," he found legally significant madness. Changes in medical theorizing about madness therefore materially altered the juror's job description. The great achievement of common sense *medical* psychology was to depict mental derangement in images not only in the conceptual moral coinage of the day but exquisitely tuned to legal notions of culpability.

The Lay Witness's
Testimony

"He came to my house, and laid his head on the counter, crying
'My head, my head, I shall go mad—his forehead and head were
as if he had taken it out a pail of boiling water, smoking with
perspiration, and the perspiration was dropping on the floor quite
in a pool . . . he did not appear to know at all what he was doing."
—*OBSP,* 1839, case 2101, 9th sess., 541–42

ICHAEL MACDONALD'S ASSERTION "INSANITY IS DE-
fined by experts but discovered by laymen" was never more clearly revealed than in the testimony lay witnesses offered at the Old Bailey.[1]
Complementing the competing schools of medical psychology, each with
its own view of the cause and experience of madness, a seemingly inex-
haustible supply of the signs and symbols of madness poured forth at the
Old Bailey. Whether it was a neighbor who "bounced out of the room
in a mad freak," an assailant who preceded his attack by falling to his
knees, lifting his hands skyward, and exclaiming, "Jesus, come down from
heaven and take this evil spirit from me," or a lodger who "knocked his
head against the wall, came down stairs without his clothes, and rolled
his head in the kennel," ordinary folk did not have to consult a Haslam
or a Prichard to determine what condition they were facing.[2] To be sure,
not all madness "sightings" were so theatrical: a man might "hide behind
the door . . . looking down upon the ground with his hands up to his
mouth," and still convey an unmistakable aspect of distraction.[3] And even
when not dramatic, such quieter episodes could still be Dramatic: "[H]e
would get out of bed in the middle of the night and recite pieces from
Hamlet and Richard."[4]

What did early modern Londoners think about madness? A review
of the *OBSP* reveals that they thought just about everything and did

not keep their opinions to themselves. Casual acquaintances and close friends, employers and fellow lodgers, neighbors and relatives, and victims and constables regularly testified about the aimless wanderings and distracted conversations of the deranged. Lay witnesses testified in approximately 70 percent (232 trials) of the insanity cases tried between 1760 and 1843; the remainder usually featured only the prisoner's statement or the sole participation of a medical man. The testimony of the nonspecialist could be maddeningly general—"he's insane, the whole neighborhood knows it"—or elaborately detailed, including accounts of devils, visions, and voices whose terrifying demands compelled the afflicted to commit unspeakable crimes. Witnesses used a variety of grounds to infer insanity, from a simple reference to "neighborhood knowledge" to firsthand experience with the deranged. Those who based their testimony on experience with the prisoner underscored the role of the senses in eighteenth-century thinking about madness. It is not the madman or madwoman's senses that were at issue, however, but the observer's. What did the neighbor see and hear? How did the friend's mental faculties sort impressions and accommodate the received image to the stored cultural symbol of a "lunatic"? Perception and accommodation were critical to the naming of the insane state (table 4.1).

Just how the lay witness spoke to the lay jury is explored in this chapter. Direct quotations provide a window into the nonspecialist's construction of madness—its ravages, its course, and its cause. They help us both to reconstruct the sensory world of the observer, particularly the witness's perception of how deranged prisoners behaved, conversed, and appeared, and to determine whether madness was becoming more foreign or more familiar; more opaque or more intelligible to the lay observer in these years of rapid growth of expert medical testimony.

"BOUNCING OUT OF THE ROOM IN A MAD FREAK": THE BEHAVIORAL INFERENCE

In almost 40 percent of the insanity trials in the late eighteenth and early nineteenth centuries in which lay witnesses offered testimony, jurors learned that it was the prisoners' specific behavior that revealed their insanity. Certainly any juror listening to the description given at the beginning of this chapter would be struck by the frightening histrionics of the prisoner—"my head, my head, I shall go mad," accompanied with a "smoking" forehead and perspiration dropping on the floor "quite in a pool." Indeed, one need not look far in the *OBSP* for parallel tales of deranged neighbors "halooing" and screaming in the night, or of lodgers

Table 4.1 Lay witnesses' basis for the inference of madness (by trial)

Basis[a]	%
Behavior	39
Conversation	30
Appearance	17
Physical injury	17[b]
N=232	

Notes: This is computed on a per case rather than a per witness basis for two reasons. First, my interest was in trials dominated by lay witnesses as a group. What were jurors likely to hear about the perception of madness in such trials? How might this differ from, or complement, what jurors heard in prosecutions that featured testimony by medical witnesses exclusively? Although some trials had both medical and lay witnesses, lay witnesses were far more common. Second, 525 citizens testified in these 232 trials. The sheer profusion and ordinariness of the neighbors and relatives who regularly appeared probably led the publisher to edit their comments (the testimony usually has a familiar ring once a certain theme is sounded). The thrust of lay testimony, therefore, is better represented by case rather than by witness.

 [a]Percentages exceed 100% because more than one observational basis could be mentioned per trial.

 [b]This category is discussed in connection with table 4.3.

frothing at the mouth.[5] Not all reports, of course, documented wild antics. One could be just as concerned about a relative who was becoming increasingly reclusive and noncommunicative: "He would lay awake at night, singing songs, psalms, and hymns."[6] Although on the surface this hardly seems to qualify as insanity, the key word was "awake"; witnesses often stressed the awful restlessness of the deranged, their continuing inability to sleep.[7]

Madmen and women might also startle their intimates by immodesty. As a tradesman testified in 1833, "When she came down to us she was dressed quite in an indelicate state, with her bosom quite exposed; she had nothing except a little shawl on the back of her shoulders, and her petticoat and shift on . . . [S]he did not exhibit the slightest shame at being so exposed; her bosom, down to her waist, was stark naked."[8] Such apparent disregard for the norms of polite society mirrored the social solipsism of other defendants who appeared in rags or those who, though they had a new jacket, "parted with it for an old and tattered one."[9] Madness, it seems, included more than a display of physically menacing behavior or the withdrawal into a world of plaintive singing and humming; it was also a matter of showing contempt for the norms of social advertisement. As MacDonald has noted with regard to an earlier period in England, to destroy one's symbols of social position was to commit a form of social suicide.[10] Who but a mad person would willingly surrender any claim to social position in a society so exquisitely attentive to the nuances of taste, deportment, and apparel?

Although overt behavior often conformed to stereotyped literary and theatrical renderings of the distracted, something more was conveyed in the lay witness's testimony. Apart from histrionics or sullen despondency, what was "mad" about the behavior was that it seemed unexplainable. Nakedness and willful shabbiness were distancing from conventional norms precisely because there seemed to be no *reason* for the behavior. How could a bystander in 1828 enter the mental world of the prisoner who "[talked] to chairs, tables, and things—he used to call the chairs and tables by different Christian names, and tell them to answer him,"[11] or of the woman who "frequently shaved her head [saying] it relieved her—she said the more she cut, the more service it was to her," or the man who went into a factory and "came out with his fingers almost off [having] put them into hot lead," as well as the large number of prisoners who "stamped about the house breaking china and glass"?[12] Relatively innocuous examples of extraordinary behavior also made their way into testimony. A person's "intellects" could become suspect if "before dinner was over, he . . . left the room, gone out, and not returned," without an explanation, or "threw his knife and fork away, and walk[ed] backwards and forwards in the kitchen."[13] Of course there was nothing particularly bizarre or terrifying in such behavior; rather, as one neighbor explained, "I could not account for his conduct."[14]

Although self-injury is not necessarily "inexplicable," jurors in 1808 could well wonder what was on the mind of a woman who had attempted to drown herself in a ditch "waist-deep." Short of attempted suicide, lay testimony provides numerous examples of self-inflicted wounds and intended injuries. "She beat her head against the mantle piece and tore her hair"; she "took poison" and "[picked] the skin off her lips till the blood has run down on her chin"; she "threw herself in a cold bath in the garden."[15] Whether attempting physical or social suicide ("emptying the till and throwing the money to the multitudes," "dismissing, for five months together, his favorite daughter for no cause upon earth"), the actions of the mad defined them as such because they were enigmatic, cryptic, and not least, one suspects, scary.[16]

But need the signs of madness be so demonstrative? Could not a care-

fully constructed plan also reveal the seeds of lurking derangement? By
the end of the eighteenth century, some voices on the bench and in the
nascent profession of advocacy law were questioning the growing reliance
on conspicuous behavior as the sign of madness. When a jailer in 1784
denied seeing any "marks" of insanity on the prisoner in his custody, the
court advised: "There is something a little ambiguous in that, he might
not show marks of violent insanity, yet there might be a great deal more
to be collected from that, than this man could observe; they are apt to
think no man insane that does not do outrageous things; but we must
collect his insanity from the fact—his mind seems to have turned to one
object."[17]

A far more impassioned warning of the injustice that attended a conception of insanity restricted to overt histrionics was offered in a remarkable exchange in the trial of Samuel Burt, the forger mentioned
earlier who had gone to such lengths to ensure his conviction and much-
desired execution. Burt's attorney, Mr. Garrow, implored the jury to
consider the following:

> [I]f I show he was rolling in the streets, that he was running about the
> streets with a fire brand in his hand . . . that he did not know his nearest
> relation; I should bring convincing proofs of his insanity: but I cannot
> give that evidence, may I not show that on the morning of this fact,
> that he conducted himself as an ideot, that he did that which no man
> in his sound mind could do, that at the same time he was writing this
> draft, he wrote a letter to his master to show that he had done it with
> a design to be brought to justice, that soon he hoped to meet his friends
> in eternity (to be relieved of the troubles of life) . . . [I]f I might show
> that he was running about with a sword to murder his own father and
> mother, may I not show this. [By "this" Garrow meant not only the
> prisoner's death wish but the existence of hereditary insanity in the
> Burt family and the prisoner's earlier attempt at suicide.][18]

Garrow's comments are particularly interesting in light of an opinion
he expressed to a jury in another insanity trial the year before. On this
occasion, the attorney seemed less disposed to a "quieter madness," advising the jury to search for "clear and unequivocal proofs of insanity."[19]
Garrow well knew his constituency. For most ordinary folk, madness was
"spectacularly on view": reports of odd, queer, silly, indecent, flighty,
frantic, absurd, irrational, and extraordinary behaviors surface in almost
two-fifths of the trials in which lay witnesses testified. If these acts shared
one characteristic, it was their seeming inexplicability. As one witness
stated simply, "I have certainly seen him guilty of actions no sensible man
could do."[20]

"NOT THE LEAST WAY OF CONNECTING HIS IDEAS": THE CONVERSATIONAL INFERENCE

When neighbors and relatives departed from reports of the suspected insane person's behavioral excesses, it was distracted speech, incoherent conversation, and fanciful visions that usually surfaced in lay testimony. The category of conversation is perhaps best examined by separating the phenomenon of distracted speech from the occurrence of delirious ranting, because these two forms of communication resulted in very different sorts of testimony. Distracted speech focused on a particular failure: the inability to recognize that a question was asked or the refusal to answer appropriately. Late eighteenth- and early nineteenth-century Londoners could find the etiquette of their speech patterns the proper subject for an insanity inquiry along three particular lines.

First, the prisoner may have quite simply failed to respond to the questioner. "[W]hen questioned, she smiles and turns away."[21] Occasionally the blank stare that faced the questioner was accompanied by physical "signs" of derangement: "[H]e made no answer, but the blood and slabber ran out of each side of his mouth."[22] Second, the deranged individual might supply an answer to a question, but not the *right* answer. "I asked him one question, he answered me another," or "[H]is giving me such an odd answer made me look in his face to see if he was in liqueur."[23] Sometimes a "wrong" answer was the questioner's reward for persisting in an interview that had yielded few results: "If you asked her a question, she did not give you an answer; if she did give you an answer, it would not be the proper answer to the question."[24] It seems that the most common response to direct questioning by this group of offenders was withdrawal: "He seemed very dull . . . made no answer at all." Interactions like these were examples not of "incoherent" conversation but rather of *no* conversation, and individuals whose conversations were thus described were most like another subgroup whose communication was discussed in court: persons who talked to themselves and laughed for no apparent reason.

When lay witnesses characterized the conversation of the prisoner as "incoherent" they were speaking of a third subgroup of the distracted, neither the delirious nor the silent. A jury in 1801 learned from a neighbor of the accused, "when we have talked of serious affairs, he has run into other things, and deviated from what had been talked about, just as I have seen people in Bedlam."[25] Or, "[She had an] incoherent manner of asking questions. And before you would answer, she would go into some other subject."[26] Sometimes the flightiness in such conversations was generalized into speech patterns that strongly suggested the diffusion of associationist tenets into popular culture: "He has not the least rational way of connecting his ideas for any time."[27] Another witness in the same trial averred, "He has always shown confusion and irregularity with his ideas and conversation—[there is] a flightiness, an unsettledness that has convinced me that his mind has been totally deranged at times." Although few witnesses made "ideas" the explicit focus of their testimony, frequent references to "incoherent sentences" and "random speech" suggest that syntax was more than a grammatical concern. Scrambled word order, like disjointed questions and answers, was grasped as evidence of manifest derangement.

Haphazard word or thought order, however, would not necessarily convince the court. When a witness in 1806 stated, "[W]hen she was speaking to you of one thing, she would leave it and ramble to another," the attorney asked, "Is she the only woman you know to ramble from one subject to another?"[28] This was not simply an early sign of sexism in the court. Jumbled speech was merely far less theatrical than the wild, grotesque displays of madness that characterized observable behavior. Many people (men *and* women) might lurch from one topic to another in a conversation, but those who rolled their head around in a kennel, stuck their fingers in molten lead, or placed their face on a counter screaming, "My head, my head, I shall go mad," were decidedly fewer, if easier to classify. Also, a certain subjectivity entered into the assessment that answers one was receiving were not "right." Medical witnesses were particularly pressed on this issue: "Do you think that every man that does not give you a direct answer is mad?" queried one judge in 1789. "Certainly not," answered the mad-doctor, who, when pressed by the judge, was forced to admit that he could not remember the prisoner's actual answers.[29]

In contrast to rambling conversation and incoherent replies to specific questions, another form of "conversation" afforded much less ambiguous interpretation: "He said that the devil, and Captain Derby, and spirits were in the ship, and that they had been tearing his heart out. That the devil had been running after him through the ship, and wanted to put him on a spit and roast him."[30] Horrific torments by devils, witches, and spirits recur with frightening regularity in the conversations recounted to juries in the nineteenth century. Most often it is the devil as tempter, appearing to the sufferer and impelling him or her to commit unspeakable deeds. Putatively mad prisoners informed their neighbors that "the devil has been very busy with me this afternoon—

he tempted me to kill my baby," or "I have had a terrible dream, [I] dreamt that the devil came to see me and told me to kill my child . . . You must and you shall kill your child."[31] The "angel Gabriel" and other religious dramatis personae were also in evidence: "I thought he was really out of his mind; sometimes he was singing, and sometimes talking of Moses and Aaron and Jacob, and then he would look as wild as could be."[32] In 1825 a constable testified, "I have heard him, through the wall, on Sundays preaching to himself . . . [He] said he was like our Savior, and had fasted 40 days and nights. He used to hold up a gingerbread twist in his hand, and say so . . . I believe him to be insane."[33]

Political persecution was another subject of rantings relayed to the court by lay witnesses. Whether the afflicted claimed to be "an agent of Napoleon" or summoned to a personal mission to "overturn the Government [of France] and establish another," those who heard such remarks recognized the dire consequences that attended them: "I told him that if he went on with these fanciful notions, he would either bring himself to a gallows or a mad house."[34] No such ambiguity characterized the fate of the truly delirious, whose tirades blended religious and political themes:

[H]e declared then the reason he was ill treated, was, that he wished to reveal what the government wished to conceal; for that he saw a cloud come down from Heaven, that it cemented to a rock, and out of that sprung a false island of Jamaica, and because he wished to reveal it, he had, he said, been confined 163 days . . . I thought that the speech of a madman; and he said that he had wrote to the King and to Sir George Young, the Secretary of War and could receive no redress, and that they had reduced him to half pay . . . [and] that he was persecuted, and that they wanted to set him up as the antichrist, or a 4th person in the Godhead.[35]

Although such comprehensive accounts of the speech of the prisoner are rare, lay witnesses throughout the late eighteenth and early nineteenth centuries offered a plentiful and evocative list of demonic forces at work on the minds of the putative mad—devils chasing a sailor in a ship, spirits speaking through walls, tormenting visions (the "sky in flames")—and temptations by the Evil One. Increasingly after 1800, random, incoherent speech gave way to haunting, spirit-ridden tales imparted to the jury through the ear of the lay witness. Changes in the content of these conversations constituted one of the most significant shifts in lay testimony over time.

"LIKE A MAD BULLOCK":
INFERENCE FROM APPEARANCE

Elanor Cotton: I have known the prisoner seventeen or eighteen years.
Mr. Knapp: During the whole of the time that you have known him, in
   what state of mind had he been?
Miss Cotton: Like a mad bullock more than any thing else.[36]

For some lay witnesses, madness was not a specific episode of behavior
or a failure to converse in conventional ways but a state of *being*, a particular form of distraction that manifested itself in appearance. The prisoner "appeared as a lunatic," as "a man out of his senses," "as much out
of his mind as any person that was in Bedlam."[37] Simply put, the madman
looked like a madman. That terms and phrases stressing unusual appearance were offered frequently, and with little elaboration, suggests
their common intelligibility in early modern England. Their actual usefulness in court, however, was a matter of concern to judges and attorneys, who chose to use their expression as an opportunity to examine the
meaning of terms like "mad bullock." The judge in this case interrupted,
"[T]hat expression conveys nothing distinct, in which the Jury can go
by—what has been his manner and deportment?"[38]

The court responded to ambiguous appearances in a number of ways.
It could request a simple definition: What has he done that makes you
suppose him to be a lunatic? What do you mean by the terms "flighty
and disordered"? You say she was convulsed, what do you mean by that?
Witnesses answered with examples of behavior that were sometimes bizarre and extravagant ("[S]he was going to light the fire, I told her there
was a very good one, she stared and looked very wild—[putting] her
hand all over the fire")[39] and sometimes rather more ordinary ("[H]e
would come in and break a great quantity of glass"). There was no consistent usage for any term or set of terms. A lunatic was not someone
whose derangement was as labile as the phases of the moon but rather
someone who "broke glass" or "tore her clothes to pieces" or "[had] a
froth come to her mouth."[40] "Flighty and disorderly" turns out to be
synonymous with "guilty of things no sensible man would do." The "mad
bullock" turns out to be someone who roared and bit his lips. In short,
the actual terms used do not denote separate species of madness but
rather a generic cultural type, one whose appearance was unproblematically signaled by "bulging eyes," "gnashed teeth," or "a face livid with
rage." Lay witnesses appear to have employed "lunatic," "deranged,"
"flighty," and "out of his senses" interchangeably and without precision.

The lay witness's choice of the terms focusing on appearance signaled

an important subcategory of perception. Lay testimony that stressed appearance often contained compelling narratives lamenting the descent of
friends and neighbors into the appalling realm of the mad. They quite
literally have become some *thing* else. Testifying about a college friend,
Joseph Higginson responded to the query, "[W]hat were his habits of
life?" in the following manner: "A man of education, accustomed to
fashionable society, and perfectly discreet in his demeanor . . . [then, describing incidents of outrageous conduct, I] never observed such conduct
in him before; his conduct was so eccentric, so extravagant, and so wild,
that I considered him under temporary derangement . . . I then began to
think him an object fit to be confined."[41] From a friend to an object,
from a man "discreet in his demeanor" to a pitiable eccentric fit for
confinement, Higginson's acquaintance exemplified the class of prisoners
who exhibited an alteration in appearance so profound that friends were
moved to exclaim, "He was not the man he used to be when I knew
him."[42] Testifying at an infanticide trial in 1838, an acquaintance of the
accused endeavored to draw the jury's attention to the material alteration
in the prisoner's functioning: "I do not consider that she was in a sane
state of mind, nor had she been so for the last six months—I have seen
a visible change in her for the last six months in the total neglect of her
person, and never wishing to go out on any occasion, nor wishing to see
any company at all."[43] Although neither personal slovenliness nor unso-
ciability could explain the killing of the prisoner's child, the witness was
stressing the significant change from the person she had been, to the . . .
object(?) she was now. Testimony heard earlier in the trial that stressed
the prisoner's recent, frequent melancholic states was complemented by
another acquaintance's observation that she "appeared quite unconscious" after having smothered her child.[44] The totality of the lay testimony suggested the appearance of a stranger where a friend had once
been. Here a character witness in 1799 is left guessing about the accused's
capacity to discern good from evil:

> *Mr. Dalton:* He has not been so exactly steady for these two years back
> as formerly he was.
> *Attorney Knowleys:* What do you mean by his not being so steady in
> his mind?
> *Mr. Dalton:* He would fly from one argument to another.
> *Mr. Knowleys:* Do you not think he knew it was a bad thing to steal?
> *Mr. Dalton:* Yes, but if he had been as formerly, he would not have
> done it.[45]

Lay testimony based on appearance is of particular interest today as
social scientists attempt to unravel the interactional processes that re-

sulted in labeling deviance. For these witnesses, madness appears as a being, a role one inhabits, and one whose outward appearance is unmistakable and frightening. Neighbors who appear as "not the person she had been," "not as he had been formerly," and "[neglectful] of her person," are described in court as having traversed a social boundary and become something—not someone—else. Although the assertion of appearance was, to be sure, supplemented on occasion with accounts of strange behavior and rambling speech, for these witnesses at least, it was the *person* of the mentally deviant they first beheld and whose label they could recall because the common cultural consciousness embraced so many stereotypes of mental waywardness.

Witnesses like Mr. Dalton, who stressed that the accused man he had known was nothing like the present incarnation, were spared a series of questions that attended neighbors, relatives, and acquaintances who had *always* thought the prisoner to be "mad" or "lunatic." Judges responded to such blanket categorizations as "he appeared like a lunatic" and she conducted herself like "a woman out of her senses" with such questions as: Did you communicate that opinion of yours to others? If the derangement appeared to be so considerable, should you not have thought it your duty to communicate it to some person in the house? How come you to send a man perfectly out of his senses for your things? Questions like these obviously cast doubt on the accuracy of the witness's diagnosis, honesty, or perhaps sanity. Occasionally, however, the judge's probing could reinforce the witness's observations and add greater weight to the designation "lunatic" or "deranged":

> *Brother of Prisoner:* He has been afflicted in a kind of stupid, heavy way, as a lunatick; the first particular thing we observed of him, was, drinking a vast quantity of water; he had a fancy in his head he was poisoned.
> *Court:* Did you endeavor to convince him he was mistaken?
> *Brother:* Yes, but it had no effect, he consumed so for nearly a fortnight; he used to drink four or five quarts of water, one after another, he was confined in St. Luke's twelve months, and was sent away as incurable.[46]

Courtroom questioning was not limited to examining the accuracy of the witness's "diagnosis" or carelessness in not seeking a remedy for the prisoner's derangement. On occasion questioning was quite subtle, especially when the examiner endeavored to distinguish eccentricity from madness and madness from distress. In 1787 William May appeared at the Old Bailey to testify about a prisoner who appeared to be "not in his senses." He was examined by the ubiquitous Mr. Garrow, this time appearing as a prosecution counsel.

> *Mr. Garrow:* Are you able to decide whether his behavior was more
>   like a distressed man, or a man mad?
> *Mr. May:* I cannot say; it did not strike me as to his being in distress . . .
> *Mr. Garrow:* Then I ask you from his conduct, were you able to form
>   a decided opinion whether that proceeded from madness or distress?
> *Mr. May:* I did not imagine he was distressed.
> *Mr. Garrow:* Suppose it was stated to you that he was very much distressed and embarrassed in his circumstances?
> *Mr. May:* I should have expected he would be more sullen than he
>   was.[47]

Clearly Mr. May was not about to be maneuvered into acknowledging that it might have been (mere) distress and not senselessness that appeared to him. When forced to suppose the existence of a hypothetical state of distress, he continued with an equally hypothetical effect. People like William May often proved to be canny witnesses.

A final point about lay witnesses who brought their impressions into the courtroom already fitted into definitional categories: unlike their colleagues who based their inferences of insanity on overt, extravagant behavior or garbled, incoherent conversation, those who cited appearance seemed attentive to two themes that would find greater expression in medical testimony and medical theorizing. First, unique to these witnesses is an effort to pair appearance with a mental state of consciousness: "She did not appear to know what she was doing"; "He appeared quite unconscious of his acts"; "She is of an absent character of mind, she scarcely knows what she is about."[48] Lay witnesses who stressed appearance were unique in alerting the juror to consider the distance between the prisoner's crime and the contemplation of such behavior. Lamentably, these witnesses were not cross-examined, so there is no way to determine what they might have meant by "consciousness." Still, the frequent use of expressions like "absent character of mind" or "wandering mind" suggests the presumption of gradations in mental awareness. There is an intriguing resonance here with the testimony of putatively mad prisoners who described their mental state at the time of the crime to be "like a dream."

A second theme that emerges in testimony about appearance, one that also characterizes both the prisoner's defense and forensic-psychiatric testimony, was the haunting presence of a force beyond the prisoner's control. Lay witnesses often drew their inference of derangement from the observation that the prisoner heard threatening voices and impelling commands. A prisoner on trial for forgery in 1828 was described by his neighbor as having "seemed to imagine he was within the grasp of some superior force . . . [A]t other times he would smile, and appeared to wish that I should not speak of such matters."[49] Seven years later, another prisoner at the Old Bailey was described in a similar fashion: "[S]he would be lost in thought, and would turn up her eye balls in a wild way, as if her mind was overpowered with some overwhelming idea—this had happened frequently, more particularly lately—I considered her mind then overwhelmed—in a state of derangement . . . [W]hen I saw her, three days before, her conversation was incoherent, and her mind was overwhelmed with some idea."[50] Although it would take the actual prisoner to supply the personal experience of being overpowered—"I could get no command of myself"—and medical witnesses to address the subject of the will directly, lay testimony in the second quarter of the nineteenth century reveals the existence of treacherous forces—not all of them satanic—that rendered the afflicted person helpless. Together with an emerging notion of multiple states of awareness, the integrity of one's mental functioning was brought into sharper focus by witnesses who stressed appearance and particularly countenance in their testimony.

TRENDS IN LAY TESTIMONY
OVER TIME

Legal thinking relative to insanity changed significantly in the years 1760–1843. Beginning with the Ferrers case and its reinforcement of total insanity as the criterion for acquittal, a series of famous trials introduced a range of innovative ways of conceiving the mind that challenged, directly and indirectly, the fundamental notions of legal intentionality and self-control. Medical theorizing about madness shifted, too, often keeping legal considerations of accountability very much within its sights. Thus Haslam's writings on medical jurisprudence were founded on associationist principles, phrenologists invoked outrageous criminal acts by the normally placid to support their assertion of "character" localization, the criminological implications of médecine mentale were self-evident in such species of insanity as monomanie homicide and lesion of the will, and Prichard's concept of moral insanity sat at the crossroads of constraint and choice. If insanity was indeed "shaped from below," one would expect similar shifts in the imagery and perspectives employed by lay witnesses to "discover" its presence.

In addition to qualitative shifts in medical theorizing, medical participation in insanity trials also changed noticeably; by the 1840s the forensic-psychiatric witness had "arrived." Study of these developments can be divided into three periods: 1760–1800, 1801–1829, and 1830–1843.[51] These three divisions demarcate an era of low participation of medical witnesses and a legal criterion of total insanity; a period of gradually increasing medical participation and a successful challenge of the total insanity criterion for acquittal; and a period that features the exponential growth in the participation of forensic-psychiatric witnesses and the introduction of radically new conceptions of insanity. Among the many questions that arise is what impact medical witnesses made on the scope and direction of courtroom testimony. Did they supplant the images of lay witnesses with medical esoterica? Did medical testimony replace street perceptions and common sense? Before we can answer these questions, however, we need to ask what changes in behavior, conversation, and appearance creep into the lay witness's narrative? More important still, how might the three most common grounds for inference—behavior, conversation, and appearance—reconfigure in the words of the lay witness in these three periods? This is a question not so much of which of these bases becomes more or less frequent but rather of how variations in the way madness is perceived over time reflect changes in the observer's curiosity and attempts to articulate madness as a *lived* experience. These changes cannot be presented in quantitative form because the terms have different meanings both within and among time periods; rather, it is the context that framed particular terms that reveals changes in the discovery and understanding of madness. Though context does not lend itself readily to quantification, a number of elements can be enumerated, and they are presented at the end of this section. Narrative extracts that seem to reflect emerging themes within each period follow below. Over time, lay testimony moved from labeling to fathoming, from characterizing the conversations of the mad as madness to distilling their words and actions so as to render more intelligible the mind of the mad.

1760–1800: The Rule of Stereotypes

Testimony from the last half of the eighteenth century reveals the enduring cultural stereotype of the recognizable madman or woman within one's midst. The "speech of a madman," "walking around like a man deranged in his senses," standing "like an idiot, picking his nose" was the most frequently heard testimony of lay witnesses. In 1780 Thomas Haycock came to trial at the Old Bailey, having been indicted for rioting. No fewer than six lay witnesses testified on his behalf.

Acquaintance #1: I have heard that he was insane.
Court: Has he shown marks of insanity?

Tavern Cook: He's a madman; was confined for some weeks.
Neighbor: He was much afflicted with insanity.
Acquaintance #2: He is out of his mind.
Acquaintance #3: He is called "Mad Tom."
Acquaintance #4: He is an honest and peaceable man—has some fits
   of insanity about him when in liquor.[52]

These witnesses employed stock eighteenth-century terminology—calling
him insane and out of his mind, using familiar nicknames—but they
provided no insight into the prisoner behind the label. Even a question
asking for "marks of insanity" is answered by pointing to the fact of his
incarceration, as though that was proof of derangement. In a way, of
course, it was: one immediately thought of tattered clothes, disheveled
hair, matted straw about the feet.[53] When a witness in a trial later that
year described the prisoner "as much out of his mind as any person that
was in Bedlam," he was doubtless borrowing from the same cultural
storehouse of images—not to mention Hogarth prints.

It was the *fact* of the prisoner's madness, not the experience of derangement, that juries considered in the late 1700s. No attempt was made
to connect the prisoner's derangement with his or her criminality; the
derangement was not examined at all. No effort was made to convey the
way the prisoner looked at the world. The law remained relatively un-
challenged because there was no divergence between a moral and a legal
wrong. Until at least 1800, it was the specter of the insane, not their
world, that the lay witness imparted to the jury.

1801–1829: "Insane . . . upon This Subject"

Philip Bond, gunsmith: My opinion was, that his mind was not quite
   right upon the very point which brings him to this unfortunate situation.
Attorney Knowleys: What is that point?
Mr. Bond: The attachment.
Mr. Knowleys: Love?
Mr. Bond: Love upon this subject, though he has discovered a sanity on
   other points, on that point he has always shown some degree of insanity; that has been uniformly my opinion.[54]

On 15 April 1803, John Grant fired a pistol at Spencer-George Townsend because Townsend had refused to supply Grant with documents
that would have assured a Miss Ward that Grant was a suitable suitor.
Grant had never been "confined as a lunatic," his friends thought "he
knew it was a criminal act to fire at a person," and his employer testified
that he was a "well behaved man." But, the employer added, "[H]e
always showed some degree of insanity" on the subject of love. Grant's

trial affords one of the earliest glimpses of the meeting between the conventional legal standards for assessing accountability and the particularistic species of insanity that was narrowed to one subject.

> *Attorney Knowleys:* Do you believe him to know the difference between good and evil?
>
> *Acquaintance (some duration):* Perhaps he may, except in the question of this unfortunate attachment; certainly it is not the same in any topic not connected with that circumstance.
>
> *Attorney Fielding:* What was his conduct in respect to that attachment?
>
> *Lifelong friend:* It was extremely absurd and irrational in every degree.
>
> *Mr. Fielding:* Did his conduct lead you to conceive he was deranged?
>
> *Prisoner's friend:* On that subject, I believe he was.
>
> *Mr. Knowleys:* Did you conceive him conscious of moral good and evil?
>
> *Prisoner's friend:* I think he was, except when this subject comes across his mind, he was quite wild.
>
> *Mr. Knowleys:* Do you think he was so deranged, as not to feel that it was a dreadful crime to fire at a fellow creature?
>
> *Prisoner's Solicitor:* I think his mind was so distracted as not to know what he was doing, and that he might fire at Mr. Townsend without knowing whether he was doing right from wrong, or even fire at myself, or anybody else, when his mind was on that subject; I conceive he was entirely incapable of knowing what he did.[55]

Throughout the early nineteenth century, lay witnesses brought forth a host of subjects for the juror to consider: obsessive love, political victimization, spirit-world tempters. Although the steadfast insistence on circumscribed derangement that one finds in the trial of John Grant was rare, trials of the early 1800s are remarkable for the refinement in the lay witness's conversations with the accused: they begin to afford a glimpse into the mental world of the distracted. Where the eighteenth-century prisoner "spoke like a madman," the nineteenth-century prisoner apparently inhabited a universe of demons, desires, and—post-Hadfield—delusion. Although it would remain primarily a feature of forensic-psychiatric testimony, delusion as fanciful notion and mistaken impression was also present in lay testimony. In 1827 a defendant's employer repeated a story the accused prisoner had told him: "I was very ill a long time, but once, when I got to the center of London Bridge I met the devil, I took him in my arms, and threw him over into the water."[56] Although it was a surgeon who actually characterized the prisoner's mental functioning as "some delusion" and affirmed that delusions were indeed the "test" of insanity, the story was supplied by the layman.

Certainly not all trials were occasions for a peek into the world of the allegedly mad defendant. Some eighteenth-century testimony patterns continued: random speech, nonsensical answers, inexplicable antics. But the world of the putatively insane offender was recast in the years that followed the Hadfield trial. The insane offender was no less mad, but he or she was much less a madman or woman, if that term signified an inhabitant of an unknowable world. Grant's derangement centered on the subject of love, Bellingham's concerned political persecution in a Russian prison, and a series of other offenders were subject to an insanity that revealed their acts to be no less horrific but perhaps less mysterious. The person behind the mask was becoming a little more visible.

1830–1843: "He Believed That He Must Murder"

Lay testimony in the 1830s and 1840s continued to transport the ideas of the mad into the courtroom, often providing quite graphic evidence of the existence and the sway of *circumscribed* derangement. In 1833 one jury at the Old Bailey heard the remarkable tale of ship's captain Noah Folger, who had been tormented by the unshakable conviction that the ship's owner was planning to "ruin him in character and fortune." At the very mention of Mr. Mellish's name, Captain Folger was capable of the most extravagant acts, including breaking windowpanes with his bare fists, dancing on the broken glass, and then jumping on the back of a passing whale. Captain Blisson, master of another ship, informed the court: "[H]e always appeared under great excitement when he had spoken of Mr. Mellish; he was quite calm and collected till Mr. Mellish's name came into question—I have seen much of persons who are insane; the disorder begins when the subject which caused their malady is raised."[57] Interestingly, it is not the witness who names Folger's condition but the judge. "When persons in a calm state have gone off when a subject has been named, have not these been cases where the mind has been under some delusion?" The witness, who had "been with two or three masters of ships in similar cases," asserted that "there has always been something which operated on their minds." Although the unfortunate Captain Folger apparently had a general history of "nervous excitement" and extravagant—indeed threatening—behavior, witness after witness affirmed the immediate effect produced by the mere mention of Mr. Mellish's name. Indeed, there seemed to be an Ancient Mariner quality to Folger's obsession: "[H]e began talking about [Mr. Mellish] with nine people out of ten." The tales of his circumscribed derangement brought to the court by lay witnesses were in fact so graphic and apparently so convincing that even the testimony a medical witness who denied the existence "of any symptom which he has exhibited to make me come to the conclusion of his being of unsound mind" could not keep the jury from acquitting.[58]

Not all lay witnesses could depict such abrupt changes in the afflicted person's behavior the minute the subject of the derangement was raised, but the term *delusion* was still used occasionally to delineate particular fears and torments. "He has labored under a delusion about witches and lizards ever since I corresponded with him," testified one prisoner's sister. The prisoner's landlord reinforced her testimony: "I have heard him speak about witches; he repeatedly said he was tormented with witches . . . he told me he fired this shot . . . intending to be taken, that the public might know his troubles concerning these witches."[59]

The case of this unfortunate man underscores a development in lay testimony that characterizes delusion and other forms of circumscribed derangement in this period: the connection lay witnesses were beginning to draw between the derangement and the crime. Where neighbors and relatives in the early 1800s cited fanciful notions and tormenting visions as "signs" of madness—clues to the presence of derangement—by the 1840s people were attempting to find a link that connected the torment and the eventual act—not necessarily between the actual victim and the derangement but rather between the type of crime and the distraction. In 1835, for example, William Whiskard was brought to trial for the felonious assault of Jane Burn. His wife gave the following account of Whiskard's distress: "[H]e frequently complained to me that he was haunted by ghosts—between five and six years ago he told me he saw the devil at his bed-side—he has told me frequently that old *Tom Paine,* the writer, and the devil, have appeared to him when he was in bed, and told him he must commit murder."[60] Whiskard's choice of victim was not as important as the implication that he believed "he must . . . murder." Of course, some delusions (or hallucinations) dictated the exact crime as well. In an instance of satanic compulsion reported in the 1830s, the prisoner claimed she was told: "[Y]ou must and you shall kill your child."[61] Lay testimony linking tormenting voices and explosions of violence were beginning to draw criminality and derangement into a much tighter circle.

The search for a connection between a particular form of derangement and the crime seems to have been part of a growing lay interest in uncovering an underlying reason for the madness. Whereas witnesses in the late eighteenth century rarely cited causes of the insanity they were naming, lay witnesses in the 1830s and 1840s were increasingly turning their attention (and presumably the jury's) to a search for the agent responsible for the derangement (table 4.2).

In the late 1700s, barely one trial in ten contained speculation from

Table 4.2   Cases in which lay witnesses mention the cause of mental
derangement

Years	%	N
1760–1800	9	74
1801–1829	22	86
1831–1843	36	72

Note: As in table 4.1, the trial is the unit of analysis. Although the overall proclivity
of lay witnesses to speak in terms of causation is worth considering, whether the jury
heard a "causal statement" once or several times in a trial is less important than
recognizing that in these trials the court was increasingly hearing a view of insanity
based in something other than the crime. Included are only those factors that witnesses
appeared to advance as a reason for derangement: sometimes a causal relation was
unambiguously asserted; at other times a strong association was made between a
physical disturbance and later derangement; and sometimes various physical and mental
ills were indexed by the witness with no attempt to relate them to the derangement.

lay witnesses regarding the agent responsible for the madness. Jurors
learned little of the prisoner's past, his accidents, fevers, or the skull
fracture that might have brought on the derangement. By the 1830s, a
third of all trials in which lay witnesses appeared featured testimony linking the derangement to some cause, not all necessarily physical (table
4.3).

Witnesses blamed madness on everything from bad falls to bad hus-
bands, from strokes to religion—although physical causes outnumbered
emotional stress three to one. The assertion of either a physical or an
emotional cause was a straightforward affair. Rarely were lay witnesses
questioned in depth about the nature of the causal relation; indeed, one
could have assumed that fits were themselves a sign of derangement,
although the way in which they were invoked clearly signaled that they
were responsible for causing the derangement. One prisoner's neighbor
in 1768 stated, "He is subject to fits, which have disordered his head very
much."[62] A jury in 1804 heard an attorney ask a witness: "[Are] the
prisoner's senses, by means of an apoplectic fit, at times affected?"[63]

Although such examination and testimony hardly constitutes sophisticated commentary about the etiology of mental pathology, it provided
critical support for the defense of mental derangement by affirming that
the prisoner's insanity had a reality in something other than the crime.
However indirect and implicit the relation they were citing, lay witnesses
were according the prisoner's distraction an independent existence, often

Table 4.3   Causes of insanity cited by lay witnesses

Physical	(49)
Head wound	8
Fits	7
Liquor	4
Brain fever	4
Fever (unspecified)	3
Fall	3
Heredity	3
Accident	3
Fractured skull	2
Paralytic stroke	2
Head sore	2
Sunstroke	1
Paroxysm	1
Milk flow to breast[a]	1
Poison	1
Drugs	1
Bleeding	1
Disease (not specified)	1
Violent passions	1
Emotional and other	**(17)**
Death of family member	4
Family distress ("bad husband")	3
Moon	3
Delusion	3
Sorcery	1
Voyage	1
Ill treatment	1
Religion	1

Notes: Sixty-six lay witnesses offered possible causes of the prisoner's insanity in the 57 trials that comprised table 4.2; the data are presented in terms of witnesses, not trials, as in tables 4.1 and 4.2, because witnesses sometimes offered more than one cause.

[a]Problems attendant with nursing

combining organic injury with mentalist consequence. As jurors learned from one witness in 1839, "I have heard from his family that fourteen years ago he fell down a ship's hold, and was insensible for three days, and there are now pieces of lint and things in his head; I knew he is subject to such fits of aberration, that he will set for hours together with

his head on his hand, and beat his head to get sense in it." The prisoner's
injury was described by his brother as a skull fracture, "and ever since
that he has been rather singular." Unlike assault or murder, which might
appear as the logical consequence of a specific delusion, a particular physical injury and the resulting insensibility did not lead *inevitably* to a particular result. In the case cited above, the prisoner's skull fracture, "pieces
of lint in the head," and consequent "insensibility" convinced the jury
that his foolishness subsequent to the crime—"sitting around with two
jackets on" and making no attempt to hide the stolen goods—was not
mischievousness but madness.[64]

Domestic woes also "turned [the prisoner's] brain" (see table 4.3).[65]
Among these, the death of a family member was most prominent. A
longtime acquaintance of a prisoner in 1842 testified, "Since the death
of his wife, about fifteen months ago, he was quite a different man to
what he was before."[66] Several years earlier, jurors at the Old Bailey heard
a similar sentiment: "He has had a great tendency to wandering in his
mind since last March, which I attributed to domestic calamities." Explained the prisoner's neighbor, "I have noticed that he had lapses of
memory, and an aberration of mind since last September, when his sister
died and left him with two small children." Another acquaintance discovered the cumulative effect of these woes: "I have noticed him falling
into a kind of stupor."[67]

It did not take lint in the head or "brain fever" to leave one demonstrably altered, of course, nor did insanity necessarily require domestic
calamities. One could be subject to "violent passions" that appeared to
be autonomous and unpredictable:

> I have known the prisoner for four or five years, he was in a very bad
> state of mind; at times quite deranged: he is always so when he is
> subject to violent passions, and takes dislikes, and uses violence; most
> chiefly to his father and mother, and his nearest friends; I know of no
> provocation which he received on these occasions; I believe him a
> deranged madman; at times a raging madman, he is quiet and peace-
> able at other times; it comes on suddenly without notice; his father and
> mother can always discover something in his countenance when it is
> coming on, he is kind to his family when he is not so.[68]

The victim of the prisoner's assault, his father, explained to the court
that his son "is very rational at times, but goes off all of a minute."[69]
Again, no injury, or fever, or disease was posited as the cause for the
accused man's intemperate assault; rather, some unaccounted-for violent
passions swept over the prisoner "suddenly without notice."

Like physical causes, emotional spurs to derangement are merely recounted: witnesses make no attempt to explicate a possible underlying relation. On the infrequent occasion when lay witnesses were asked to expand on their comments, elaboration, not explanation, was solicited.

> *Sarah Leech:* About two years ago he received news from Gibraltar that his friends all died in the flames; that turned his head rather lunatic.
>
> *Attorney Knapp:* Did it appear to you, after he had received this intelligence with respect to the loss of all his family, that he possessed his senses?
>
> *Miss Leech:* I am certain it turned his head; I had constant opportunity of seeing it; he has been brought here by a parcel of boys several times, with a rope tied around his waist . . . he said he would go to Gibraltar . . . I asked him if he knew me, he said he knew nothing of me.[70]

On trial for stealing church property, the prisoner described above perfectly fit the description of the foolish thief who, confronted with the deed by a constable, uttered simply, "Oh God, I be so wicked."[71]

The trend in the 1830s and early 1840s to attribute the crime to illusory voices and mistaken impressions appears to reflect a growing tendency for lay witnesses to speak generally in terms of cause and effect. Thirty-six percent of lay witnesses mentioned a cause of insanity in their testimony in this period (see table 4.2). Although this is not an overwhelming frequency, it does represent a fourfold increase over the tendency of witnesses just thirty years earlier simply to declare that the prisoner was "out of his mind" or "not in his senses." Perhaps this change in testimony reflected a greater confidence among lay witnesses in their courtroom role; perhaps it was a reaction to the type of testimony they were hearing from medical witnesses, who were becoming a regular feature of insanity trials. Yet the rise of expert testimony in insanity trials certainly did not lead to the marginalization of lay witnesses' observations. In contrast, these trials contain more elaborate and expansive consideration of the mental world of the afflicted. Lay witnesses were hardly being silenced; in many ways, they were just beginning to find their voice.

THE LAY WITNESS'S UNDERSTANDING OF MADNESS

Does the frequency of such statements as "spoke like a lunatic," "behaved like an idiot," and "appeared as a madman" suggest a pervasive cultural agreement regarding how each of these *things* spoke, behaved, and appeared? Lay witnesses expressed little diffidence: they rarely couched their inferences in expressions like "I might be wrong, but . . ."

or "Of course, it's only my opinion, still . . ." Rather, they spoke clearly and with self-assurance, and there seems to be every reason for this. Madness, in Roy Porter's words, was not only "spectacularly on view," it was ubiquitous—at least by common cultural assent. One could spot insanity in speech, in dramatic alterations in behavior, and in casual conversation. London's citizens might attest to common understandings about madness with phrases that clearly assumed "everybody knows" ("It is often the case that insane persons are sometimes mischievous, sometimes melancholy") or they might cite their own experience with the deranged as a *class* ("I have seen much of persons who are insane; the disorder begins when the subject which caused their malady is raised").[72] Questions from the bench or posed by attorneys also conveyed the notion that insanity was hardly an unknown commodity: "[Y]our notion was, that he was at that time acting, as is very common for a madman, under mistaken impressions?"[73] Perhaps Attorney Mr. Raine gleaned this insight from William Battie's *Treatise* of 1758, or even from Locke's *Essay Concerning Human Understanding,* but early modern England certainly offered him a seemingly limitless trove of cultural beliefs about madness that he could employ to alert both witness and juror to the workings of the distracted mind.

Lay opinion concerning the etiology of mental derangement provides an analogous situation, ranging from earthly to heavenly realms. Several judges interrupted testimony to inquire if the moon was full on the night of the crime. Testifying about daytime hazards, Captain Horatio Nelson appeared in 1787 to attest to the ravages of the sun on one of his sailors. "[A]t the Island of Antigua, I think it was, he was struck with the sun, after which time he appeared very melancholy; I have been affected with it; I have been out of my senses; it hurts the brain."[74] *How* the sun affected the brain was neither explained nor queried. Indeed, one would be surprised to see any systematic questioning or sustained consideration of organic irritation and mentalist result. These were not medical witnesses; their opinions were *only* those of neighbors, lovers, and acquaintances. Still, the testimony could be elaborate: "[H]e had a paralytic stroke 7 years ago which affected his instep and leg . . . the cause of his leaving that employ was the rupture of a blood vessel, but I do not know where, there was a great discharge of blood—his conduct was materially altered since that, he gave many evidences of derangement of mind."[75] In sum, mind-body relations were asserted throughout the years of study, implicating brain fevers, blows to the head from a sledge-hammer, skull fractures, and "the rupture of a blood vessel" among other events. Popular culture appeared to accept the results of such easy traffic between mind and body unproblematically and, given the silence from the bench, uncritically, too.

When lay testimony came under judicial scrutiny, it was not at the level of the ambiguous perceptions regarding behavior or conversation but whether this altered state necessarily affected the afflicted person's capacity to distinguish right from wrong. Such queries were understandably difficult to answer and usually ended with the witness conceding that the prisoner most likely had retained sufficient capacity to know that "stealing was a bad thing." Exceptions can be found in cases where the prisoner had undergone a substantial alteration in functioning. In these trials, a lay witness could in all candor assert that the prisoner may *not* have been able to discern right from wrong, just as he or she apparently was unable to control any violent tendencies. Previous evidence of discretion and sound judgment were of no predictive value for these prisoners. The other question commonly asked of lay witnesses concerned their failure to take steps to ensure the prisoner's confinement. Neighbors usually responded that they expected the derangement to "go off again," but sometimes their answers could be quite effective, especially when they defended their inaction by asserting that they could minister to the mad more effectively than a mad-doctor could. The mother of one prisoner in 1843 testified, "If I had consulted a mad doctor, it would, in my opinion, have been likely to excite him very much indeed—I found that soothing him and treating him with kindness, was a much better remedy—he has frequently entreated me, if ever he went out of his mind, not to send him to a mad house."[76]

Witnesses who were not asked either whether the prisoner could tell right from wrong or why they had sought no medical advice might be challenged to consider signs that the prisoner actually knew very well what he or she was "about." A judge in 1784 asked a witness, "Do you happen to know that his wife has a little money of her own, independent of him?" suggesting an all-too-understandable motive for a supposedly motiveless crime. Alternatively, the bench might choose to highlight the considerable skill the prisoner had manifested in eluding detection: "Then he was not so mad but he wanted to keep out of the way?"[77] Indeed, the court was not above snide suggestions that the prisoner was *counterfeiting* madness. When a witness testified that the putatively mad prisoner impressed him as a "clever" woman, the judge sneered: "I dare say she was the cleverest woman you ever saw in your life?"[78] These few comments notwithstanding, lay witnesses did not encounter a legal culture that was unremittingly hostile to a defense of insanity. Questions from the bench could expose glaring gaps in the basis for one lay witness's inference of insanity but could also coax another to concede that a person perfectly collected at one moment could go "perfectly mad" the next.

If one steps back a bit from the issue of insanity per se, it is clear that neighbors, lovers, and relatives of allegedly mad prisoners were appearing in court under much the same rubric as acquaintances of any prisoner whose past behavior might be thought to have a bearing on the jury's deliberation—that is, as *character* witnesses. After all, acquaintances of sane prisoners appeared not as "experts" in human character but as intimates of the accused, informing the court of the prisoner's habitual functioning. The testimony of such character witnesses filled in the moral outlines of the prisoner, providing a standard the jury could consider as it gauged the likelihood that the accused was capable of committing the act. Although his or her testimony was technically a "fact" in the eyes of the law, the lay witness's assertion about the character of the accused prisoner was every bit an opinion about the prisoner's essential nature. The witness's "facts" about a neighbor's "appearing like a mad bullock," flighty conversations, or "bouncing about the room in a mad freak" were opinions in the guise of facts. Judicial inquiry probed the accuracy of fact—the impression the prisoner's behavior or speech made on the observer's senses—but not the capacity of the witness to judge. Madness was too much in the public domain, too accommodating to the individual proclivity of the listener, to require the bridge between cause and effect to be built plank by plank. What judges and attorneys could effectively question was the bridge between the prisoner's damaged perceptual cognition and any consequent moral pathology. "Do you think he was so deranged as not to know that it was a dreadful crime to fire at a fellow creature?" "Do you mean to swear that he was in that state of mind, as not to know right from wrong; or that he did not know it was harm to cut a man's throat?" "Do you think he knew it was a bad thing to steal?"[79]

There really was only one way to answer such questions persuasively in the affirmative. Beginning in the first half of the nineteenth century, multiple states of consciousness began tentatively to be asserted: "He did not appear at all to know what he was doing."[80] To be sure, this is hardly a deafening cri de coeur from a phalanx of lay witnesses, most of whom answered such questions as "Do you think he was so insane as not to know right from wrong?" with a simple "No." To answer "Yes" required a third alternative: a state of being in which one's usual capacity to distinguish right from wrong was overridden. Lay witnesses lacked sustained familiarity with a universe of distracted people to establish any experiential basis for this generalization. Their testimony was restricted to their observations and, one suspects, their imaginations. Prompted by the court, however, witnesses were encouraged to consider *how* it was possible to place "on hold" an habitual abhorrence of violence or cruelty to enable one to cut a man's throat. Of course, the neighbor and prisoner knew such an act was a crime. The question became, however, did John Doe know he was cutting a man's throat when he was doing it? In the simple declarations "[H]e appeared quite unconscious of his acts" and "[S]he is of an absent character of mind, she scarcely knows what she is doing," is an echo of yet another "cultural understanding" concerning madness: the growing separation of a physical act from its mental contemplation.

To the list of how madmen and madwomen appeared, behaved, and conversed, lay witnesses—prompted by cross-examination—were beginning to add more trenchant information: what it was like to *be* mad. This was more than a matter of reporting the tales of satanic voices and spirit-filled walls, although such extrasensory events were also part of it. It was rather the *experience* of madness that lay testimony was beginning to address, revealed early in the century by a nascent interest in circumscribed derangement and delusion. Although it would await the testimony of prisoners to describe the subjective experience of derangement in more detail, and the testimony of medical witnesses to draw out the implication of "unconscious" behavior, lay witnesses were showing an interest in the more subtle and recondite features of derangement, features that the jury would have to confront as there appeared to be more to madness than "behaving like a lunatic."

Medical Testimony
in Insanity Trials, I

HOW THE PRISONER MET THE DOCTOR

THE CASE OF THE MAD APOTHECARY

In 1785 Apothecary John O'Donnell appeared at the trial of his business partner, John Elliott, who had been arrested for firing two pistols at Mary Boydell, a spinster. O'Donnell made no secret of his partner's derangement: "[M]y opinion given of him to others has been, that he was mad, and on very slight provocation, he would go out of his mind and kill himself . . . [T]here was that excentricity about him that made him appear insane." O'Donnell nevertheless continued his professional association with Elliott; over the past six months, "[H]e attended my patients; prescribed for them; he directed the making of medicines." Mr. Garrow, appearing for the Crown, asked if the prisoner "gave directions for bleeding and blistering," and the witness willingly acknowledged: "In that respect, I saw no insanity, but in particular points the man was always insane." This answer was apparently too much for Mr. Garrow, who questioned O'Donnell as follows:

> *Mr. Garrow:* How many of [your patients] might he have poisoned in the course of that six months?
> *O'Donnell:* I do not know that he poisoned any. He was getting into his own back parlor stamping, and swearing, and d——n——g like a madman, and had every appearance of a madman; in short he was a madman.
> *Mr. Garrow:* But during all this time he was a mad apothecary, attending all his patients in partnership with you, and taking care of his patients?
> *O'Donnell:* Men are partially insane.
> *Mr. Garrow:* And that does not make them worse apothecaries perhaps?
> *O'Donnell:* Perhaps not.
> *Mr. Garrow:* Then I am sure I will not ask you another question.

At this point the judge interrupted,

> *Court:* I am a little at a loss what to understand from you.
>
> *O'Donnell:* I have been so bullied; witnesses should be examined with candor, and not put out of temper, and out of their senses, so as not to be able to understand what they say.
>
> *Court:* You describe this man as capable of going about his business, and prescribing for his patients; and as a man of philosophical well turned mind [O'Donnell had earlier described Elliott as "addicted to his experiments"]; yet you say you considered him a madman. Why do you so consider him?
>
> *O'Donnell:* From his general conduct . . . he would get into his back room, and then stamp and swear, and drive things about, and nobody knew from what; and he frequently walked about melancholy, with his hands folded; it was my opinion [that he was insane] before this affair.[1]

O'Donnell was not the only medical witness to appear at Elliott's trial. Samuel Foart Simmons, physician to St. Luke's, had known the prisoner for fifteen years and had recently looked on him as "somewhat disordered" in consequence of a letter he had received announcing that the sun was "a very comfortable and habitable spot." The prisoner's missive, grounded in "the theories of Dr. Priestly, phlogistication, and calcination," concluded that "a fruitful imagination may easily conceive [the sun] to be by far the most blissful habitation of the whole system." If Dr. Simmons thought such a letter constituted a prima facie proof of derangement, he was mistaken, for the judge observed archly: "I think I could point out a passage in Buffon, that would prove him as much insane." Garrow pressed the questioning further.

> *Mr. Garrow:* Is the argument well pursued to establish the point which the author labours?
>
> *Mr. Simmons:* I think not; the argument itself appears to me absurd.
>
> *Mr. Garrow:* But a man intending to establish such a conclusion, absurd as it may be, has he argued it rationally?
>
> *Mr. Simmons:* He has argued it ingeniously.[2]

Simmons tried to extricate himself from this obviously equivocal basis for inferring madness by switching to more familiar signs of madness—Elliott's "irritability of temper" and "general inconsistence of conduct"—but here, too, he found himself eventually cornered because he had to acknowledge that he had done nothing in response to his friend's increasingly deranged behavior, implying that the behavior, though bothersome or even troubling, was not sufficiently threatening to warrant restraint.[3] Indeed, nothing in either Simmons's or O'Donnell's testimony could not have been uttered by a neighbor, an employer, or a relative, though both were medical men. Lay witnesses reported their neighbors "stamping about" and employed the terms *melancholy* and *insane* in their testimony. In fact, lay witnesses probably came off looking much less foolish than these two men of medicine.

The Case of the Mad Apothecary is selected here not to reveal the ineptitude of medical witnesses in eighteenth-century medical trials but to illustrate a significant point in the early stages of forensic-psychiatric testimony. At the conclusion of his testimony, Simmons was asked a seemingly ordinary question: "Do you mean to state it as your opinion, solemnly delivered, that he was a lunatic?"[4] Although neighbors and relatives were routinely asked to characterize the accused's behavior or conversation in such terms as "Was it the speech of a lunatic?" and "Did he behave like a madman, quite *gone?*" medical witnesses alone faced questions regarding the ultimate question: the prisoner's *membership* in a specific class of humanity—the mad. Not surprisingly, an affirmative assertion led to spirited questioning regarding the basis for the diagnosis, the precision of the medical definition, and the unequivocal legibility of the supposed symptoms. The language of medical witnesses eventually diverged from lay images grounded in common community perceptions to reveal a distinctive professional voice that clarified the previously impenetrable and mystified the seemingly obvious.

FACT OR OPINION? THE SPECIAL CASE OF FORENSIC MEDICAL TESTIMONY

The difference between asking a witness "Was he only violent when he heard Mr. Mellish's name?" and "Is it a common symptom of derangement for madmen to be moved to violence under a derangement?" is the difference between asking a witness to report a fact and asking him or her to express an opinion. All witnesses are ostensibly precluded from giving an opinion; persons not related to the dispute are called into court only to inform the jury of facts surrounding the case that they alone could have known. Jury members originally needed no such factual input. They had been selected precisely because, as neighbors of the accused, they were in the best position to be familiar with the circumstances surrounding the crime. Over time, as the jury evolved into a very different kind of body—with jurors chosen specifically for their lack of knowledge pertaining to the crime—the court grew increasingly reliant on the testimony of witnesses: community members who had heard or seen something that implicated or exonerated the prisoner.

Witnesses in English courts were traditionally permitted to impart only such "knowledge" of the crime as they had apprehended though sensory impressions. Only "facts" that the witness had directly experienced— that he or she *saw* the accused fleeing the scene, *heard* the gunshot, *smelled* the sulfur escaping from the pistol barrel—could be reported to the court.[5] From hearing these firsthand experiences of on-scene witnesses, the jury was charged to determine the true circumstances surrounding the offense. In the words of a noted jurist, "A Witness swears but to what he hath heard or seen, generally or more largely, to what hath fallen under his senses. But a juryman swears to what he can infer and conclude from the testimony of such witnesses."[6] The direct observations of immediate bystanders or actual parties to the crime, however, might not exhaust the information the jury needed to render an informed judgment. For example, on-scene witnesses could inform the court whether the accused party had actually signed a bond, but it might take a "master of grammar" to decipher ambiguous words in the agreement or to translate and interpret the bond's actual meaning "when the court's Latin halts a little."[7] Likewise, a bystander could testify to having found a drowned man floating in the Thames, but he could hardly answer the court's query regarding why the victim's lungs were free of water. To render a judgment in a case where the facts were unclear or in dispute, the jury's inquiry extended to hypothetical questions, requiring a familiarity with the phenomenon that could be provided only by someone with unique experience or learning. Beginning at least as early as the fourteenth century, London courts summoned skilled persons to advise the jury in a range of civil and criminal matters.[8] What the "master of grammar," skilled craftworker, or insurance broker shared was the possession of particular knowledge that transcended the life-events of the ordinary citizen. Either special occupational experience or unique, systematic learning enabled these *expert* witnesses to interpret evidence that the untrained or unknowledgeable could not.

The opinion expert witnesses offered was distinguished from the lay witness's fact by "a practical consideration, i.e. whether the inference [was] within the fair range of dispute, or whether, given the impressions of sense, the inference from them [was] so self-evident as to make any effort to question it frivolous."[9] It might have been "frivolous" to ask if an apparently deceased infant was in fact dead, but determining whether it had been stillborn or born alive and later smothered brought the circumstances surrounding the death into the "fair range of dispute." Similarly, it would be frivolous to question if a stone-cold body was dead but inquiring why his wounds "gave no blood" raised the possibility that death had preceded the stabbing, thus shifting the lay witness's perceptions—*facts*—again into the "fair range of dispute." When surface sensory impressions were ambiguous or potentially misleading, the court called on the peculiar experience of the expert. Alone among witnesses, the expert was able to broaden the court's inquiry from the specific incident to the general category: the *anticipated* course of a fever, the *expected* lethality of different types of wounds, the *usual* symptoms of a particular disease. Also alone among witnesses, the expert witness need have no direct knowledge of the crime under review. Training, special learning, and occupational experience legitimated such a witness's opinion just as the lay witness's experience legitimated his or her "facts."

Although it appears to have been a settled practice for the English court to avail itself of expert advice in evidentiary disputes, legitimacy was a negotiable commodity, easier claimed by some experts than others. Eighteenth-century English physicians, surgeons, and apothecaries, for example, did not find quite the same acceptance in the courtroom as their European cohorts. Courts of law on the Continent traditionally sought medical advice on a range of criminal matters, including poisonings, infanticides, murderous assaults, suicides, and insanity. Further, the pursuit of expert knowledge was not ad hoc, as in England, but mandated by statute. Beginning with Charlemagne, codes of law stipulated the oath courtroom physicians were to take, their qualifications, and their fee for testimony.[10] Although proof of the prisoner's culpability necessarily rested with the court, formalized statutes within the *Bamberger* and the *Constitutio Criminalis Carolina* codes in Germany and the Napoleonic Code in France signaled the recognition that in certain kinds of criminal cases, medical opinion could be pivotal. Medical assistance was rendered in the form of either pretrial reports or sworn testimony delivered at trial. By the sixteenth century, medical advisers to European courts could avail themselves of a rich corpus of medico-legal writing beginning with Ambroise Paré's *How to Make Reports, and to Embalme the Dead* (originally published in French in 1575), followed in the next century by the nine magisterial volumes of Paolo Zacchia's *Quaestiones medico-legales.* Both authors addressed the issues specialists in legal medicine were likely to face, such as how to determine the cause of death in infanticide, how to recognize the signs of drowning, and how to determine fetal age. Organized series of lectures on medicine in relation to law began at the University of Leipzig in 1650.[11]

The edicts that created a niche for medico-legal expertise and, by extension, a ready market for the growing body of medico-legal tracts also fashioned a privileged forensic role for European medical advisers. In France, medical practitioners served not as mere witnesses but as *chirurgien jurés,* almost as subordinate judges. French law offered to these sworn surgeons both exalted professional status and guaranteed remuneration. They might be consulted on the annulment of a marriage on the ground of impotence or on the presence of idiocy, insanity, or disputed identity.[12] Even such modern-day professional concerns as discerning malpractice and estimating the costs of medical treatment could fall within their province. Whatever the issue, only sworn surgeons were permitted to testify, a privilege highly prized in the seventeenth and eighteenth centuries.

The development of forensic medicine and of the role of the forensic witness in England presents a sharp contrast. Before the nineteenth century, a medico-legal literature was virtually nonexistent, lectures on the subject were not offered until the late 1700s, and the status of the medical witness was anything but exalted. This has recently been attributed to the manner in which proof was assessed in the English courtroom. Whereas the Continental court focused primarily on adjudication by rational, demonstrable methods, based on proof methodically assembled by experts, the English court emphasized adversarial confrontation between the parties, and trials centered on persuading a lay jury to believe one or the other account of what had happened. As Crawford notes, "English law preferred lay consensus respecting justice over rigorous demonstrations of truth."[13] Since the mode of proof carried no statutory requirement for medical examinations, the conditions that favored the creation of a medico-legal specialty on the Continent were conspicuously absent in England. Although physicians, apothecaries, and surgeons certainly participated in criminal courts in early modern England, they enjoyed no special status and received no remuneration. Indeed, they were *compelled* to appear, like any citizen might be who possessed information germane to a criminal prosecution. With few medico-legal texts to draw on, with the prospect of facing embarrassing cross-examination,[14] and with no financial benefits to encourage participation, medical men in the late eighteenth century could hardly relish the prospect of appearing in court.

In the space of a few short years in the nineteenth century, however, English legal medicine acquired both a number of important forensic texts and, perhaps more important, the enthusiastic advocacy of medical writers. In part, the rapid development of a corpus of writings in medical jurisprudence appears to have been a defensive move sparked by the professional humiliation forensic witnesses faced at the hands of an advocacy bar. Lawyers and judges seem to have been better informed on matters of medical evidence than clinical practitioners, which is not surprising given their regular attendance at lectures on medical jurisprudence and their authorship of some early medico-legal tracts.[15] Further, the evolution of the lawyer's role from questioner of witnesses to adversary meant a heightened scrutiny of evidence and the essentials of proof. Although such sustained inquiry would necessarily mean even closer examination of forensic witnesses, many medical authors intent on reforming haphazard professional diagnosis and classification welcomed the medico-legal courtroom interchanges. "[O]f all the medical sciences," one medical author averred, forensic medicine was "the most precise and exact."[16]

The demands for evidentiary rigor and the threat of public humiliation through blatant exposure of professional ignorance were therefore much-needed spurs to the general practitioner's quest for knowledge about areas of medical jurisprudence he was likely to encounter if subpoenaed to appear in court. Beginning in 1816, with George Male's *An Epitome of Juridical or Forensic Medicine: For the Use of Medical Men, Coroners, and Barristers,* and continuing into the 1820s with the publication of important forensic treatises by Smith, Paris and Fonblanque, and Christison, professional designs and defensiveness were reflected in both the quantity and the quality of medical writing.[17] Medical periodicals that often highlighted developments in legal medicine flourished in the 1820s, and the first university chair in legal medicine in England was established in 1829, when John Gordon Smith was appointed chair of medical jurisprudence at what is now University College, London. Andrew Duncan, Jr., had been appointed to Britain's first professorship of medical jurisprudence at the University of Edinburgh in 1807.

Medical witnesses participated in dramatically increasing numbers in London's homicide trials in the 1820s. In his survey of London killings between 1729 and 1878, Thomas Rogers Forbes uncovered evidence that whereas medical testimony was given in slightly less than 50 percent of homicide trials at the Old Bailey in the mid-eighteenth century, medical participation had grown to approximately three trials in four by the 1820s and to nine in ten by the late 1840s.[18] The questions asked of medical witnesses were designed to elicit their professional *opinion;* subjects ranged from whether a simple fall could produce a bruise that resembled a blow from a blunt instrument to how much poison had been administered to the victim. Medical witnesses commented on a range of forensic matters: from wounds caused by sharp or blunt instruments to injuries to the central nervous system, from sexual offenses to infanticide, from poisonings to asphyxiation.[19]

Although lay witnesses were of course also familiar with bruises, wounds, and fevers, their *knowledge* did not extend beyond their own experiences, restricting their ability to speculate on the natural course of a fever or the relative lethality of different types of wounds. If medical opinion sometimes seemed inexact or equivocal, it was nonetheless true that lesions, poisons, and fevers were mysterious entities whose characteristic course was arguably a matter of professional opinion rather than straightforward lay "fact." One area of pathology, however, though mysterious and unpredictable, was not peremptorily consigned to the medical expert. Although medico-legal writings sought to isolate and classify the clinical varieties of insanity and medical witnesses claimed a privileged voice in detecting its hidden properties, the boundary separating opinion from fact was never more in question than when expert testimony turned to the prisoner's alleged madness.

In 1817, John Haslam, apothecary to Bethlem, published *Medical Jurisprudence as It Relates to Insanity,* the first English work on the forensic aspects of mental derangement. As we have seen, a host of late eighteenth-century texts endeavored to define and classify various forms of mental impairment; some even speculated about the wider implications of mental distraction. Haslam's treatise, however, was the first to combine a classification of types of insanity with the assertion of occupationally based expertise in deciphering insanity's more recondite character. Medico-legal authors writing in the area of mental medicine faced the task of convincing a dubious public (and court) that their particular area of expertise was not intrinsically intelligible; that the lay witness's "facts" were often misleading or simply erroneous.

> Ordinary persons have been much deceived by the temporary display of rational discourse . . . [exciting] a doubt in the minds of learned and intelligent persons who have merely speculated about the disease . . . but let him protract the discourse [with the mad person], let him touch the fatal string which throws his mind into discord; let him draw the hair-trigger which inflames the combustible materials of his disease, and he will be surprised if not alarmed by the explosion . . . [T]he experienced will . . . find that by some unaccountable association, even ordinary topics are linked to his darling delusions—the map of his mind will point out that the smallest rivulet flows into the great stream of his derangement.[20]

Not only was the lay witness likely to be duped by appearances of "surface rationality," he or she was also apt to be taken in by the madman who "overacts his part." What concerned the public and the courts most, after all, was not the error of mistaking reason for insanity but the possibility that sane prisoners might actually counterfeit insanity. On this point Haslam was emphatic: since the public's only experience with deranged persons was gained by visiting Bethlem or witnessing stage performances, they could very likely be deceived by momentary histrionics and exaggerated emotionalism. The *trained* observer, however, knew that it was beyond the power of the sane person to sustain the character of a paroxysm of active insanity (hence the need to persist in the interview). Once alone, once confident that they were unobserved, the counterfeiters drop "the deception . . . unable to prevent sleep." Only the experienced observer knows that the play-actor is deficient in "the presiding principle, the Ruling Delusion." Like the modern-day detective who sifts through false confessions and recognizes the genuine article because only the real culprit could have known the nonpublicized, incriminating detail, the early mad-doctors claimed to share knowledge that only truly mad persons could possess. The lay witness stood conspicuously outside this "knowing circle" and was therefore easily fooled by either extravagant display or apparent calm. Medico-legal tracts concerning insanity therefore asserted privileged insight as they disparaged the acuity of the public's discernment.[21]

Over time, authors of medical jurisprudence challenged not only lay perceptions of derangement but the law's traditional notion of insanity and mental functioning. In *The Medical Jurisprudence of Insanity* (1840), J. M. Pagan extended the consideration of insanity beyond impaired intellectual faculty to include derangement of the passions and affections: "disease of the moral faculties may exist when it is impossible to discover any intellectual disorder."[22] Criminality that flowed from such insanity knew no motive, and its perpetrator made no attempt to avoid detection. Pagan set aside the law's traditional criterion for finding insanity—the incapacity to distinguish right from wrong—as he sought to incorporate the emerging conception of moral insanity and homicidal monomania that had been popularized by the schools of médecine mentale and common sense philosophy. At stake was the entire question of insanity as a matter of intellectual delirium, whether global in its mental reach or particularist, as in delusion.

Although Pagan did not explore the implications of "nonintellectual" insanity in this early text, the attention he gave to such issues as the lack of motive and absence of precaution caught the eye of the *British and Foreign Medical Review,* which warned medical witnesses to stay away from judging the "adequacy of motives." A better question—indeed, the only question—was whether the prisoner had the power to resist the "horrid impulse" that led to the crime. The *Review* therefore took exception to Pagan's formula for discovering the existence of moral insanity (the lack of motive), but its unmistakable emphasis on control signaled a public acceptance on the part of medical writers that insanity could be a matter of immoral impulse quite apart from what the defendant "understood" regarding the difference between right and wrong. The "true test of responsibility," concluded the reviewer, was whether the actor retained "sufficient power to control his actions."[23]

The effort to expand medico-legal inquiry into a disease of the moral faculties also included a critical scrutiny of traditional "intellectualist insanity"—specifically, the assumed centrality of delusion to madness. Thomas Erskine's initial caveat that the exculpatory delusion must bear a direct connection to the crime—"the act must be the immediate unqualified offspring of [the] disease"—came under increasing scrutiny. Suppose no connection could be found between the delusion and the crime; did this mean that none existed? Suppose a link could be discerned; to whom should it appear "logical" or "rational"?[24] What, after all, does it mean to say that a deluded person found his or her delusion logical? A good measure of this assault on delusion appears to have been motivated by the belief that circumscribed derangement was an obstacle to the acceptance of an insanity of the will unaccompanied by intellectual delirium. Writing in 1842, James Cowles Prichard complained that it was "a settled doctrine of English Courts that there cannot be insanity without delusion." Like Pagan, Prichard believed that mental derangement not only affected intellectual faculties but extended to understanding, "implicat[ing] the moral affections, the temper, the feelings and the propensities, [affecting] the moral character even more than the understanding." His contention that "the act of the madman is for the most part without motive" drew criticism from the *British and Foreign Medical Review,* very much along the lines of the "sufficient delusion" criterion. The failure to discover a motive could be taken to signify its nonexistence, when in fact a motive may well exist for the "most atrocious crime without our being able to discover it." Does the existence of a rational motive—revenge, for example—necessarily mean that the prisoner was sane, hence responsible?[25]

The editors of the *Review* also revealed a certain uneasiness with the idea of a moral insanity devoid of intellectual confusion. Although they freely admitted the possibility that the affections could take a pathological turn, the necessary coupling of such moral insanity with clear-headedness they found unacceptable. In every case of true insanity "some latent disorder of the intellectual powers" had to obtain.[26] Like the originators of monomanie homicide and related forms of derangement that implicated the will exclusively, medico-legal writers often found fierce opponents not only in the legal community but from their medical brethren as well.

The "cause" for a moral insanity was taken up in full force in 1843 with the publication of *The Plea of Insanity in Criminal Cases.* Forbes Winslow, a member of the Royal College of Surgeons, "wish[ed] to direct the particular attention of the reader, inasmuch as it has not hitherto been recognized in our English courts of judicature, . . . to a disordered condition of the moral affections and propensities, unaccompanied by any delusion of the intellectual powers."[27] Locating the condition's origin in Pinel's manie sans délire, Winslow reviewed a series of cases, including Georget's discussion of the trial of Henriette Cornier, to substantiate his claim that there was a form of insanity, "the principal symptom of which [was] a morbid desire to sacrifice human life [and in which] no intellectual delusion was perceptible." Winslow's focus was desire, not motive. It was in fact the absence of motive that distinguished the moral maniac from the real criminal, who revealed sanity in attempting to conceal intent, secure a means of escape, and elude detection. None of this was true for the *morally* deranged person, who killed as a result of morbid propensities and diseased passions. Winslow underlined the need to attend to questions of impulse control in his advice to medical witnesses. "Never forget, [you have] nothing to do with the legal definition of the term." Avoiding the question of whether the alleged lunatic was competent to distinguish between right and wrong, the witness should confine himself to one "legitimate point: had [the prisoner], at the time he committed the offense, sufficient control over his actions?" But Winslow provides no helpful hints regarding how such a determination was to be made.[28]

An unmistakable tone of defensiveness in Winslow's text suggests something more than interprofessional rivalry. It was not only that lay witnesses were routinely asked to give their opinion regarding a prisoner's insanity that annoyed him: "No man is considered competent to give an opinion on a complicated question of mechanics who has not paid some attention to the science [and yet] medical knowledge is thought to come by intuition." Never having had the opportunity to study the diseases of the mind, the judge and the jury "must depend principally upon the evidence of the medical man" although it is clear from Winslow's tone that he did not believe this to be the practice. What seemed to rankle him much more deeply were the outdated legal doctrines represented in judicial instruction and opinion. "Has not our knowledge of the disorders of the mind advanced during the last fifty years? Do we not know more of insanity than our professional brethren did who lived in the days of Coke, Mansfield, and Erskine?"[29]

On reflection, the "plea" in Winslow's book appears to have been the entreaty of the mad-doctor for the legitimacy to proffer an opinion in an area of human functioning misunderstood by the public. Winslow's opinion, like Pagan's, was not geared to intellectualist insanity; widespread acceptance of madness as profound confusion or delirious rantings hardly needed to be negotiated. Winslow and Pagan were mapping cognitive territory that extended into areas of the human soul that medicine was only starting to claim as its rightful preserve. Pagan and Winslow represented a generation of mad-doctors who were actively expanding expert opinion into the possibility that intellect, will, and the passions could function independently. By the late 1830s and 1840s, therefore, the assertion of medical *opinion* over lay *fact* was taking place against a profound shift in what medical men believed themselves capable of understanding about the range of madness.

The task of convincing the public, as well as the legal (and perhaps, the medical) community, that insanity was indeed the most recondite of phenomena was complicated by the fact that insanity traditionally constituted the one area in which the common law permitted lay witnesses to venture an opinion. According to Wigmore, "Whenever a person presented himself as having acquaintance with, and therefore observation of a testator or an accused person whose insanity was in question, i.e., whenever the witness had the fundamental testimonial qualification of personal observation no one thought of objecting on the score of the opinion rule [the rule that restricted witnesses to direct observation]."[30] The reason for the court's active soliciting of lay opinion is not hard to fathom. Madness, after all, was not a physical *lesion* requiring a surgeon or an apothecary. In most cases, personal observation—the traditional basis for the lay witness's fact—apparently afforded sufficient experience to support any acquaintance's opinion. Such opinion, however, was restricted to the particular prisoner on trial and any specific signs of derangement. No opinion was ventured on the properties of madness: the probability that it could subside at any moment or return with renewed ferocity. The lay witness's opinion was therefore circumscribed by his or her familiarity with the prisoner's conventional way of behaving. When the witness deemed madness to occur, common cultural stereotypes and definitional tools constituted the basis for that opinion: the speech of a madman or madwoman, the look of a lunatic. As long as insanity remained a matter of delirious ranting and conspicuous incoherence, one hardly needed a specialist to "find" distraction.

What lay witnesses could not address with their limited frame of reference were the questions about mental functioning that courtroom inquiry increasingly probed. Granted that they considered their neighbor, relative, or fellow worker to be "senseless"; did they further believe the accused capable of committing the crime without knowing what he or she was doing? Acknowledging that the prisoner was traditionally capable of distinguishing right from wrong, did they believe that such capacity could be suspended in a particular *paroxysm of rage?* Having just smothered her child, did the accused appear to "feel what a person in

her right senses ought to feel"? Of course, not many medical witnesses
could (or can!) answer such questions either, but what distinguished
mad-doctors' court appearances from lay witnesses' was that doctors
were questioned concerning the dynamics of the supposed disease first
and the characteristics of the prisoner second. The novel feature of Dr.
John Monro's testimony in 1760 was that its focus was not the prisoner,
Earl Ferrers, but lunacy itself: its symptoms, the likelihood that lunatics
"knew what they were up to," and how often lunatics were "apt to be
seized with rage." These were points lay witnesses could not speak to
because their only frame of reference was their neighbor's or friend's or
relative's antics and their own idiosyncratic understanding of madness.
Between the years of Monro's appearance and the publication of Winslow's treatise in 1843, the broadening of courtroom questions from "how
Ferrers acted, when angered," to "how lunatics acted, when seized with
rage," transported the lay witness's fact into "the fair range of dispute."
The issue was no longer whether the neighbor was "knowable" to intimates but whether he or she belonged to a species of persons whose
behavior was decipherable only by the expert observer.

ACQUIRING THE BASIS FOR EXPERT OPINION

The appearance of the physician superintendent of Bethlem, John
Monro, in 1760 represents a critical juncture in the history of forensic
psychiatry because it marks a moment when testimony about lunacy was
conceived in terms of professional experience, not common cultural consciousness. Although it would be decades before medical witnesses would
begin their testimony with such statements as "Among my patients at the
asylum" or "Having 85 patients under my care," the centrality of occupationally based training was fast distinguishing the "impressions" of lay
witnesses from the experience of the practitioner. Of course, asylum superintendency was only the most conspicuous work-related basis for singular experience with the mad. Particular knowledge could also be
claimed by the general medical man who, in the course of his regular
practice, would very likely encounter madness in either its temporary or
permanent manifestation. Indeed, eighteenth-century medical testimony
bearing on insanity was offered by just such men—physicians, surgeons,
and apothecaries—who happened upon a case of mental derangement
every so often and appeared in court to venture an opinion on the "general case." At least to the end of the eighteenth century, the more extended experiences of the asylum superintendent were not deemed to be
essential to support the assertion of professional opinion. All medical
practitioners could theoretically claim expertise by virtue of their pro-

fessional training. Madness was not regarded as a separate pathology with distinctive physical or interactional symptoms and a discrete place in the medical curriculum. The first lectures on the medical jurisprudence of mental derangement were held in London in 1825 and even then were sparsely attended.[31] For most medical men, madness was an aspect of general organic pathology. Expertise was most often demonstrated by situating the derangement in a fever or in the effects of a head injury. As we have seen, such "explanations" were routinely put forward by lay witnesses as well.

Not surprisingly, then, it was not the general medical practitioner who eventually distinguished himself from the lay witness in insanity trials but the asylum physician, surgeon, or apothecary who could cite a wealth of experiences in treatment and case management, differentiating himself not only from the lay witness but also from his fellow medical practitioners who could refer to only one or two cases a year. The more experience in treatment, the more assertive the opinion, even to the point where (mere) practitioners began in court to defer to their brethren with "greater numbers" of patients.[32] This sort of acknowledgment, however, is absent in the early years of medical testimony bearing on insanity, when any professional familiarity with madness could support an opinion on the general case. Only in time did medical testimony reveal the importance of texts written from the specialist's gaze and professional opinion grounded in more than general medical training. When John Monro mounted the witness stand in 1760, few observers in the House of Lords could have predicted the eventual emergence of the role of asylum practitioner cum forensic-psychiatric witness that his appearance would initiate.

Few observers could also have predicted how difficult it would be for medical witnesses to justify their privileged voice in this category of disease. Whether it was a surfeit of folk wisdom that attended the experience of madness or a belief that it was not particularly mysterious but decipherable by the "inexperienced" eye, mad-doctors in court faced special obstacles. The observations of lay witnesses were apparently given the aura of officially sanctioned opinion. If neighbors, lovers, or relatives considered themselves something less of an expert on *all* features of madness, they nonetheless felt perfectly qualified to pronounce a particular prisoner insane. What, then, was the medical man doing in the court in the first place? Weren't the signs of insanity self-evident? Wasn't it just plain frivolous to question what the lay witness had seen or heard?

The first question concerns the entrance of medical witnesses into the ordinary trials heard at the Old Bailey. Were they standard witnesses—character, on-scene, familial—who happened to be medically qualified

Table 5.1   How the doctor met the prisoner (in percentages)

	1760–1800	1801–29	1830–43
Private acquaintance	33	14	7
Professional acquaintance	61	37	22
Prison or jail interview		40	58
On-scene witness			7
No previous contact			3
Insufficient data	6	9	3
N	(18)	(35)	(74)

Note: Several medical witnesses testified more than once; each court appearance is represented as a single occasion to examine the basis for prisoner-practitioner acquaintance.

(like O'Donnell and Simmons in the case of the mad apothecary), or were they medical practitioners whose prior treatment of deranged patients enabled them to advise the court on the *particular* characteristics of insensibility? Were these early forensic witnesses merely interested professionals who believed it was their duty to address the court in matters of their expertise, or had they formed a professional association with the accused? Were they perhaps prison surgeons or asylum physicians whose familiarity with the accused began with confinement? Each of these forms of association was represented in the years 1760–1843, although the relationship between the medical practitioner and the prisoner shifted significantly over time. To address the larger question concerning how medical men were able to establish a voice separate from the lay public, it is vital first to answer the more immediate question: What brought medical men to court in the first place?

HOW THE PRISONER MET THE DOCTOR

Catherine Crawford's investigation of medical witnesses at the Old Bailey between 1730 and 1830 affords a convenient starting point to examine the special case of the mad-doctor as forensic witness. Her analysis of the participation of "general" medical witnesses revealed three forms of association: attending (having had a professional acquaintance with a person who subsequently became embroiled in a legal dispute), pretrial (having performed a postmortem or been called to determine whether the prisoner stood mute "through obstinacy or through visitation of God"), and pure (lacking firsthand knowledge of the particular case, appearing in court to offer an opinion on evidence submitted at the trial). Crawford concluded that pretrial association was most common, while pure medical testimony was rare in the eighteenth century.[33]

Interactions likely to generate forensic-psychiatric testimony include Crawford's categories as well as a range of other forms of associations particular to mental medicine. Some medical men certainly appeared to testify about patients who manifested symptoms of delirium and mania, but others reported their casual conversations with neighbors as grounds for their inference of derangement. From 1760 to 1843, 98 physicians, surgeons, and apothecaries made a total of 127 court appearances in 78 trials (table 5.1). Most testified only once, although a few offered opinions in several trials. Prominent among them were prison surgeons.

A Private Acquaintance

I am the apothecary at Bethlem Hospital. I have been conversant with complaints of insane persons about twenty years, I have in that time had the opportunity of seeing many thousand cases. In November last, by desire of Mr. Haigh, the prisoner was introduced to me under a feigned name, rather against my will; I had one interview with [the prisoner] for near two hours, my opinion is that he is absolutely insane; on my certificate he was put into Hoxton mad-house . . . [H]is mind was in a state of insanity. I delivered the opinion that he was a incurable lunatic.[34]

In his only appearance at the Old Bailey, John Haslam admitted in 1813 to a rather unorthodox diagnostic procedure that nonetheless reveals one way in which persons in early modern England might encounter the medical *gaze*. In the early years of medical testimony—particularly in the late eighteenth century—medical witnesses were likely to have had no previous professional association with the mad. Acquaintances, neighbors, and fellow-lodgers appeared in court and testified very much in the capacity of a character witness, except that they prefaced their comments with a reference to their medical qualifications. Much like the prisoner who was kept from knowing Haslam's real name and intent, the accused in these trials listened as their neighbors acknowledged their position as a "Physician to St. Luke's" and then added, "I have for some time past looked upon him as a man somewhat disordered." The encounters that could generate subsequent testimony varied widely.

In 1805, Frances Lowndes, a "medical gentleman," appeared in court to testify about a defendant who, years earlier, had completed some work for him at his house. "I knew the prisoner about seven or eight years ago. [H]e talked perfectly incoherent, I never could make anything [of it], he talked so frantic, he was running out of one thing into another, fancying that he had made a gun superior to all in the world."[35] This physician's testimony contained nothing remarkable—nothing sets it apart from that of any other previous employer. In another case, in 1774, a witness who "studied medicine" described his fellow-lodger, now on trial, as "sometimes frantic, sometimes melancholic." In this case, his perceptual skills had been sharpened by having once lived near a mad-house, spending his days conversing with the inmates who were "chained to the trees."[36]

In each of these trials, medical witnesses appeared, cited their professional background or occupation, and answered questions on the type of madness they perceived the prisoner to be suffering from. Although their testimony was indeed unremarkable, their simple presence in the witness box constituted an important stage in the early acceptance of medical testimony bearing on insanity because they closely resembled witnesses who normally appeared at insanity trials: friends, employers, co-workers. Their knowledge was mediated through a personal relationship with the particular prisoner: "the one who was in the best position to know" was gradually transforming into "the one who was in the best position to judge." Fully one-third of medical witnesses in the eighteenth century enjoyed a personal acquaintance with the prisoner before the crime, and one suspects that it was this rather than the court's ready acknowledgment of medical expertise that facilitated the acceptance of the new expert.

Professional Acquaintance: "Out-patient"

A second form of association between the accused and the medical witness was clearly professional, although here, too, years of casual acquaintance often preceded the eventual consultation for derangement: "I am a surgeon and live in Hackney-road. I have known the prisoner six or seven years—she has not been of sound mind during that time—she was not always unsound, but occasionally so—I attended her about four years ago, in consequence of hypochondria—I have attended her several times in a similar way."[37]

A long-standing acquaintance was also described by a Dr. Willis, testifying in 1800, who informed the court, "I have known the prisoner at the bar for twenty-five years, I have prescribed several times for him, and attended him for the purpose of assisting a derangement in his head."[38] On occasion, an ostensibly physical complaint was revealed to have mental consequence: "I attended the prisoner two years and a half ago for a bodily disorder; I perceived her to be a woman of melancholy temper.

She had symptoms which indicate a predisposition to insanity which is at times hereditary in families, it is very susceptible to break out at particular intervals."[39] Regrettably, most medical witnesses did not reveal the circumstances under which they were called to see a deranged person—whether it was at the individual's or the family's instigation. Explicit reference was occasionally made to a third party, such as a charitable organization that paid local physicians to visit the poor and ailing of their congregation. One such organization was the Society for Visiting the Sick and Charitable Deeds, which was sponsored by London's Sephardic Jewish community. The society had employed Daniel Jacob de Castro to see a prisoner a little more than a year before trial. Testifying in court, de Castro reported, "I am secretary to the Jewish communion; this man's friends applied for relief, in consequence of his being in a state of lunacy; I looked back to my books, and I found in consequence of that, two guineas were granted. March was a twelve-month."[40] Joining Dr. de Castro in attendance was his brother, Benjamin, and a third physician, Joseph Hart Myers. Myers's examination reveals the type of questioning that often attended the proffering of expert opinion.

> *Dr. Hart Meyers [sic]:* I am a physician—I have attended [the prisoner] in the character of a physician . . . I was called in to him about two years ago, under a great delirium, he had every symptom of insanity . . . after attending him four or five weeks, his fever yielded to the treatment we administered; but there was a perfect degree of idiocy, which remain a fatuity, absolute fatuity.
> *Court:* [H]ow long did you attend him after his fever had abated?
> *Dr. Hart Meyers:* His fever intermitted and returned with as much severity as the first: I attended him often after his fever was removed.
> *Court:* Is it not uncommon for a state of weakness and wandering of mind to remain for some time after a fever, for a delirium to remain?
> *Dr. Hart Meyers:* Yes.
> *Court:* Were you able from attending him for a week after his fever had left him, to form any judgment whether his disorder was a permanent nature or not?
> *Dr. Hart Meyers:* From his having been deemed incurable by other professional men, I was convinced his disorder would not yield to the treatment. I believe this disorder was of the kind called idiocy . . . he had a ticket I believe from St. Luke's, to which I recommended him.[41]

What set Dr. Hart Myers's testimony apart from the lay witness's was not the terminology he employed—delirium, fever, and insanity were long familiar to the court by way of any neighbor's observations. Hart

Myers's appearance differed in terms of the questions he was asked: "Is it not uncommon" for delirium to linger after fever? "Were you able . . . to form a judgment whether his disorder was a permanent nature or not?" This physician's testimony—and his credibility—were grounded in his occupational experience, particularly his report of the course of the prisoner's derangement, which suggested the possession of knowledge beyond the ordinary lay witness's.[42]

As long as medical witnesses invoked some unique experience or specialized training, they were unlikely to meet hostility on the bench, unless of course they happened to share an apothecary shop with a madman and continued to ask him to mix medicines! A medical witness was likely to expose himself to ridicule not in the arrogant assertion of esoteric knowledge but in just the reverse: the mundane recital of "conventional wisdom" from his privileged position as a medical expert. Following Dr. Hart Myers in the 1789 trial was Benjamin de Castro, brother of the first witness, whose assertion that the prisoner had not given him a "proper answer" led to the following uncomfortable exchange.

> *Court:* How came you to judge it not a proper answer?
> *De Castro:* I knew he did not give me a proper answer.
> *Court:* Why not?
> *De Castro:* I remember it was not and I have seen him since that in the street.
> *Court:* Had you any conversation with him?
> *De Castro:* None at all, I judged of the state of his mind, by his raving about, jumping about the street; not walking in a manner that a man in his senses should do, he walked in a harum scarum manner.
> *Court:* Now describe a little.
> *De Castro:* Just as a madman does.
> *Court:* I really do not know how a madman walks till you tell me; I want to know.
> *De Castro:* By his raving and jumping about.
> *Court:* Did you see him jumping?
> *De Castro:* Yes, about the street.
> *Court:* In what manner, do describe a little.
> *De Castro:* Why, jumping from one place to another.
> *Court:* What to try how far he could leap?
> *De Castro:* I do not know . . . I asked him how he did and I do not recollect what his answer was, but it was not a direct one.
> *Court:* Do you think that every man that does not give you a direct answer is mad?
> *De Castro:* No, certainly not; I think that the answer he gave me was not a direct one.

Court: You cannot tell us anything like his answer?
De Castro: No, I cannot.[43]

Although few lay witnesses could ever expect to face questioning about the meaning of such ambiguous terms as "flighty" or "incoherent" in their characterization of the prisoner's speech, when Dr. de Castro cited a parallel sign—an "improper" answer—the completely subjective nature of this opinion was clearly grist for the examiner's mill. What exactly made an answer improper (or proper, for that matter)? How precisely does a madman "jump about"? Lay witnesses could advance such observations as "facts," but the same perceptual cues fell woefully short when they were cited as the basis for experienced-based opinion. What, after all, made this an expert appraisal? No standards of diagnosis were given to the jury, no professional experience was invoked either implicitly or explicitly to justify the use of the term "madman." In sum, although previous professional association between medical practitioners and prisoners provided an obvious basis for the proffering of experienced-based opinion, the expert witness had to take care to phrase his testimony in a manner consistent with a knowledge-base gained through occupational insight or specialized learning. Lay witnesses could speak in "medical terms" but the medical witness who borrowed lay vocabulary did so at great professional risk.

Professional Acquaintance: "In-Patient"

By the mid- to late eighteenth century, some prisoners were entering the Old Bailey not only with prior experience with mad-doctors in "private attendance" but with a previous commitment to a mental institution as well. Consequently, medical personnel from Bethlem and St. Luke's were well represented among the cadre of medical witnesses, as were medical practitioners from private asylums. Some of these men had been instrumental in institutionalizing the prisoners. In other cases, a charitable organization appears to have taken the initiative. A Mr. Gosner, apothecary at Bethlem, testified in 1784:

> *Mr. Gosner:* [The prisoner] was sent to Bethlem by the Commissioners of sick and hurt seamen, as insane, and was in a state of insanity for some time, but got well, he was there to the best of my recollection seven or eight weeks.
>
> *Court:* What did you judge of the condition of his mind about that time?
>
> *Mr. Gosner:* I had about ten minutes conversation with him, he appeared in his perfect senses then; he appeared in great distress, and wanted me to recommend him to an apothecary.

Court: Do you know enough of his case to know whether it was a kind to be subject to a relapse?

Mr. Gosner: Most of these cases are subject to relapses, we frequently have them over and over again.[44]

The possibility of relapse—of particular significance to a legal tribunal—was often addressed by asylum personnel because they were in the best position to witness re-admission. Thomas Warburton, soon to give his name to the largest private madhouses in England, acknowledged to a jury in 1805 that the prisoner had, at some time earlier, been placed under his care at Hoxton House:

Warburton: [The prisoner] was then in a low desponding state of mind; then he was admitted to St. Luke's Hospital, upon what they call the cure establishment; he remained a year there, the usual time . . . re-admitted [later] into St. Luke's Hospital in the incurable establishment. [H]e was, however, very ernest to be set at large . . . against my own conviction, we complied with his request . . . [and placed him at a house nearby]. [H]e conducted himself with very great propriety, he was calm and very honorable, which is his natural disposition when he is right . . . I saw him after he was committed to the House of Correction; there I saw him completely outrageously mad, scarce a rational word to be got out of him.
Court: You were examined before the Magistrate and told him all this?
Warburton: I did; [the prisoner] was in a strait waistcoat then; he told me a long history that he had been Bonaparte, and had conquered him and his brother Jerome . . . I am thoroughly satisfied from the questions I put to him about Bonaparte, that he is labouring under mental derangement.[45]

The juxtaposition of calmness with "outrageous" madness sat at the center of inquiries regarding relapse. Although Warburton clearly believed that the prisoner had *returned* to his natural disposition—betokened by the restoration of calm—other asylum keepers interpreted such composure as camouflage. George Man Burrows explained to the Old Bailey why he was suspicious of "calm" as a sign of restored reason.

Court: I believe Sir, you keep a house at Hoxton for the reception of lunatics?
Burrows: Yes; I am in partnership with my mother . . . [the prisoner] was confined there three weeks and four days.
Court: In what state was he when under your care?
Burrows: Some times quiet and some times outrageous; we were obliged to put a strait waistcoat on him frequently.
Court: Have you the slightest doubt that at the time he was deranged?
Burrows: Not the smallest.

Court: Now Sir, would it be the course of a person afflicted with that
kind of malady to do strange things when they appeared to be very
calm?

Burrows: Yes, they are most full of mischief when they are calm.[46]

Burrows's testimony is instructive as an early example of the argument
that medical witnesses increasingly made: surface impressions—by implication, the lay witness's "facts"—could mislead. Calm did not necessarily reveal a return to sanity; it might instead mask deranged
mischievousness lurking just below the surface. "Ordinary persons," in
Haslam's words, failed to detect this because they didn't "protract the
discourse." Burrows, however, claimed to detect "the seeds of insanity"
lurking about the prisoner even when he appeared to be better. The
capacity to "pierce sanity's smokescreen" was fast becoming a claim of
early mental medicine, particularly among practitioners who earned their
stripes in the asylum. Increasingly in the nineteenth century the asylum
brought practitioner and prisoner together, producing the "professional
acquaintance" referred to in court.

The Prison Interview

I am surgeon of the gaol. I have been in the habit of seeing a good many
cases of lunacy . . . I have had almost daily conversation with [the pris-
oner] . . . I have taken pains continually to observe him, thinking it
probable I might be asked my opinion . . . [T]he clerk of arraigns told
me it was very likely I should be wanted; and I had better be in attendance, on one occasion the Lord Mayor met me and said, Mind you see
that prisoner, for it is very likely we shall want your evidence. [In answer to the question, "You are employed by the Corporation," the witness assured:] Yes; I go to the Compter daily to see the prisoners.[47]

Gilbert McMurdo, surgeon to Newgate Gaol, was accompanied on
his rounds by several medical assistants—Mr. Olding, Mr. Harding, and
Messrs. William J. and William H. Box—who also testified at the Old
Bailey as expert witnesses. Appearing in seventeen trials between 1830
and 1843, McMurdo was not only the most frequent medical witness to
testify at insanity trials of this period but also the most likely to assert
"shammed madness." Testifying in 1833 at the trial of an accused forger,
McMurdo reported these prison observations: "[S]he appeared to know
what I was saying, but would not answer me—I have observed her manner at the bar, she can conduct herself different at times in the gaol; and
when I was sitting in the box just now, the moment I spoke to her, to try
the effect of my observation, she instantly began to assume the position of
the eye . . . she was perfectly right before, and she began moving her

mouth as she does now."[48] Like the asylum doctor (and unlike the general practitioner, who saw the prisoner only once or twice, and the neighbor, whose eye was inexperienced and untrained), the prison doctor was schooled in multiple observations and had a "base line" of knowledge to inform his opinion. Surgeons of Clerkenwell, Newgate, the Giltmur Street Compter (a debtors' prison) and other unspecified compters, and London's House of Correction regularly appeared in court to report impressions gathered from jail interviews. Prisoners also received visits from medical men at the instigation of relatives, who often asked practitioners who had previously attended the accused to record and compare the earlier impressions with derangement in its current form.

Sustained Observation and the "General Case"

How did the early modern Londoner suspected of mental derangement come under the medical gaze? In the late eighteenth century, the relative informality and neighborliness of medical scrutiny made courtroom diagnosis seem almost inadvertent: fully one-third of medical witnesses testified about casual acquaintances or friends. Their associations took place within the context of employment or such common leisure activities as taking tea; nothing would have alerted the unsuspecting neighbor that a medical acquaintance was storing up idiosyncrasies for future testimony. The remainder of the witnesses were engaged in a professional capacity, but here, too, the reason for the initial consultation was usually a physical complaint that only with time revealed itself to have a mental consequence. These interactions were not initiated because of obvious psychological distress, and the medical witnesses who eventually appear in court display no clinical specialty in mental medicine. In the early nineteenth century, however, there was a significant development within the category "professional acquaintance" that can be grasped from courtroom testimony though it is not apparent from the array in table 5.1. Professional acquaintance increasingly took place in the asylum setting; almost half of the initial meetings between the prisoner and the practitioner began in a madhouse. Non-institutional meetings grew less common as "private acquaintance" dropped by more than half, and jail or prison interviews constituted two-fifths of all contacts. The trend toward institutional settings continued into the 1830s and 1840s; in these years four-fifths of all associations between prisoner and practitioner took place in some confined space.[49] At the most basic level of how the prisoner and the practitioner met, the asylum and the prison assumed growing significance in the formation of forensic psychiatry.

The institutionalization of social deviants in the early to mid-nineteenth century appears in retrospect to have been a precondition for the rise of the "corrective" human sciences. Criminology, penology, and certainly psychiatry could hardly be envisioned in their modern-day incarnations had it not been for a captive population and the opportunities such a setting provided to examine and classify. In terms of *mental* medicine, never before had there converged a confined community *and* a generation of keepers eager to delineate distinct classifications and categories of derangement. The first cohort of asylum physicians—Arnold, Battie, and Perfect—had argued that disturbances in thought process and behavior constituted distinctive problems outside the experience of practitioners trained in general medicine.[50] The medical keepers who followed them—Haslam, Winslow, Burrows—elaborated the notion of insanity as a discrete entity that required training for accurate discovery and treatment. General medical training no longer sufficed. Knowledge about insane persons required the opportunity to compare and contrast like cases, especially when distinguishing between mere eccentricity and madness. Professional insight required daily scrutiny. Only in asylums and prisons were the deranged subjected to close inspection and repeated observation.

Prison surgeons apparently took advantage of the opportunity to draw out conversations. Gilbert McMurdo, for example, explained in 1831 how he had originally entertained doubts about a particular prisoner's insanity: "I have seen the prisoner daily since he has been in custody . . . and he has related his adventures to me so connectedly and so consistently that I entertained some doubts as to his insanity, but with these last two or three days my conversations with him have been longer, and I have some doubts of his being of sound mind."[51] Jails also provided the occasion for surprise inspections: "I have found when she has thought she was not observed, that she has been calm and collected in appearance, [but when she knew she was observed] she has put on all these grimaces and actions."[52] Most often, the insights into madness associated with the prison cell inhered in an enhanced capacity to detect shammed or counterfeited madness.

The asylum was emerging as the institutional setting that generated the most consistent claim that insanity existed, in the tradition of medical testimony, in the "general case." From the institutionally linked medical witness, the court learned that there was indeed a disease of insanity: an *acknowledged* proclivity to relapses, the *fact* that in "this kind of malady . . . they are most full of mischief when calm," the *recognition* of a form of insanity in which the mind itself was not affected. The prison doctor's self-proclaimed insight into counterfeited madness also attested to peculiar knowledge of the "general case." He knew what to expect precisely because he had seen insanity in its *true form*. When lay witnesses learned that their observations were likely to have been shallow and misleading, it was the asylum superintendent or the prison surgeon who brought them the news. "Surface calm" was no more an indication of sanity than the forger's "wild eye" betokened insanity. Behavior that might suggest a "lucid interval" to the casual observer revealed a *paroxysm of mania* to the mad-doctor trained and experienced in the general case of derangement. The testimony of mad-doctors whose familiarity with insanity transcended the immediate case increasingly challenged the surface impressions of the casual observer, whether lay witness or general practitioner.

Before we turn to the content of medical testimony, it is important to underscore the importance of social setting in generating the increasingly assertive voice of the forensic-psychiatric witness. Among the mad-doctors who made the strongest *professional* statements—David Uwins, John Conolly, Forbes Winslow—one finds asylum keepers and, not coincidentally, authors. Other keepers, authors, and *witnesses*—George Man Burrows, Edward Thomas Monro, Alexander Morison—further exemplify the medical specialist whose asylum experiences were expressly brought into the courtroom. Together with colleagues in both public and private asylums, these early forensic-psychiatric witnesses were attempting to become more than mere custodians, to become scientific observers and chroniclers of the essence of insanity. A qualitative change was thus taking place in what these keepers believed themselves capable of understanding. One patient's derangement might be the immediate issue in court, but it was the *class* of derangement that intrigued the asylum doctor cum forensic-psychiatric witness. Could the prisoner's condition be classified? Did it conform to other types of disease? Was it knowable at all? These men were challenging common cultural perception regarding the legibility of madness. Their conceptions of insanity transported the prisoner's derangement into the realm of the general case, where properties and elements of derangement were apprehended only after repeated interviews and comparisons. It is the asylum doctors (and in some cases prison surgeons) who shifted the "facts" of the lay public into the "fair range of dispute."

Medical Testimony
in Insanity Trials, II
WHAT THE MAD-DOCTOR SAID IN COURT

*T*O UNRAVEL THE DYNAMICS THAT PRODUCED A NEW forensic role for medical witnesses in the late eighteenth and early nineteenth centuries requires more than a consideration of the changing forum that brought prisoner and practitioner together. Whatever new insight and professional confidence the mad-doctor gained from sustained observation of deranged persons, forensic-psychiatric witnesses found themselves in a criminal courtroom with a purpose and cast of characters all its own. Most conspicuous among the Old Bailey's participants were members of a newly emerging advocacy bar whose ambitious efforts to fashion a defense and prosecution "case" would have profound consequences for the tone and texture of witness examination.

Although we have come to assume that relations between medicine and law are inherently fractious, the first forensic-psychiatric witnesses faced no initial hostility from either the bench or the prosecuting counsel. They certainly found skepticism, but so did lay witnesses. To their great surprise—and, one suspects, to the historian's as well—mad-doctors also found carefully crafted questions that elicited articulate opinions, implicitly affirmed their observations, and in general added immeasurably to their appearance in court. Before speculating on the role of professional designs in the mad-doctor's assumption of a forensic role, one should consider that such designs were likely to be the attorney's. An analysis of medical testimony over time reveals the near-perfect fit of the interests of a rapidly evolving advocacy bar with the conceptually expanding realm of professed medical expertise. Conspicuously absent from this mutual-admiration society was the judiciary.

1760–1800: *"I HAVE LOOKED UPON HIM AS A MAN INSANE"*

Although three out of five medical witnesses in the late eighteenth century could cite a pre-existing professional relationship with the accused individual as the basis for their inferences regarding mental derangement, a third of the medical men knew the accused only informally through casual, episodic meetings (see table 5.1). The testimony of these medical experts was indistinguishable from that of the prisoner's other neighbors. Insanity itself appears as an additional element for the jury to consider, and the medical witness as just one more character witness to listen to. Of course, he was permitted to give his opinion about the prisoner's functioning, but then, so were the other character witnesses. This is not to suggest that there was no difference between the two types of witnesses: the questions posed to the medical witness clearly expanded his opinion from the particular case to the general. The direction of the testimony, however, at the court's instigation, not the witness's. He did not present himself to the jury as an expert but only as a neighbor. His observations and language were therefore culturally, not professionally, contoured. Although professional association was certainly cited in most of these early appearances by medical witnesses, it is important to note the very gradual transformation that *some* neighbors who happened to have medical credentials were making into the role of expert witnesses and the critical part that such familiarity played in effecting this transformation.

From medical witnesses who could cite a pre-existing professional relationship with the accused the court learned that derangement "discovered itself" in the routine daily work of a navy surgeon, an apothecary at a hospital, a physician sent by a charitable society to visit the ailing poor. In a few cases, the medical man was attached to an asylum. When asked, "[I]n attending the prisoner, what complaint did he labour under?" late eighteenth-century medical witnesses said simply, "[H]is insanity, he was quite mad," or "[H]is mind was deranged."[1] These men described episodes of distraction; they did not endeavor to explain the grounds for their inference. In fact, one is immediately reminded of the lay witness's reliance on cultural stereotypes in support of a finding of insanity. Appearing usually at the end of the trial, the medical witness legitimated previous witnesses' observations. "He was seized with insanity on board the Salisbury"[2] was uttered very much as one would say, "He received a wound" or "He suffered from scurvy." To be sure, such pronouncements were often followed by questions that addressed, for example, the surgeon's use of "flighty" to characterize the prisoner's conversation, or the time lapse between the physician's observation and the date of the crime. But with rare exceptions, medical witnesses were not asked to specify the grounds for their diagnoses. Employing such terms as "insane," "mad," "mental derangement," and "delirium," medical witnesses were denominating a universe of disordered beings who were capable of inflicting harm but not of displaying cleverness or surprising ingenuity.

The *professional* task for medical men in the late eighteenth century was restricted to speculation concerning whether the disease was curable, bore some relation to the moon, was brought on by "a little drink," or was subject to relapse. Their unelaborated testimony was not particularly enlightening, probably because it did not stand in sharp relief from that of other witnesses. Medical men were neither startling the court with something that was counterintuitive nor claiming a capacity to pierce the veil of madness. Their words are unexceptionable: "I have looked upon him as a man somewhat disordered."[3] The question, "Have you looked upon him as a man who could distinguish right from wrong?" carried no greater significance when asked of a neighbor than when solicited of a medical attendant. Indeed, in the late 1700s, these were often the same person.

Had the witness described a mental condition sufficiently *alien* to the lay understanding of how deranged people functioned, the court might well have evinced greater skepticism and probed more deeply. As it was, the eighteenth-century medical witness and the lay public shared a common conviction that insanity was indeed a discoverable, recognizable condition. Medical witnesses also appear to have met little hostility in the court because they didn't always find insanity sufficient to warrant either St. Luke's *or* an acquittal. Asked to explain if his characterization of one prisoner's conduct as "flighty" meant "flightiness so as to approach madness, or madness itself," Thomas Reynolds replied simply, "neither . . . [H]e seemed in many instances very inconsistent in his actions in life, but nothing I could collect, as a medical man, that was approaching to madness."[4] In 1796 a surgeon, Mr. Ramsden, appeared at a hearing to determine "whether the defendant stands mute through a visitation of God, or through obstinacy," and advised the court: "There was always something very odd about the man, but I never perceived him so deranged as not to know what he was about . . . the first thing I heard of him was that he shammed madness . . . I have seen him perfectly aware of what he was about."[5]

Evidence could hardly be more damaging than this, and although few medical witnesses were so declarative of the prisoner's *sanity,* few of these early forensic medical witnesses were unequivocally convinced of the prisoner's insanity either. They described prisoners as flighty, deranged, or delirious—rarely and definitively as "insane." Again, these were terms the lay witness shared, and distinguishing a state of disorder short of full-blown madness was also well within the lay witness's practice. Both elements—a shared language, and a willingness to say what madness was not—increased the credibility of the courtroom appearance and may explain the usually tepid cross-examination of early medical witnesses. It may also explain a rather unexceptional beginning for a new courtroom expert.

1801–1829: "'THAT OLD DELUSION' HAS HIM IN ITS SPELL"

The forums that brought the medical witness and the accused together changed substantially in the years following the Hadfield trial. Although previous "professional acquaintance" continued to predominate, casual acquaintance with the madman or madwoman now supplied only 11 percent of all associations. Taking its place was a new category of medical witness: the prison doctor and the jail surgeon. Although it was thirty years before the prison cell became the forum that generated the greatest number of expert witnesses, the discovery of mental derangement was already shifting from the casual neighborhood conversation to the house of correction interview.

Even within the category of professional association the place of medical attendance was changing. The private and public madhouse was quickly becoming the institutional point of contact for the shaping of professional opinions later delivered in court. Surgeons and apothecaries from Bethlem, St. Luke's, and Hoxton appeared in court with greater frequency. This institutional affiliation became fundamental in later claims to experience-based authority, but it also reminds us that people were not committed to asylums for life; indeed, several prisoners at the Old Bailey had a history of multiple visits to St. Luke's. Even so, a history of civil commitment was not prima facie evidence of derangement sufficient to exonerate someone from criminal culpability. For a jury to find that the accused was insane at the time committing of the crime, something beyond a previous finding of lunacy was required, as medical witnesses in a trial in 1812 soon learned.

Having suffered a fit of apoplexy in consequence of a riding accident, Thomas Bowler increasingly worried his family because of his memory lapses, incoherent conversation, and unprovoked quarrelsomeness. Bowler's erratic behavior grew so vexing that only the fear that "the world might say that we locked up the man for the sake of taking his property" had initially kept his son-in-law from instituting a lunacy hearing. It was in fact the prisoner's preoccupation with his property that appears to have fueled his suspicion and growing hatred of his neighbor and erstwhile good friend, William Burrows. As Burrows approached London Market on 30 May 1812, he observed Bowler hiding behind a tree. Stopping his horse to speak to Bowler, Burrows was instantly presented with a blunderbuss aimed directly at him and held by the prisoner, who cried out, "[D]amn your eyes." Burrows dropped to the ground, escaping the full fusilade, but he sustained injuries to the back and neck.

At Bowler's trial the court's attention was drawn to a riding accident that appeared to have left the prisoner with apoplexy. The first medical witness to appear was the surgeon-apothecary who had treated him immediately after the accident. Hyatt reported that in consequence of the bleeding he prescribed, the prisoner "recovered, by degrees . . . I don't think he ever [fully] recovered . . . He has complained of something in his head . . . [H]e complained that he had an uneasiness in his head." It seems, however, that Bowler was only periodically deranged. When asked if Bowler's symptoms were likely to continue, Hyatt responded with a less-than-definitive: "Either more or less." Asked if the prisoner had the appearance of a man incapable of looking after his own affairs, Hyatt replied, "He certainly has, latterly." In short, Hyatt's cross-examination is a study in equivocation.

> *Court:* My question is: during the whole of that time, whether he was not in a state to exercise his mind, to know whether he was doing right or wrong.
> *Mr. Hyatt:* I do not think he was, perfectly. His recollection was much better at times than others.
> *Court:* Then you do think, at any part of that time, he was a man that knew what he was about?
> *Mr. Hyatt:* Not entirely.
> *Court:* He might have a complaint in his head: do you mean to say that it was to that extent that he was incapable of acting as a rational being?
> *Mr. Hyatt:* I think he was, a greater part of the time.
> *Court:* Can you distinguish what part he was, and what part he was not?
> *Mr. Hyatt:* At times, as I observed before, he was better than at others, but never had his intellects perfectly clear.[6]

Nothing in these questions and replies could not be found in an examination of any reasonably alert neighbor or friend. Clearly, few acquaintances bled their neighbors in consequence of a fit, but at the level of providing the court with insights into mental derangement and its effect on human functioning, Hyatt could hardly serve as anything more than a character witness. In this respect, his testimony exemplifies the increasingly apparent limits of the general practitioner: his knowledge about delirium and fever may have set him apart from the lay public, but his capacity to speculate on the twists and turns of derangement was circumscribed by his infrequent treatment of distracted individuals and lack of experience in *managing* the deranged. "Expert" he may have been in terms of general medicine, but mental medicine was fast constituting another field of expertise.

Consider the testimony, and particularly the questioning, of the physician who followed the hapless Hyatt.

> *Mr. Gurney:* In the course of your practice you must have seen a great number of persons deranged.
> *Dr. Ainsley:* Certainly, a great number.
> *Mr. Gurney:* From the experience that you have acquired, did it appear that his derangement might have been of considerable standing?
> *Dr. Ainsley:* I have no doubt of it.

When asked if the nature of Bowler's derangement was "such to act constantly, or subject to lucid intervals," Ainsley replied:

> Not to lucid intervals, but subject to various acts of violence, where there is a delusion on the subject; upon all other subjects the man can act as well as any person. Upon all subjects, except the subject of delusion they would think rationally and clearly. In the present state these parts of intellect are considerably weakened, and his memory imperfect, so that, perhaps, he has not a sound mind upon any subject, in any case where the derangement remains.
> *Mr. Gurney:* The old delusion, acting on his mind, will lead him to do any act.
> *Dr. Ainsley:* Undoubtedly it will . . .
> *Court:* Not conscious that he is doing wrong.
> *Dr. Ainsley:* Most likely.[7]

Ainsley's appearance in 1812 marked the first time a medical witness at the Old Bailey invoked delusion to characterize a prisoner's mental state. Although the attorney Thomas Erskine had introduced the concept of delusion into English jurisprudence in 1800, no witness—medical or lay—had employed it in court before the Bowler trial. Its importance in criminal hearings is well illustrated in the present case, because Ainsley skillfully sidestepped the forced choice "acts constantly [mad] or is subject to lucid intervals" by suggesting a third possibility: rational and clear thinking, unless and until the subject of a delusion was raised, at which juncture derangement ruled.[8] The prisoner's calm was not a lucid interval; rational thinking and rational action would attend all functioning where no delusion obtained. Such calm, however, was neither a lucid interval nor a *return* to sanity. Insanity was present, though not active. Lay witnesses were doubtless familiar with madness that could flare up and suddenly dissipate. What Ainsley was asserting was a localized form of insanity that could exist alongside rational functioning.

Further, what might strike the lay observer as a return to sanity—the purposeful hiding behind a tree to sneak up to the victim and catch him unawares—might actually reveal a man in the throes of delusion that could "lead him to do any act." Purposeful action might not be all it seemed; one was capable of deliberate mischief even under the sway of circumscribed, delusional derangement. The doctor's conviction that delusion best described Bowler's particular affliction was endorsed by a third medical witness, Thomas Warburton, who had appeared at the Old Bailey seven years earlier. Prefacing his remarks with "I have seen many thousand [insane persons] in my time," Warburton testified as follows:

Mr. Gurney: Does his derangement consist in delusion of mind?

Mr. Warburton: Yes.

Mr. Gurney: Is it common for deranged persons to conceive a dislike against some particular persons—

Mr. Warburton: It is a character of mental derangement, brought on by epilepsy. In that it is more characteristic than any other.

Mr. Gurney: It is most common for them to conceive that enmity to the most dear friend—

Mr. Warburton: Frequently.

Mr. Adolphus: You apprehend that he did labour under some particular delusion—

Mr. Warburton: I am satisfied it applied particularly to Mr. Burrows. He imagined Burrows to be his secret enemy; he had instigated the whole country against him; that he could not pass from his own house to the next village without being insulted by the women and children, in order, as he imagined, so to deprive him of his property.

Mr. Gurney: From the opportunity you have had many years of observing insane persons, have you any means of discerning whether they are deranged, or whether they are not—

Mr. Warburton: I have not the least doubt, in this instance, that he is insane. He is uniformly the same, since the commission of lunacy as before, from all my observations. I am quite satisfied that he has not imposed on me.

Mr. Gurney: It is not a common symptom of derangement of one man to suppose that another man means to deprive him of his estate, and, under that delusion of mind, they would proceed to vengence.

Mr. Warburton: No doubt, they uniformly do, if not taken care to prevent it.[9]

Although Thomas Warburton effectively sketched in details of the case to fit with Ainsley's use of delusion and the inherent compulsion that attended mistaken belief, one can't help noticing the pivotal role the questioner played in unambiguously affirming the existence of delusion both in the abstract and as illustrated in this case. Such deft questioning reminds contemporary historians that any attempt to reconstruct the conditions that favored the acceptance of forensic-psychiatric testimony must keep in mind that the immediate trial concern was the prisoner's defense, not the abstract certification of "expert knowledge." The recitation of broad experience and claims to expertise may have bolstered the physician's claims to a privileged role in the courtroom, but its main purpose was to render the testimony credible and *useful.* Professed expertise is therefore inextricably bound with advocacy: deftly phrased questions carried an implicit affirmation of the possibility of states of consciousness that left the accused "out of the pale of self control."[10]

The last medical witness to appear at the Bowler trial was the surgeon of Clerkenwell Prison, Mr. Webb. Asked whether the prisoner was "sensible [that] his killing and shooting Mr. Burrows was a wrong thing," Webb responded, "I don't think he had any idea he had shot Mr. Burrows, My Lord, or that he had done a wrong thing. He said he had not seen Mr. Burrows, but had shot his cow, a sow, or a child."[11] Webb's testimony extended earlier opinion regarding circumscribed derangement to include a fateful implication for criminal law: the very real possibility that the actor was unaware that a crime had been committed. One is reminded of the eighteenth-century judge who instructed the jury to consider if the prisoner was "a mere instrument in the hands of Providence." Now, in the nineteenth century, Providence has been secularized into overwhelming suspicions that "will lead [the prisoner] to do any act."[12]

Delusion as circumscribed derangement was not new to the court or to theorists contemplating its significance for medical jurisprudence. What was novel, however, was its having acquired two fateful implications: blind force and virtual unconsciousness of action. One could go through the motions of a complex behavioral activity—securing a firearm, hiding behind a tree, executing a plan to ambush one's nemesis— and yet know no more of who one actually shot than a "cow, a sow, or a child." Of course, not all delusional actors had "total absence of thought."[13] Hadfield's intended victim, after all, was fundamental to his plan. Yet delusional individuals shared one vital characteristic: profound derangement on a particular subject that precluded them from comprehending the criminal nature of their acts and, by implication, left them prey to the powerful forces that propelled them to act. The exact nature of these forces, their autonomy from global intellectual delirium, became by the 1830s the focus of a generation of medico-legal authors.

In the early years of the nineteenth century, medical witnesses found themselves answering questions that attributed to them a level of insight into human functioning that was in fact new to their specialty. Fully experienced in matters of fever and delirium, they were the logical specialists to ask regarding the significance of derangement that persisted long after a fever had subsided or treatment for apoplexy had ended. Had Mr. Hyatt confined his comments to or, more to the point, faced questioning solely on physical injury or disease and any consequent intellectual confusion, he might well have appeared a more sure-footed witness. Courtroom questioning, however, transported him into a realm of speculation for which he was unprepared.

No such failure of nerve inhibited the surgeon who had treated "a great number of such afflicted prisoners" or the asylum superintendent who spoke with such confidence on the relation between delusion and vengeance. The full implications of circumscribed derangement were only too familiar to them. Guided skillfully by attorneys in pursuit of an acquittal, medical witnesses began to take tentative steps into elements of human functioning that few other courtroom participants included in their testimony. As they extended their inquiry into the necessary course of mental disease, medical witnesses like Ainsley, Webb, and Warburton cast doubt on conventional assumptions about the extent of volition that must attend human action. Asylum keepers, prison surgeons, and medical men experienced in treating mad people were beginning to move the will—heretofore unproblematically inferred from the prisoner's seemingly purposeful action—into the "fair range of dispute."

With or without its behavioral implications, delusion continued to interest medical witnesses particularly in the 1820s, when the delusions associated with particular somatic disturbance were the focus of medical testimony. In 1827 surgeon Mr. Houghton responded to the question whether delusions were the test of insanity as follows: "Certainly; I have heard the woman's account of his bowel complaint, its being attended with bleeding would be very beneficial to his state of mind; it would improve it; and on his getting stronger, the delusion would be likely to return."[14] Although jurors did not learn how bleeding would affect the intensity of the prisoner's delusion or what necessary connection the specific delusion bore to the crime, the medical witness was able to situate the presence of delusion in the widespread cultural notion of the easy traffic between physical change and mental function. The association of delusion with blood flow was made by another surgeon who, when asked about the relation between the prisoner's fits and his derangement, responded: "I was called to attend the prisoner in February 1827, and found him suffering from a violent hemorrhage from the nose, in consequence of a termination of blood to the head, which was very probably caused by great excitement of the mind."[15] Traffic between the mind and the body not only traveled both ways but sometimes made return trips.

Not all physical changes were of course associated with delusion, although its association with melancholy and perpetual torment can sometimes be glimpsed from medical testimony.

> I attended the prisoner two years and a half ago for a bodily disorder: I perceived her to be a woman of melancholy temper. She had symptoms which indicate a predisposition to insanity, it was a species of insanity which is at times hereditary in families, it is very susceptible to break out at particular intervals. I have known an attempt to wean a child and not accomplishing it, produce insanity; if it was lurking in the habit it would be more likely to break out at that time. When I attended her [three years before], she repeatedly made use of the words, "I have no peace at all," and in notes which I have of her case, those words repeatedly occur. I was not at all surprised when I heard she was the subject of insanity. At the time of weaning, the breast remains extremely full of milk, which always produces a degree of irritation. I believe she was an affectionate wife, and had correct parental feelings.[16]

Surgeon Dalton's words carried immediate relevance because the prisoner was on trial for infanticide. His connection between the outrageous act and a physical irritation is particularly noteworthy, as is his final statement, which neatly combines the roles of expert and character witness. This trial in 1822 also provides the first instance of a gender-specific psychophysiological debility: puerperal insanity. The precise link between mental and physical irritation is left unexplored in the case of a breast "extremely full of milk." What is significant, however, is that unlike eighteenth-century medical witnesses, who "announced" the prisoner's condition as insane, delirious, or deranged, medical witnesses in the early 1800s endeavored to provide a context, if not always an explanation, for the prisoner's madness.

A thorough knowledge of the mind per se was not required to venture into this realm. Indeed, in contrast to mad-doctors who spoke about a "paroxysm of mania" or the autonomous power of a delusion, the three examples of physical correlates cited above were professed by medical men whose only familiarity with the mad was in attending these prisoners. Although the most pronounced change in early nineteenth-century forensic-psychiatric testimony is the change in the institutional forums that brought prisoner and doctor together, a second theme is evident: the introduction of mental disturbance in a broader somatic context. The grounding of medical opinion in sustained exposure to the mad would have fundamental significance for the extension of derangement from intellectual to emotional and moral realms of functioning. Eventually, medical opinion would extend its expertise to assert a physical cast to a metaphysical concept: a *lesion* of the will.

1830–1843: Triumph of the Will?

> Among my patients at the Institution, they have gone through the same process of reasoning for the object they have in desire, as a sane person would—the act itself, I should not call an act of insanity, but should conclude that an individual, being insane, could perform that act; there may be considerable imbecility of mind, and yet the process of reasoning exist—I conceive it possible for an individual to act as the prisoner did with respect to this cheque, without knowing the degree of responsibility which she must stand in reference to it.[17]

At the request of her relatives, physician and author David Uwins visited Elizabeth Wratten in her prison cell in 1833. Like most medical witnesses at the Old Bailey between 1830 and 1843, he knew the accused only through the prison interview, but, as his words reveal, his experience with institutionalized patients afforded him the opportunity to learn that the "act" was not a sufficient basis for inferring insanity. What sort of mind could house both imbecility and a "process of reasoning"? How could the asylum physician freely acknowledge that "all this stratagem might be employed without a consciousness of there being anything wrong with it"? How could Uwins state unequivocally to the court: "I don't think she was in a state to distinguish right from wrong at the time of this affair"? When compared to medical witnesses just thirty years earlier, Uwins represented a qualitative departure in forensic-psychiatric witnesses: experience-based, experience-informed, and not at all reluctant to challenge the fundamental tenets of criminal responsibility—intention and choice.[18]

When late eighteenth-century and even early nineteenth-century medical witnesses appeared at the Old Bailey, their broad characterizations of the prisoner's state ("I have looked upon him as a man insane" or "Her faculties are deranged") addressed the consequences of mental functioning for actual behavior only by implication. They did not engage the issue of intent or even the practical significance of mental derangement for one's ability to "know what he was about." Rather, the focus of their testimony was global delirium, which, if substantiated, precluded responsibility. Eighteenth-century witnesses therefore broke no new ground in terms of the legal consequences of medical testimony because the actual world of the mad prisoner was left unexamined. Beginning in the nineteenth century, however, states of mental derangement often termed "partial insanity" (though not in its traditional legal context) suggested a gauzy consciousness in which the afflicted person yet retained sufficient awareness of what he or she was up to. The thrust of delusion's place in the nineteenth-century trial was that the prisoner was conscious of his or her actions at some level, yet failed to understand their moral wrongfulness or was incapable of self-restraint. A review of medical testimony between 1830 and 1843 suggests that medical witnesses tried to account for the legitimate acquittal of the "partially insane" through an innovative rendering of the mind of the mad. Where medical psychology had long maintained a unity of the mind—the intellect reigning sovereign over the passions and the will—new thinking emanating from France and Scotland challenged this notion. Medical witnesses were beginning to claim that derangement resulted not in intellectual or emotional pandemonium but rather in a methodical, purposeful, and *insane* pursuit of an objective. Intellectual powers could therefore suffer derangement confined to one subject, leaving the person perfectly capable of rational thought and purposeful behavior in all other areas.

The early characterization of this single-minded quest, oblivious to the consequences of the act and therefore to responsibility in reference to it, was very much the meaning that "monomaniacal" had come to symbolize. In the case of Elizabeth Wratten, even a physician who contradicted Uwins's inference of insanity conceded, "It is known that insane persons have pursued an object with a degree of cunning which belongs to very few except the most exalted talents."[19] Such cunning was most assuredly not a lucid interval but evidence that madness and reasoning could coexist in the mind: a condition Gall had called partial alienation.[20] What was *partial* about it of course was that Mrs. Wratten was not a wild beast but a cool, calm forger whose "contrivance" Uwins seized upon to reinforce the point that imbecility and reasoning could exist side by side. In fact, it was in answer to the judge's query "Would such degree of contrivance be consistent with the absence of reason?" that Uwins gave the statement cited above. The prisoner's pursuit of the cheque's value was clearly disconnected from related faculties of judgment: though capable of devising a plan, Elizabeth Wratten was incapable of appreciating the moral context in which she executed that plan.

Throughout the 1830s and early 1840s, delusion and, to a lesser extent, monomania were the most frequently cited terms among medical witnesses to support an inference of insanity.[21] Most often the delusion concerned a conspiracy, usually implicating members of the prisoner's family. As Edward Thomas Monro—fourth generation of his illustrious family to find himself in "the mad business"—testified in 1841: "[H]e heard them speaking of him under his window and they were determined to have him out of his bed, and he barricaded his house against them . . . that he heard them speaking up the chimney, and heard them repeatedly on the roof of his house, and he had had hemblane and hemlock put into his beer by his mother—he was full of delusions and fears . . . [A]t times he thought his head was on the wrong way, with his forehead behind."[22] Family conspiracy was also the subject of Gilbert McMurdo's testimony eleven years earlier, when he summed up his opinion of a prisoner's insanity by saying: "[W]e consider delusion a very common test of insanity; and that of a man's family conspiring against him to be the most common, and what we are apt to regard as a test of an unsound mind."[23] But where did delusions come from, and how was the jury to conceive of these strange suspicions? Were these merely false beliefs willfully indulged in or the secular possession of the prisoner's mind by some organic pathology?

In 1840 the Old Bailey heard an intriguing trial that compellingly resembled the Case of the Mad Apothecary. The prisoner, William Pearse, was himself a medical man whose professional advice one of the expert witnesses continued to seek even after he had concluded that Pearse was deranged. Pearse came to trial for the attempted murder of his wife, who, according to the prisoner, not only failed to show appropriate concern for his heart ailment but was poisoning him as well. Questioned alternately by judge and prisoner, surgeon and apothecary Samuel Taylor answered queries regarding the prisoner's delusion.

> *Taylor:* He thought his disease was more important than it was, he considered he should die and he had sleepless nights . . . I have seen him in bursts of crying—he would come to my house and talk of his indisposition, and suddenly burst out crying.
>
> *Prisoner:* Did you not sometimes see me three times in the course of a day?
>
> *Taylor:* I have, during the time I have been mentioning—I bled you largely one morning, by desire of Dr. Scudamore—you had blisters applied to the nape of your neck many times—you passed many nights without sleep.
>
> *Prisoner:* Did not you remark of the unfeeling conduct of Mrs. Pearse in leaving me entirely to the servant, never coming into my room to inquire how I was, nor come to give me medicine?
>
> *Taylor:* I believe the question was first put to me by you, and I replied, it was unfeeling, but I was not privy to the fact . . . [eventually

switching topics to another subject] I have called you in to assist me with your advice, as a medical man, when Dr. Kerrison was attending a young man who had mortification in his arm; I have called you in to see three of my patients—one was a person who fell down suddenly with cholera.

Attorney: If you had been aware that he was under the delusion of being poisoned by his wife, and subject to fits of delusion, should you have thought him a man whose advice should be taken . . . ?

Taylor: I should not—I merely called him at the moment—I have no doubt he is a clever surgeon—I did not consider him a confirmed maniac.[24]

Taylor was followed to the witness box by Sir Charles Scudamore, who had directed the prisoner's bleeding. Scudamore reported having "examined him carefully, both by queries and by my eye, to ascertain whether his representations were correct or not." He concluded that Pearse's heart was indeed not "the seat of the disease," even though it was "very naturally increased." Instead, he averred that "the brain was the chief seat of the morbid excitement—I had not been made acquainted with the delusion respecting his wife's infidelity, or attempts to destroy him. If I had known it, it would certainly have strengthened my opinion that the brain was the seat of the disease." There was, in fact, "a general and very marked disturbance of the whole nervous system, indicated by the remarkable absence of sleep most nights, by the most gloomy state of spirits, and by the most unreasonable ideas of the nature of his case."[25] The attorney's question, which again demonstrates how persuasively a query could recapitulate the case for the defense, was followed by the prisoner's examination of the physician:

Attorney: Regard being had to the state of mind in which you left him and what you heard today, his suspicions of his wife, and shutting himself up in a dirty room, having a belief of her intent to destroy him, and his conduct of his wife at the time in question, what should you consider to be the state of his mind when he discharged the pistol at her?

Sir Charles: Most assuredly that he was not in a sane state of mind—I should say that most confidently . . . although in the beginning of his disease I might assign false ideas to the state of the delirium, but it went into a chronic form, and he continued to indulge false delusions, I considered him in a state of monomania, in which case he would very readily have his ideas perverted, and take up with any delusions that might engage his thoughts and feelings.

Prisoner: You say my pulse was extremely high—did you consider my complaint was only a nervous one?

Sir Charles: That term would not describe your case when I first saw

you—I think in the continuation of the illness the nerves were ultimately distinctly disturbed—I mean in that the excitement of the
fever, and the disordered state of the stomach and liver, which were
so remarkable in the commencement of the illness . . . I advised a
loss of blood . . . I considered the indication of the brain, at my first
visit, to be your inflammatory nature, and with which I thought the
heart sympathized—I judged it expedient and necessary to direct
the removal of blood—although you never recovered, you got into
a better state of health . . . except as related to your disorder, I did
not find any irregularity of mind.[26]

The trial of William Pearse represents the most concerted attempt by
a medical witness to situate delusion in general somatic disturbance. How
exactly bleeding was supposed to relieve brain inflammation and how the
release of pressure on the brain would interact with the prisoner's false
suspicions were not addressed by the witness or queried by the judge (or
indeed the attorneys). Still, Pearse's trial is memorable not only for the
compelling specter of a medical witness explaining (justifying?) treatment
protocol to his former patient—a medical man on trial for attempting to
kill his wife—but also because the intensity of delusory beliefs was once
again linked to blood flow. The nebulous link between delusion and
somatic changes resonated with several other occasions in which medical
witnesses invoked injuries or disease in their testimony. The usual culprits, brain fever and head injury, certainly were in evidence, but there
might also be a disturbance—only hinted at earlier in the century—that
was now specifically named.

In 1838 Elizabeth Hodges was indicted for the willful murder of her
infant daughter, Sarah. James Hayes, a surgeon who had been attending
Mrs. Hodges, testified at her trial that he had discovered the child's body
wrapped in a blanket. The prisoner had been able to describe how she
had smothered her daughter but was perfectly mute when asked why.
The following questions were put to Mr. Hayes:

Attorney Clarkson: Had you observed anything with respect to her
milk?

Mr. Hayes: She had no milk for a fortnight previous to that—I understood so from inquiries—that would very likely have an effect on
the head of a person so circumstanced.

Clarkson: What is your opinion of the state of her mind?

Mr. Hayes: At that time I consider she was not at all aware of anything
she did—she was not conscious—she was very ill for some time
afterwards, so much so, that her life was despaired of.

Cross Examiner: You have been consulted on the propriety of suffering
her to plead to-day?

Mr. Hayes: Yes—I am of opinion that she has to a considerable extent recovered her self possession—I think her in a state of perfect consciousness now, and fit to take her trial—it is not unfrequent for women during parturition, and shortly after, to be affected with a mania peculiar to that state—it is called *puerperal mania*—deficiency of milk, and the milk flowing upwards, would probably cause such consequences.

Court: You have seen many instances, probably, of that?

Mr. Hayes: Yes.

Clarkson: Except at the period of pregnancy and parturition, and immediately after, has her conduct been rational, and like other people?

Mr. Hayes: Quite so—I have known her from a child—the mania is only during the time she is pregnant, and a short time afterwards.

Clarkson: While confined to her bed was there a greater flow of milk than afterwards?

Mr. Hayes: Yes; then the milk left her.

Court: The sudden leaving of milk is very commonly the consequence of determination to the head?

Mr. Hayes: Yes.[27]

The form of insanity said to afflict Elizabeth Hodges had been familiar to the English courtroom since at least the sixteenth century. Mental disturbance associated with childbirth could understandably play a critical role in the prosecution of infanticide, although acquittals following the mere mention of distracted behavior attendant to labor or delivery were by no means automatic.[28] Eighteenth- and nineteenth-century verdicts in trials of infant murder do suggest, however, jurors' willingness to entertain the possibility that the physiological effects of parturition left the woman with "an unusual excitement through the nervous system."[29] Contemporary medical writings likely reflected popular notions about physical strain and female psychology: "[T]he female constitution was so weakened by trials of labour and the nervous system so excited, that disorders of the mind could easily supervene."[30]

Disorders attendant to childbirth were apparently not limited to confusion or disorientation; one might be *driven* to murderous fury. Indeed, one of the particular features of puerperal insanity was an "impulse to destroy the newly born child."[31] The association of mental derangement with irresistible impulse reminds one of the states suggested by such terms as *manie sans délire* and *monomanie:* a level of functioning in which one was carried away by fear, impulse, or ruling passion. In retrospect, the grounding of puerperal mania in an unequivocal physical base and its considerable history in matters pertaining to medical jurisprudence might well have eased acceptance of the nineteenth-century species of impulsive manias, but there is little way to know this for certain. What one can say with confidence is that mental derangement expressed in irresistible spurs to action had profound legal implications. The exercise of choice seemed far removed from such human actors, regardless of the shred of consciousness they could yet cling to. When such concepts were invoked in court by medical witnesses, one observes a fateful move on their part beyond the limits of confused intellect and gauzy consciousness as the defining conditions of insanity. Medical testimony by the year 1840 clearly revealed the medical expert's embrace of an expanded conception of impaired human agency that directly challenged the legal construction of intent: *willfully* chosen behavior.

With its departure from traditional notions of madness as intellectual delirium, the French school headed by Pinel had given a new significance to the will and the passions. Emotions *themselves* could be perverted; the will *itself* could be diseased. Two members of the second generation of French médecins mentales, Etienne-Jean Georget and Charles-Chrétien-Henri Marc, named a particular affliction unattended with intellectual delirium as "lesion of the will." By 1840 this term found its way into the Old Bailey during the trial of Edward Oxford for an assault on Queen Victoria. As Dr. Hodgkin, a lecturer on "morbid anatomy" and the self-described author of "some works on pathological anatomy," informed the court, the prisoner's "becoming suddenly insane, whose conduct had been previously only eccentric," was the result of a

> *Lesion* of the will, it has been called by Le Marc, insanity connected with the development of the will—I should not consider a headstrong person to be under such an influence—I mention *lesion* of the will, as a term which a highly reputed writer on insanity has chosen to designate as a form of insanity . . . it means more than a loss of control over the conduct—it means morbid propensity—moral irregularity is the result of the disease . . . I have had cases under my observation, in which this form of insanity existed . . . I think that committing a crime without any apparent motive, is an indication of insanity.[32]

Hodgkin's testimony is noteworthy for a number of reasons, not least because "lesion of the will" appears to fit all the particulars of the Oxford case. Although lay witnesses gave the court a clear picture of a decidedly bizarre, erratic, even violent man, it was generally conceded that Oxford not only lacked any motive to injure the queen but had committed the crime in broad daylight, took no steps to elude detection, and freely acknowledged his actions once apprehended. To Hodgkin and the four other medical witnesses who appeared at the trial, Oxford's behavior was far from mysterious: it was a clear sign that a *moral* insanity could exist—

that reason could separate from will, and will from reason. Reason, in fact, could remain intact as the insane were swept into furious states by a pathological turn of the passions or the will. Complementing the French school's conceptualization of discrete forms of monomanie, James Cowles Prichard's "moral insanity" also resonated with Oxford's crime: "some ruling passion seems to have entire possession of the mind."[33] The impulsive will impelled the afflicted into motiveless, atrocious criminality.[34] The want of a motive, not the want of intellectual coherence, sat at the root of this species of insanity.

A hundred or perhaps even fifty years earlier, a clearly motiveless attack on a sovereign might have been ascribed to treason or baseness, but hardly one thinks to disease. By the mid-nineteenth century, however, the human passions and the will had entered medical theorizing about insane criminality. In the process of giving such metaphysical concepts a physical reality—conspicuous in the use of the term *lesion*—the growing field of mental medicine and the emerging cadre of medical witnesses were casting themselves as arbiters of the human heart, distinguishing themselves qualitatively from their earlier role as "certifyers" of the insane and "legitimators" of lay opinion. These were not neighborhood acquaintances or medical men who happened to attend the prisoner for a stomach ailment and chanced to observe mental derangement. As the preceding chapter revealed, medical witnesses in the fourth and fifth decades of the nineteenth century first made their acquaintance with the accused in the prison cell, and not all were prison surgeons. More and more, and especially in the celebrated trials, these witnesses were authors, lecturers, and asylum superintendents whose reasons for visiting the prisoner can be glimpsed from the ambitious claims to insight and knowledge they put forward in court.

Hodgkin's diagnosis of Oxford's "lesion" was corroborated. A physician and lecturer on medical jurisprudence at Charing-Cross Hospital, Dr. Chowne, informed the court:

> [A] propensity to commit acts without apparent or adequate motive under such circumstances is recognized as a particular species of insanity, called in medical jurisprudence, *lesion* of the will—I do not know a better term—it is an old term—it has been called moral insanity; may I be allowed to give you an example? It is by no means an uncommon thing for me to have patients who complain to me that they are impelled with a strong disposition to commit suicide, of the madness of which there can be no doubt, and yet there is no one symptom about those people indicating mental disease . . . [these patients will say:] "I have nothing to complain of, I have no unhappy news, I have no disappointment. I have no unsatisfied wish, my husband (if the case

be so) is kind to me, I have nothing at all to impel me to the act but a strong impulse.[35]

Oxford's indifference to his fate extended beyond his free acknowledgment of the attempted killing. When Dr. Chowne visited him in prison, he reminded the accused that his crime "was a terrible one, and that in all likelihood it would end in capital punishment, and if he knew whether that was decapitation." Oxford apparently replied that "he had been decapitated a week before, for he had a cast taken of his head."[36]

Accompanying Dr. Chowne in the prison visit were two medical men who elaborated on the prisoner's insanity. John Conolly, physician to Hanwell lunatic asylum, announced that he had 850 patients under his care and "some experience in the treatment of disorders of the mind." To Conolly, the evidence of Oxford's unsound mind was compelling. He read his case notes to the court: "[A]n occasional appearance of acuteness, but a total inability to reason—a singular insensibility as regards the affections—an apparent incapacity to comprehend moral obligations, to distinguish right from wrong—an absolute insensibility to the heinousness of the offense . . . a total indifference to the issue of the trial; acquittal will give him no particular pleasure."[37] Although Conolly's testimony muddied the waters of "lesion of the will" by including "a total inability to reason," his words spoke directly to the law's fundamental concern: intent. Oxford's explicit failure to understand the "heinousness of the offense"—something more than a vague inability to distinguish right from wrong—challenged the jury to find a basis for the pronouncement of moral wrongdoing. Not only was the prisoner oblivious to the moral context of his actions, he was the victim of an impulse beyond his control. James Fernandez Clark, honorary secretary to the Westminster Medical Society, next informed the court that there were medical witnesses who had predicted when an insanity such as Oxford's was likely to "break out": "In that kind of insanity, particularly, which is connected with acts of violence Escoreaux [Esquirol] says, in several cases which bear great analogy to the one which we might suppose to exist at present—in six of these cases I think that three of them took place at the age of puberty, between the ages of perhaps fourteen and twenty."[38] The Oxford jurors were thus informed that the prisoner's type of insanity had already found its way into print. Although the jury was probably not familiar with the author of *Maladies mentales,* Clark's confident citing of a medical text suggested that there existed a body of opinion that conceived of a species of insanity that might heretofore have betokened nothing but plain wickedness.

Why was explanation required? It was not motive, after all, but intent that concerned the law. If someone could be shown to be in control of his or her faculties—to understand the consequences that surrounded a criminal act—the actual reason for committing it was relatively unimportant. Motive, of course, *does* become an issue when intent is unclear. In instances where the offender stands to profit from the action, motive can be used as shorthand to discern intent. But how can intent be discerned when an action seems devoid of purpose? The medical witnesses in Oxford's trial appear to have found an avenue into the vagaries of the accused's mind by arguing that a form of insanity existed that could be recognized by its very *irrationality*: the fact that it put the perpetrator at risk for no discernible purpose. Moral insanity's very irrationality revealed its diseased character: only the insane would destroy their own happiness.

The impact of lesion of the will extended beyond the Oxford case as other medical witnesses in the early 1840s began to incorporate notions of volitional insanity into their testimony. Surgeon John Hunter reported to the Old Bailey in late 1840, for example, that when he had asked the accused his motive in attacking his brother:

> —[H]e was dogged, and would give no answer, but said he would go to prison—I reasoned with him, whether it would not be better to remain in his father's house and behave better in the future—he disclaimed all idea of good behavior, saying he would do the same thing again and over again, and wished to go to prison—his look was not furious, but it was the look of an insane man, to my judgment—I have seen insane persons—he had that peculiar look which is indescribable, a coward-like quivering of the lip, and his face effused with blood— [Hunter next tells how he had been sent by the prisoner's parents to elicit a promise from the prisoner that he would not attempt another assault, to which the prisoner responded,] "No, I will give no pledge, I will do it again, and again, I will go to prison"—this makes me feel that he is labouring under a blind influence, which he considers he has no power to counteract, and that he is morally not guilty, because he says, "I cannot help it."[39]

At the Old Bailey, medical witnesses employed a host of terms to convey the image of a prisoner powerless to think clearly and act morally. In 1843 Samuel Gardner spoke of the prisoner's being "out of the pale of self-control . . . not answerable for his actions."[40] Two years earlier, another surgeon, John Gouldsmith, had found the prisoner "labouring under an hysterical affection, screaming and sobbing . . . [I] think there is a perversion of the moral feeling, disposed to delusion."[41] Gouldsmith's pairing of delusion and perversion of the moral feeling signaled a fateful turn in medical testimony, inaugurated in the trial of Daniel Mc-Naughtan.

Although delusion always carried at least the implication of future action, medical witnesses before 1843 stopped short of giving the precise crime a sense of inevitability. Perhaps the reason was that not all strange beliefs found their ineluctable expression in a particular crime.[42] The prisoner described as "out of the pale of self-control" was on trial for the theft of postal letters, not a violent assault. The man who believed his mother was putting hemlock in his beer actually assaulted a man not named in his delusional conspiracy. In such instances, delusion was a barometer of the prisoner's derangement, not part of a "cause-and-effect" formula to explain a particular crime (pace Erskine). For most prisoners who suffered from delusion, however, one could usually infer a connection between the mistaken belief and the choice of victim. And yet the precise linkage was an inference for the jury to draw; the motor that drove the delusion was never made explicit.

During the celebrated trial of Daniel McNaughtan, the inherent force of a circumscribed derangement found its voice. The following interchange reveals that the deft phrasing of questions was a vital conduit of evidence for the jury to consider, that delusion's potential found its voice in the interrogation as well as in the response.

> *Mr. Solicitor General:* Is it now an established principle in the pathology of insanity that there may exist a partial delusion sufficient to overcome a man's moral sense and self-control, and render him irresponsible for his actions, exciting a partial insanity only, although the rest of the faculties of the mind may remain in all their ordinary state of operation?
>
> *Edward Thomas Monro:* Yes, it is quite recognized . . . [A] person may have a morbid delusion, and yet still know that thieving is a crime, or that murder is a crime, but his antecedent delusions lead to one particular offense or another . . . [I] think that delusion of this nature [political persecution] carries a man quite away—I mean that his mind was so absorbed in the contemplation of the fancied persecution, that he did not distinguish between right and wrong.[43]

Accompanying Monro in his visit to McNaughtan at Newgate was Sir Alexander Morison, who testified about the prisoner's delusion "impelling" him to act, a conviction shared by William McClewer. According to McClewer, the prisoner "was not . . . under the moral restraint by which persons in general are bound in their conduct; his moral liberty was destroyed."[44] A fourth medical witness, William Hutchenson, was asked, "Connecting that act with those delusions, are you of opinion that at the time the man committed the act, he was capable of exercising self-control, and of resisting the impulse to which he yielded?" Hutchenson, physician to the Royal Lunatic Asylum at Glasgow, responded, "He was perfectly incapable of exercising control in any manner connected with the delusion—I am decidedly of opinion that the act flowed immediately out of that delusion . . . [and that it was] an irresistible one—the impulse was so strong that nothing short of a physical impossibility, would prevent him from performing an act which his delusion might impel him to do."[45] Perhaps the nature of delusion (and its historic, indeed ancient, association with melancholia) was most effectively characterized by Aston Key, surgeon to Guy's Hospital, who had not even interviewed the prisoner. "Regarding delusion, I mean that black spot on his mind . . . if the delusion impels him to any particular act [and in McNaughtan's case, his intended victim was the subject of the delusion] the commission of the act is placed beyond his moral control."[46] Taken together the images and phrases were unequivocal: a delusion "grinding" on the mind "impels," "destroys moral liberty," and "carries a man quite away."

Once a localized thought disturbance or false belief, by the 1840s delusion had acquired the power to remove self-control, in a sense rendering the prisoner—in the words of an eighteenth-century judge—a "mere machine." Rational inquiry—indeed, sober and deliberate interpretation of the reality of one's surroundings—was vitiated by the autonomous and overwhelming force of one's groundless suspicions. Of course, delusion had always been associated with powerful fears and suspicions; what was new was the independent power of the will to "modify the association among ideas,"[47] producing not intellectual confusion but moral anarchy. The concept of base motivation was hardly new to a discussion of crime: it was after all the intent to harm—the will to harm—that was the crux of the criterion for culpability. And medical witnesses were hardly new to the court by 1840. From at least 1760 they had indirectly addressed the court's fundamental concern with intent by *announcing* a finding of delirium, derangement, distraction, or insanity, leaving the jury to bridge medical pronouncement and moral outrage. By 1840 no bridge was required. Where derangement had existed, "moral irregularity" reigned. Where delirium had been reported, "morbid propensity" ruled. And where a paroxysm of mania had been diffidently asserted, a "lesion of the will" was confidently claimed. The medical and the moral had become one.

THE "FAIR RANGE OF DISPUTE"

It is one thing to appropriate the philosophico-legal concept of moral choice and claim it as within one's realm of expertise; it is quite another to convince the court that this claim is legitimate. How did the judiciary at the Old Bailey respond to expanding claims to "cognitive inclusiveness"? After Dr. Hodgkin introduced "lesion of the will" to the Oxford jury—pointing out the significance of motiveless behavior as an indicator of insanity—the judge interrupted to ask, "Do you conceive this is really a medical question at all which has been put to you?" Hodgkin answered:

> *Dr. Hodgkin:* I do—I think medical men have more means of forming an opinion on that subject than other persons—I am supported in that opinion by writers on the subject, by Loura [Leuret], and by Le Mark [Marc], who I have alluded to, who is a particularly eminent writer—my reasons for thinking so is, because it is so stated by those writers.
>
> *Court:* Why could not any person form an opinion whether a person was sane or insane from the circumstances which have been referred to?
>
> *Dr. Hodgkin:* Because it seems to require a careful comparison of particular cases, more likely to be looked to by medical men, who are especially experienced in cases of unsoundness of mind.
>
> *Court:* What is the limit of responsibility a medical man would draw?
>
> *Dr. Hodgkin:* That is a very difficult point—it is scarcely a medical question—I should not be able to draw the line where soundness ends and unsoundness begins—it is very difficult to draw the line between eccentricity and insanity.[48]

For all practical purposes, Hodgkin answered the court's query as if it had been phrased "Do you consider this is really a *professional* question at all which has been put to you?" At first glance, there was nothing traditionally *medical* in Hodgkin's reply—nothing that spoke to damaged nerve endings, fever, or the enlargement of a cerebral organ. He employed medical authority and medical experience in a professional context: since we are the experts who treat the deranged, derangement is a medical question. The conflation of professional experience with medical authority reveals in fact just how "medical" nonphysiological treatment of the insane had become by the mid-nineteenth century.[49] Subsequent questioning of this witness revealed the court's only real concern to have been the rightful division of labor regarding medicine and the law, and on this point Hodgkin displayed exquisite sensitivity to the forum in which he found himself: "it is scarcely a medical question." His response, however, must strike us as a more than a little disingenuous: he had just finished declaring "moral irregularity [to be] the result of the disease" (that is, a lesion of the will). What does the court's apparent willingness to accept medical explanations of "moral irregularity" suggest about the understanding of madness in nineteenth-century English jurisprudence and the role of forensic-psychiatric testimony in effecting its placement?

Medical witnesses in the early to mid-1800s persistently attempted to scrutinize allegedly mad prisoners through signs and symptoms of insanity common to their culture. Their interviews did not necessarily lead to routine discovery of derangement where the layperson might see only eccentricity—far from it. Instead, they testified at the Old Bailey that, on examination, they found "great agitation" but not insanity, "distraction" but not derangement, outright fakery rather than lunacy. One can be just as persuasive in claiming privileged insight when one denies that madness exists—exposing lay errors in assuming the legibility of conventional symptoms—than by steadfastly insisting that derangement reigns everywhere. To this end, some of the most spirited testimony at the Old Bailey was heard when a medical man refused to budge on the "obvious" signs of madness.

> *Q.* Supposing you had a patient who exhibited great want of sleep, should you not attribute that to some affliction of the brain, to the diseased action of the brain?
>
> *Drewry:* Not in all cases, certainly not—continual excitement will keep sleep away—it is not always to be attributed to inflammation, because in affections of the brain we have *coma,* and a perfect *comatose* state of the body.
>
> *Q.* If a person showed great wakefulness beyond that of an ordinary person, would not you attribute that to an extraordinary and unusual action of the brain?
>
> *Drewry:* It would depend very much on circumstances—a constant stimulant will some times keep persons awake, but in affection of the brain we have a very different state—the brain would not be wrong in all cases of wakefulness . . .
>
> *Q.* Supposing the absence of any artificial stimulant, and a person in an ordinary degree of health, showed great wakefulness, should not you attribute that to something wrong in the brain?
>
> *Drewry:* Yes, it may be, but not in all cases . . . [I]f a person exhibited great wakefulness for years, without any symptom of disease, I should not attribute that to an affection of the brain—some people can do with 2 or 5 or 6 hours' sleep out of 24—and go on that way for years—I should say that was natural, unless explained in some other way—we have so many cases of that sort—I should attribute sleeplessness beyond the ordinary course of nature to a good mental activity.

Failing to induce the witness to budge with the criterion of "wakeful-ness," the attorney decided to pitch a hypothetical question that would guarantee a finding of insanity:

> Q. Suppose an individual in apparent good health exhibited great
> sleeplessness, was excessively ravenous in his appetite, very dirty in
> his habits, said he was converted and a child of God, called himself
> Dick Turpin and King Richard, and wanted to dig his father out of
> his grave because it was no use he should lie there, would you be
> prepared to say he was in a sound state of mind?
>
> *Drewry:* It would depend very much on the circumstances—if satisfied
> those things existed, I should say there might be some peculiarity
> about him[!]—he might have some of those symptoms without hav-
> ing his mind affected at all—if they all existed, I should say he was
> not in a sound state of mind—an alienation of natural affections, a
> person fond of his relatives at one time; and subsequently exhibiting
> great violence to them, is one symptom of insanity—continual ex-
> pressions of weariness of life is not always a symptom of insanity—
> it is at times certainly.[50]

Surgeon Drewry's obduracy was clearly animated by his refusal to con-cede the "self-evident" symptoms of insanity, whether they were wake-fulness, filth, or even the prisoner's desire to "dig his father out of his grave." Although the last "symptom" suggests at least *some* peculiarity about the prisoner, the witness carefully phrased his rejection of the other symptoms in the context of multiple causes leading to the behavior, not all of them symptoms of derangement. How did he know this? He an-swered, "We have so many cases of that sort." Echoing Hodgkin's as-sertion that "it seems to require a careful comparison of particular cases," both the denial of madness and the uncovering of its more hidden "seeds" needed the steady professional gaze: the experience of the med-ical man.

The thrust of Drewry's comments followed a pattern that was fast becoming a hallmark of medical testimony. He was shifting wakefulness and filth out of the column of self-evident symptoms of insanity and into the "fair range of dispute": the territorial preserve of opinion. No less than the claim that "contrivance" need not be attended with conscious-ness, that the cunning of the insane "would surprise anybody," that the mad could so cleverly ape the actions of the sane, ordinary folk were increasingly learning that they simply could not believe their eyes and ears. Sensory impressions—the "facts" they were bringing to court— were increasingly unreliable guides because madness could be infinitely subtle and recondite. Of course, raving delirium still existed, as did the occasional "mad bullock." The legibility of insanity's other forms,

however—its delusions, its monomania, its "contrivance without consciousness"—required something beyond even intimate, long-term acquaintance. It required specialized occupational experience.

Medicine's claims to expertise, however, concerned more than arro-
gating to itself a privileged voice in the courtroom; it concerned the
substance of what it chose to address. Medical witnesses in the late eighteenth century confined themselves to blanket pronouncements
of derangement: delirium, insanity, madness. They appeared as quasi-
character witnesses, announcing a nonproblematic, commonly agreed-
upon condition with a certain medical gloss. It was left to the jury to
infer intent from such "opinion," which at such a mundane, ordinary
level hardly threatened the sovereignty of the ultimate judges. Indeed,
eighteenth-century medical opinion fit comfortably with Judge Mansfield's contention that "this kind of witness's 'opinion' really has a flavor
of fact about it to suffice." It was (just) one more element for the jury to
consider.[51] Although the famous jurist may have been speaking more
wishfully than realistically, it was certainly true that little in eighteenth-
century medical opinion could not just as easily be considered fact.

How different one finds the medical testimony just forty years later!
Mania has become *reasoning* mania; cunning is now *monomaniacal* cunning; insanity takes on a fateful prefix to become *moral* insanity. No
longer is intellectual coherence the subject of medical speculation; rather
it is the retention of human agency once seized with mental pathology.
Of course a behavioral component was always associated with forms of
mental pathology: the medical literature is replete with examples of bizarre antics of the delusional.[52] What distinguished this generation of
medical witnesses at the Old Bailey was their willingness to seize on the
antics themselves and to endow them with a force—a perverted will—
that had little to do with mental incoherence at all. What remains end-
lessly intriguing in their images is that a realm of human behavior
so traditionally mysterious—indeed, spiritual—should come under the
medical gaze and be rendered *understandable.* Traditionally common law
had ascribed a "wicked will" to wicked persons. Biblical references and
centuries of religious commentary demonstrated that evil simply existed.
But in the nineteenth century no longer are evil thoughts one's own; they
are the residues of *diseased* emotions or morbid pathology of the will
itself. The court's query to Hodgkin could not have been more apposite:
Is this a medical question at all?

Of course, the witness could have replied more honestly, "It depends
on how you define medical." Medicine would appear to have actively
relinquished any claims to an exclusive materialist rendering of insanity
with a concept such as "lesion of the will," but in fact medicine's fran-

chise in "the mad business" had never been limited to organic pathology and materialism. Insanity could originate in causes ranging from the somatic to the astrologic, the satanic to the alcoholic, and yet medical men steadfastly maintained that their profession was insanity's rightful interpretive healer, or at least its *moral* manager. The increasingly adventurous scope of medical theorizing drew on experiences gained in this professional supervisory capacity, particularly in asylum superintendency. It is no coincidence that the bearers of delusion, contrivance, and moral irregularity were asylum managers who transported their experiences from Warburton's madhouse to the witness box.

The implicit invoking of institutional experiences and the opportunities thereby afforded to refine the classification of insanity treads, for some historians, dangerously close to Whiggish interpretations of the history of psychiatry. Jan Goldstein, who analyzed French psychiatry's abandonment of the category monomania, expressly rejects the notion that the accretion of clinical evidence prompted the theorists' revision. Having uncovered the testimony of médecins aliénistes who (belatedly) confessed that the highly explosive concept of monomania had been externally driven from the outset for a variety of professional and humanistic reasons, she clearly and forcefully lays out the case for externally driven nosology. Seen in this light, relinquishing monomania appears to have been both an exercise in professional self-abnegation—a sort of "now the truth can be told"—and a form of damage control, given the French judiciary's utterly dismissive contempt for its claims.[53] Although Goldstein's account is brilliantly researched and positively compelling—she has unearthed contemporary voices who were only too willing to paint a nascent profession's claims in strokes that made the whole enterprise look suspect—one still wonders where monomania emerged from. It may well have been that overeager classifiers cum forensic psychiatrists perceived an ideal type where there was only a "variation on the theme," but with only the voices of the recanting physicians, there is little way to determine what the patients "supplied" (in terms of raw evidence of clear-headed mania without confusion) and how much the professional interests contributed to the construction of a legally significant mental affliction. Deranged patients are not plants, after all: they talk back, they describe their torments, they fit uncomfortably into discrete categories. Monomania in whatever form may have reified nondelirious criminal impulse beyond reasonable clinical reality, but that does not mean that day-to-day interaction with, and observation of, incarcerated people produced nothing but an imaginary concept, cooked up to accomplish professional ends. The history of psychiatric classification still awaits material evidence of these early sustained interactions between the keepers and the kept if we are to realize the limits of Whiggish notions concerning the role of clinical evidence in conceptions of insanity.

An important legacy of Goldstein's illuminating study is the reminder to keep ever alert to the possible impact of professional interests on psychiatric claims to insight. For our present purposes, we must ask: Did the generation of mad-doctors who entered the Old Bailey in the late 1830s transport professionally driven psychiatric concepts along with their oft-cited professional ambition? Certainly they "brought" ambition, probably about as much professional appetite as the attorneys whose questions drew them out, shaped their answers, and phrased delusion for its greatest effect. Of course, medical witnesses were on much weaker footing professionally, yet attorneys were also trying out new adversarial techniques and were very much in the business of proving their worth to their clients and, one suspects, to *potential* clients. It is important, however, to remember that medical men did not flock to the court en masse in obvious quest of professional dominance. Their participation in the courtroom was actively subpoenaed by the lord mayor, the prisoners and their relatives, and the defense attorneys who employed asylum superintendents and lecturers on medical jurisprudence to reveal the inadequacies of lay witnesses' facts. That the court's zeal to employ medical assistance met with expressed medico-legal writers' ambition to marginalize lay testimony does not lead to the inevitable conclusion that testimony regarding the autonomous power of the will or the passions constituted medical categories that had been externally produced by nothing more than *profession-envy*. Without the substance of what transpired in asylums and in the particular interaction between patient and clinician, one is left with little way of knowing how critical evidence was screened out to make way for professional advancement.

Fortunately, the *OBSP* contain statements made by prisoners either to medical visitors in the prison cell or during their trial, and these provide a glimpse into the ways prisoners described their torment. Not only do these testimonies provide the historian of medicine with haunting evidence of how, through images and metaphors, patients sought to make sense of what was happening to them, but these voices also help the historian reconstruct the material from which medical observers might well have constructed an insanity of the will, which by the 1840s was fast becoming the substance of forensic-psychiatry testimony at the Old Bailey. The prisoner's defense, to which we now turn, therefore provides further compelling evidence of the extent to which not only psychiatry but *forensic* psychiatry was "shaped from below."

The Prisoner's Defense

Prisoner: From what do you form your opinion that I am insane?

Mr. Nevly [apothecary to St. Luke's]: From your action, and ideas, and your general conduct told me that you were an improper person to be at liberty.

Prisoner: You judge from ideas; you have a good opinion of yourself.

Mr. Nevly: I could see from your general conduct that you wished to do away with your uncle.

Prisoner: Why did I not shoot my uncle when I was there [on an earlier date]?

Mr. Nevly: I conceive you had not a fair opportunity for doing it.

Prisoner: Do you think a madman is so considerate as to think of that?[1]

*T*HE REMARKABLE CHARACTER OF THIS DIALOGUE—THAT the cross-examination of the medical witness was conducted not by a prosecuting attorney or the judge but by the prisoner himself—reminds the twentieth-century historian that putatively mad defendants in early modern England not only could take an active role in their own trial but, even more surprising, could use the prisoner's defense to *deny* their madness. The participation of deranged prisoners in their own trials should not be surprising. English trials were adversarial contests, and with little room permitted for an advocacy defense even in the early nineteenth century, prisoners who sought acquittal were in effect compelled to speak.[2] An examination of trial narratives, however, reveals that the defense counsel had emerged in a form easily recognizable to modern eyes: he examined witnesses brought forward by the prosecutor and character and medical witnesses who appeared on behalf of the prisoner. Although he was proscribed from directly addressing the jury, his carefully crafted questions could affirm the existence of insanity and effectively convey the subverting power of delusion.

Still, it would be wrong to conceive of insanity trials at the Old Bailey in the late 1700s and early 1800s as dominated by an emergent defense counsel and forensic-psychiatric witnesses. Although few prisoners engaged medical or lay witnesses directly, the allegedly mad prisoner was hardly a tabula rasa on which witnesses of any description could write their diagnosis. One could argue that the most compelling voice to emerge at the Old Bailey in the years 1760–1843 was neither that of the medical witness, who eventually professed a nosology all his own, nor that of the close acquaintance, whose years of familiarity yielded myriad vivid episodes of distraction. No such witness could convey the immediacy of mental derangement from the vantage point of the afflicted individual. This chapter adds to the testimony of lay and medical witnesses the last voice the jury often heard: the prisoner's. Whether brief or expansive, articulate or ranting, the testimony of the defendant in an insanity trial gave jury members a range of debilitating mental states, physical injuries, and unbidden forces to consider when they faced the law's ultimate concern: the prisoner's capacity to act with intent . . . a "will to harm." To the historian of forensic-psychiatric testimony, the prisoner poses an even more penetrating question: What do images employed by the defendant tell us about the mentally afflicted person's capacity to describe a world of inner turmoil in conventional, intelligible language?

THE EXPERIENCE AND EXPRESSION OF MENTAL DERANGEMENT

How does one convey the experience of an extraordinary state of being? Medical witnesses and neighbors could of course employ conventional cultural language to make sense of their observations, but neither had directly experienced mental derangement. For the prisoner tormented by visions, propelled into motiveless, self-destructive criminality, or fatefully deluded regarding the intentions of intimates, what distance existed between the derangement and the *name* of the derangement? Is an all-pervasive feeling of dread even retrievable in the language of the sane? Allan Ingram cautions, for example, that "the experience of pain and mental suffering must always proceed in a region that is remote from language"; that what the listeners hear is the madman or madwoman's "capitulation" to the language of the rational which the deranged must use if they are to impart anything meaningful to us.[3] Yet must we assume that a conceptual gorge separates experience from language, that some vast expanse divides genuine sensation from imposed linguistic conventionality? Ingram's conviction that we cannot hear the true voice of the mad stems in part from the dismissiveness of eighteenth- and nineteenth-century mad-doctors concerning the speech of the distracted. From such prominent practitioners as John Monro and John Haslam there is ample evidence that the language of the mad was simply discarded: because theirs was not a "disease of ideas," what insight could the mad possibly impart by their speech?[4] Although he stops short of Foucault's characterization of medicine's effect on the mad as "resolute linguistic repression," Ingram forcefully contends that medical writers "sanitized" the affliction they tried to address.[5]

Without knowing what patients said to their keepers, we have little way of knowing what was sanitized, and how. That one finds madness described in the language of the sane is not prima facie evidence that conversations have been robbed of their authenticity and spontaneity. Psychic pain is doubtless experienced personally and subjectively, but the notion that this experience therefore exists devoid of cultural meaning is merely an assertion, and a questionable one at that. One could just as easily argue that deranged sensation is rendered intelligible from the onset by cultural signifiers that "name" the experience. The delusional outpourings of Old Bailey prisoners reveal specific religious and contemporary political content that suggests direct cultural shaping of the delirious experience rather than simply the *expression* of mental derangement. One hardly suspects that religion was used by the mad to make their torment comprehensible to their listeners. Why must we characterize religious discourse as a "borrowed robe"? Why could religious torment not constitute the experience of madness?

Ingram is on much stronger footing with his other charge: that maddoctors, in their writing at least, paid little attention to the ideas expressed by their charges. The most vivid examples of nineteenth-century thought disorder—delusions, for example—were seldom examined by clinicians for fear of "contagion" or owing to a belief that the false ideas would only be reinforced by discussing them. Delusions and other forms of concretized erroneous beliefs were taken as evidence of derangement, not as an opportunity to enter the world of the distracted.[6] What survives in the medical literature is therefore the clinician's thinking *about* madness: its causes, likely course, and possible remediation. Occasionally a practitioner left behind a chronicle of case histories, but again, these are written not from the perspective of the sufferer but from that of the listener cum systematizer. One looks in vain for a sustained treatment of the patient's thought-world.[7] In addition to medical texts, there also exist memoirs of recovered patients—usually well-educated melancholics—that document the "natural history" of the mental ailment. Perhaps the most famous of these is *Perceval's Narrative,* whose author captures a mental world replete with delusion, tormenting commands, and mysterious external forces: "the blow was involuntary, as if my hand had been moved by a violent wind."[8]

Memoirs are by definition retrospective constructions, and these seem to have been ways for the newly recovered to display insight into the course of their distress. "As I came gradually to my right mind," Perceval writes at the end of his memoir, "I used to burst into fits of laughter, at the discovery of the absurdity of my delusions."[9] One rather suspects that the material has been worked to support a particular point. Such serendipitous discovery and insight are claimed in modern times by the now-recovered victims of child abuse, parental alcoholism, or drug dependency; popular memoirs routinely carry a narrative theme retrospectively grasped from the outset. Just as Perceval learned to "recognize" his religious delusions for what they were and to construct a narrative that made sense out of his torment, so contemporary categories of abuse, "co-dependency," and "learned helplessness" will doubtless structure the past experiences of recovered victims for years to come.

Whether sanitized by medical authors or editorialized by restored melancholics, the language these recovered melancholics employed to make sense of aberrant mental states was chosen to make a point, and one can only assume that a similar effort was at work when prisoners on trial for capital offenses endeavored to substantiate a plea of insanity. These men and women were attempting not only to impart a mental world but to convince a jury of mental derangement sufficient to escape blameworthiness—though, curiously, not sufficient at the time of trial to preclude its clear articulation. Given the law's criterion of total insanity—a complete want of memory and understanding—as the basis for acquittal, it might seem remarkable that allegedly mad defendants could utter any form of coherent defense, since the display of reasonable speech seems to fly in the face of "Wild Beast" imagery.[10] Total and permanent insanity, however, were not the same condition (the solicitor general in the Ferrers case of 1760 had in fact stipulated the sufficient condition as a "total permanent want of reason" *or* a "total temporary want of reason"),[11] so it is not surprising that recovered prisoners could have sufficient mental composure to describe their derangement to the court. Further, in many trials the prisoner was the only "witness" to speak on his or her behalf. Considering the spotty representation by legal counsel until the second quarter of the nineteenth century, the prisoner's defense takes on great importance. Whether caught red-handed with stolen goods or clearly observed by on-scene witnesses, a prisoner who asserted mental derangement as a defense mounted the witness stand and uttered a range of statements in an effort to make intelligible an extraordinary state of being.

VARIATIONS IN THE
(INSANE) PRISONER'S DEFENSE

In early modern England jurors usually learned that mental derangement would play a part in their deliberations only after the trial was well under way. A witness might happen to mention the accused's history of bizarre antics, or an on-scene bystander might casually mention the prisoner's agitated state, and the direction of courtroom inquiry would change abruptly. On occasion a trial that had proceeded rather straightforwardly concluded with a surprise when the prisoner uttered a defense that clearly invoked mental derangement. Such statements could range from the un-elaborated "I was in a state of utter insensibility" to the more detailed "As I sat by the fire something came over me, I could give no account of it, I could get no command of myself."[12] To be sure, a number of "ranters" who doubtless conformed to the common folk stereotype of the delirious madman were also in evidence. Asked to make his defense in 1830, one prisoner exclaimed, "Rose Green Loretto, her green flags rise up ... goddess rise up! I fired at [the victim] in defense of her name."[13] Although there were also "formulaic" insanity trials, in which the intention to plead insanity surfaced at the outset and medical witnesses described the characteristics of madness and nature of the prisoner's derangement, most juries learned of the accused's derangement during a trial, often only at its end. As such, insanity appeared as (just) one more contentious "fact" for the jury to consider.

In the years 1760–1843, 170 of 331 allegedly mad prisoners made some statement in their defense during their trial—usually at the very end. The form this defense took varied considerably, although any impression that delirious, incoherent ravings were the norm is belied by an analysis of the *OBSP*. Of course, verbal pandemonium was not totally absent; several defendants offered the jury a truly bizarre construction of events surrounding the crime, claiming blamelessness and sometimes an *absence* of derangement as well. Most prisoners who spoke at trial, however, were sufficiently articulate to permit an examination of how their mental world was expressed in such expressions as "lack of consciousness," "a dreamlike state," and "lunacy ... like the flux and reflux of the tide" (see table 7.1).[14]

The great majority of the allegedly mad defendants who provided a prisoner's defense did not dispute the prosecutor's narrative or the evidence of on-scene witnesses but asserted that mental derangement had precluded their capacity either to understand what they were doing or to control their actions. Medical witnesses generally did not appear in these trials; their participation usually attended the trial of a silent pris-

Table 7.1 Variations in the prisoner's defense

Prisoners who affirmed their madness	123
Prisoners who denied their madness, the crime, or both	31
Prisoners who "ranted"	8
Prisoners who claimed self-defense	4
Prisoners who gave another type of defense	4
Total	170

oner. On occasion, however, medical witness and mad prisoner could both be heard, as described in the preceding chapter, offering a rare glimpse of the medically qualified prisoner arguing with the medical witness over the exact nature of the prisoner's ailment. Juries at the Old Bailey might also hear prisoners deny any participation in the crime or any possession of madness. In such instances, a plea of derangement had been advanced by neighbors or medical witnesses and often featured the prisoner's very dramatic avowals of innocence or sanity. The very simplicity of such disavowal of responsibility or madness set these prisoners apart from the "ranters," who claimed to be influenced by religious demons or contemporary political opponents. Other prisoners offered a defense of "wonderment," in which they seemed utterly confused by the whole allegation and proceeding. Although they clearly appeared more bewildered than bedeviled, their defense—like that of prisoners who denied both crimes and madness—still took place within the context of mental derangement because someone had questioned their capacity to comprehend the nature of their actions.

Most prisoners sought unequivocally to convince the jury of their derangement. Their testimony, at times richly metaphoric and graphic, suggests the penetrating effect of social setting on the expression of mental torment and, more intriguingly, the diffusion of socio-legal culture into the very conceptualization of what one experiences during "physical and mental invasion." From the late eighteenth-century prisoner's relatively unproblematic invoking of "senselessness" as the name for this profound confusion to the more elaborate mid-nineteenth-century effort to articulate an absence of consciousness and will, the years that separate the Ferrers and McNaughtan trials reveal not only provocative shifts in the evolution of medical and lay testimony but dramatic changes in the prisoner's defense as well.

1760–1800: "Out of My Senses"

During the earliest years of the insanity defense, the plea of mental derangement most closely resembled the simple plea of distress. Following the testimony of victim and eyewitness, a prisoner who alleged some form of mental derangement was most likely to say "I was not in my senses" or "I was insensible at the time" and to leave it at that.[15] Although no attempt was made to explain what was meant by insensibility, senselessness was frequently coupled with two other commonly heard states: "*I know nothing about it,* [I] lost my senses by the cuts I received in the last two wars," and "I was deprived of my senses, [and] I *don't remember anything I did.*"[16] G. S. Rousseau writes that in the eighteenth century, "sensibility" connoted self-consciousness and self-awareness, which certainly seems to be borne out by the prisoners' statements.[17] Insensibility also distanced the perpetrator from the act. "I was not sensible what I did, and can give no account how I did it," is not the plea of a man denying the assault but rather the protestation of one whose senses were so deranged as to render him *missing* at the time of the crime.[18] Such testimony resonated in case histories published in the late 1700s that also chronicled the possibility of sensation experienced "out of body." John Hunter, for example, wrote of a patient who appeared to "want [a] connection between the mind and the body"; the patient would become "sensible of impressions" but would suppose them "to be in any other body but his own."[19]

"Insensibility" on occasion was attributed to a cause. In addition to the defendant cited above who coupled senselessness with "head cuts," a prisoner in 1792 declared: "I had the misfortune to be thrown by my horse, and my skull is fractured—And from that time I was incapable of attending to my business . . . being deranged in my senses."[20] The unproblematic association of wounds with insensibility gives weight to the conventional acceptance of an easy traffic between mind and body, a motorway so intelligible to ordinary folk that no experts were needed to explain the route. No experts were apparently needed to explain the effects of liquor either, although prisoners who referred to this form of "voluntary derangement" hastened to couple drinking with a pre-existing injury—often fortuitously received in military service. As one prisoner in 1797 explained, "I have been in His Majesty's service many years, I have been wounded twice in my head; I served with the Duke of York the whole of the last campaign, I have had some splinters taken out of my side, which causes me to be delirious at times, especially if I get a little liquor."[21] When war wounds were unavailable, liquor was most often conjoined with physical injuries, in an effort, one suspects, to mitigate the obvious willfulness of the drinking: "I was in a state of intoxication if I [did do] it; when I was a boy, I fell out of a 3-pair of stairs window, and have a plate in my head—if I drink any thing, I don't know what I do; therefore I leave myself to the mercy of the court."[22] Of course, alcohol had long been known to inflame passions, cloud thinking, and inhibit the will. The patent voluntariness of hoisting a pint, however, suggested that drinking could not constitute a legal defense. Indeed, some jurists maintained that it should *aggravate* the seriousness of the crime.[23] Established legal opinion, however, did not preclude some prisoners' efforts to enlist the sympathy of the jury by overtly appealing to their own leisure activities.

Whether joined with injuries, accidents, liquor, or domestic woes—"I am hardly sensible of what I do, my husband treats me very ill"[24]—the mental state termed "senselessness" was apparently so familiar to the ordinary citizen that no prisoners were ever asked to explain how they knew they had indeed been deranged, or how they *now* knew they were in their "right senses." Further, it is clear that insensibility was accepted to have a transitory nature. That a prisoner could later recall the suspended state of "knowing" and attribute an uncharacteristic criminal act to this episode of utter senselessness suggests a popular acknowledgment of alternating intervals of insensibility and sanity. Of course, lunacy had long described a state of alternating bouts of derangement and lucidity. In fact, the medieval association of lunacy and the tides was graphically rendered by a prisoner in 1784: "I am sometimes afflicted with lunacy, I have been so for a series of years, and when I get a drop of liquor, I have no recollection of anything I do—it was at this unfortunate time that I committed this rash act . . . [I] have been in Bethlem, and at St. Luke's and in private mad-houses and all will not do; it comes at intervals upon me, like the flux and reflux of the tides . . . I am seized at intervals with lunacy, and I cannot account for it. I have had relapses these 12 years."[25] *Lunacy*, however, was a problematic term in jurisprudence and bedeviled medical writers and witnesses asked to specify what exactly constituted a lucid interval. As we have seen, some medical witnesses avoided the concept altogether, particularly because the state of composure that suggested either a return to or an interval of sanity could actually mask a *reasoning mania*. Prisoners in the late 1700s also avoided phrasing their condition as "lunacy," preferring "senselessness," which elicited no subsequent query regarding the interval of distraction.

For all its ambiguity, senselessness was an important first step in the prisoner's construction of the insanity defense because it introduced a mental world that challenged, however indirectly, legal conceptions about the prisoner's appreciation of the events surrounding the criminal act. "At times I have been very insensible that I have not known what I have been doing" begs a further question: How was action possible if the actor was unaware of the nature of the behavior?[26] Whose intent animated the act? Did insensibility render one unconscious? Could one retain consciousness in the pursuit of an action that was not of one's choosing? Although eighteenth-century prisoners lacked a language in which to account for actions devoid of thought, even a term so ambiguous as *senselessness* engaged the law's fundamental concern with intent and could muddy the conceptual waters that surrounded insanity and the will to harm. If conscious choice had not animated the action, what had?

1801–1829: "My Mind Was Overcome in a Moment"

The generic use of insensibility to convey derangement was refined in the early nineteenth century. Physical states that preceded the onset of distraction were described in greater detail. In 1815, for example, a young man on trial for stealing sheep told the officer at the time of his arrest that he "was determined to be hanged, he might as well be hanged for a whole flock as for 2 or 3." At his trial, however, he testified, "If there had been twice as many more, I should have taken them for I was quite insane at the time. About 16 years ago, I was bitten by a mad dog, and was dipped in the salt water at Graveshead for it, and I am always insane in the months of July and August, I really do not know how I came by these sheep at all."[27] Still unexplained by the prisoner—and unexplored by the court—was the relation between the implied hydrophobia and the sheep stealing . . . or indeed why madness contracted in this manner should become manifest in the two hottest summer months or why hydrophobia left one confused rather than foaming at the mouth and writhing on the ground. What seems clear from this testimony and numerous other examples in which physical trauma and insensibility were effortlessly combined was the reservoir of common cultural assent regarding the association between the two. When a defendant in 1810 invoked "brain fever" as the cause of his inability to "recollect" anything, no elaboration was demanded.[28]

Not all defendants were content to let matters rest there. In their efforts to describe their mental state at the time of the crime, they moved beyond physical trauma and mental effect to engage legal questions that directly surrounded culpability. On trial in 1808 for stealing, Thomas Swinton covered several bases with the following statement: "My lord, with respect to the charge that is alleged against me, I know nothing of, but with respect to the circumstance; at the time I was charged with stealing these articles, I had been drinking and when I am in such a state I am incapable of knowing right from wrong on account of a violent contusion in my head—since then, if I drink freely, I am totally deprived of my intellects."[29] Swinton was the first prisoner in the years after 1760 to introduce the expression "knowing right from wrong" directly into his defense. Whether this comment was merely off-hand or chosen for greatest courtroom effect, it is intriguing in a prisoner's defense because "knowing right from wrong" was the law's traditional criterion for attributing responsibility. Why should such a construction find its way into the efforts of a putative madman to describe his derangement?

In only one context is knowing right from wrong germane to madness, and the prisoner's awareness of this doubtless shaped his *expression* of derangement. In fact, the importance of social setting for the depiction of the experience of madness had been on view all along. One can see the resonance of the law's criterion of insanity—a want of memory and understanding—in eighteenth-century defendants who professed an incapacity to recall the act or to know what they were "about" on the day in question. Certainly madness could be described as occluded reasoning and memory loss in nonlegal settings as well. Nonetheless, prisoners who sought to affirm their mental derangement spoke not only in images and causation that were clearly intelligible to the lay juror but in terms of mental states that were exquisitely tuned to the legal context as well.

Prisoners could also provide the jury with the frightening specter of losing control of one's thoughts and actions. In 1827 a young man on trial for violent assault informed the court, "As I sat by the fire, something came over [me]—I could get no account of it; I could get no command of myself till I walked a mile and a half or two miles. I then thought I had done wrong, and was sorry for it, and have been sorry from that time till this . . . [Quoting the prisoner, the *OBSP* recorder then added,] he went to give himself up, and at times he has no command of himself."[30] Later that year, an Old Bailey jury heard one prisoner assert, "My mind was overcome in a moment . . . and of my being at the time I did so misconduct myself in a way of total absence of thought, never contemplating such a crime."[31] The phenomenon of a mind overcome marked a further shift away from the familiar though vague "senselessness" and "insensibility." The mind itself was now under assault, not by head injuries or war wounds but by mysterious, treacherous forces that flew into the prisoner's head. The result was not only confusion but a loss of self-control: "I could get no command of myself." By the late 1820s, the prisoner's defense had begun directly to address a basic tenet of culpability: intention. Defendants' statements reveal the ambiguity of consciousness: that mental functioning and behavioral act could operate more or less independently, that the mind could be overcome, that some idea could enter one's head unbidden. How was it possible to know what one did under such conditions?

The phrasing of such articulate defenses might evoke an image of the prisoner sitting in Newgate with a dog-eared copy of Bracton or Hale, busily jotting down notes regarding the essentials of inferring lack of intent. There certainly seems to be a rather serendipitous fit between the tale of distraction and the legal requirements for acquittal in some examples of the prisoner's defense. It would be a mistake, however, to infer a stepwise progression focusing on insensibility to consciousness to will. In the early 1800s "senselessness" continued to be invoked as a blanket term, as did the generic "I really do not know how I came by these sheep at all."[32] And half of the prisoners made no statement at all. Still, many defendants spoke with compelling directness to the major business of the trial: the possession of sufficient understanding to know what one was about. When "absence of thought" was joined to a "mind overcome," and when a defendant could declare quite simply "at times, I have no command of myself," the actor's understanding of the circumstances surrounding the act and any consequent capacity to act with intent were thrown into serious question.

1830–1843: "It Was Like a Dream to Me"

I solemnly declare that I never had the least intention of injuring any other person than myself. I had been for some time in a very distressing and unsettled state of mind, arising out of some pecuniary disappointments and family disputes, and these matters had so unsettled my understanding and overcome my reason, that I looked forward to an act of suicide as the only recourse left to me . . . I never had the least dispute [with the victim] and could have no possible or even imaginary, motive for seeking to do her the least injury, and much less to deprive her of life, in so shocking a manner. I came to town with an intention of using the pistol against myself, and endeavored to borrow from intoxication the resolution necessary for effecting my purpose. Of the fatal transaction I have no recollection whatsoever: my memory sank under the influence of the liquor I had drunk, and I do not remember anything of the occurrence; but I am certain that I could not have meant to destroy the deceased—I must have intended to have carried my original intention against myself into effect, and not to have destroyed an innocent and unoffending person.[33]

In addition to mentioning "intention" four times in his statement, this prisoner revealed that the contemporary meaning of intention mirrored the law's conception: what it was the actor meant to do. Rather than dwell on the precipitating causes of the mental distress, the defendant invited the jurors to consider the despair that supposedly animated his anticipated suicide but ended incomprehensibly in homicide. Such an *unintended* killing had to have been an act of insanity: since the defendant had no purpose in depriving the victim of her life, he couldn't have *meant* to do it. Intent, a concept only hinted at by defendants in the early nineteenth century, is expressed directly in the prisoner's defense by the 1830s.

On trial for forgery, another prisoner testified in 1833: "Gentlemen . . . I was labouring at the time under an aberration of mind, certainly I was not in a sane state at the time, is it likely that I should have made two people acquainted with the bill under the circumstances which would lead to immediate detection? [N]ow if I had intended to get the money, should I not immediately have gone to the banker's, instead of waiting till I had been taken into custody. [I]s it feasible that a man in his senses would have done that?"[34] This defense is particularly interesting because the prisoner used the irrationality of the act to argue his own. He challenged the jury to discover intent—purposeful action with an awareness of consequences—from an act that would inevitably lead to immediate detection. Do people of sound mind ensure their own detection? In fact, the forger's line of reasoning resonated with notions of moral insanity that were surfacing in the early 1830s. The certainty of detection was argued here as evidence of insanity: only a truly deranged individual would invite arrest and punishment.

In 1837 a man indicted for stealing explained to the court: "I will not deny that I did take the fronts, but I was not conscious of what I was doing—I was labouring under an aberration of mind."[35] The prisoner directly asserted the possibility that mental functioning and (criminal) behavior could operate more or less independently. He was pleading not a blackout or memory failure but rather an inability to comprehend how and why he took the items. Ten years earlier, consciousness was mentioned by a sailor whose "contusions in [his] head" rendered him incapable of knowing what he was "about" when he drank. He summarized his role in the theft by saying, "I was unconscious of anything till I found myself in the watchhouse."[36] Certainly one approaches the use of so significant a term as "consciousness" with caution. The prisoner may well have *intended* to signify his being "aware" or some other relatively ordinary state of "knowing." Whatever his object, there remains the very real issue of what meaning "not conscious" conveyed to the jury when coupled with "labouring under an aberration of mind." What conception of the mind explained such testimony?

Cultural inquiry into mind-body relations broadened in the last decades of the eighteenth century.[37] A host of human actions—pulse and respiration, for example—were noted to take place "unattended" by consciousness. Epileptic or hysterical displays afforded compelling evidence of physical action without conscious motor control.[38] Courtroom testimony suggests the currency of the notion of behavior unattended by consciousness, of a cultural imagination embracing the idea of variable states of "knowing" akin to sleepwalking or automatism. The prospect of assigning moral blame to such mental states had to have been daunting. How was the jury to respond to a defense phrased as follows: "It was like a dream to me, when I saw the deed was done it struck me with terror instantly"?[39]

Who or what was responsible for such an act? In testimony that resembled the young man's in 1827 who could "get no command" of himself after "something came over [him]," the following prisoner's defense featured in a tragic case of assault in 1840: "I have nothing to say; all I say is, at the time it seemed to me as if I was bidden to do it, and could not help it; I am sorry, I love my brother."[40] Although the case for "alien control" was made much more forcefully in the ravings of several quite histrionic prisoners, discussed below, it is worth remembering that poised, articulate defendants could also maintain that they were not in control of their will. It was not only medical philosophers who posited a disaggregation of mental unity into intellect, passion, and volition. In the words of some prisoners—and putatively mad prisoners at that—one could also experience a disaggregation of one's mental faculties. The integrity and soundness of one's mind was not an either-or proposition: one could be "like in a dream," one could be "not conscious" of one's actions.

Finally, and with profound implications for the question of intent, one could (calmly) assert that one was "bidden" to commit the crime; one could get "no command" of oneself. As opposed to the late eighteenth century, when defenses were based on global characterizations of mental confusion—most often termed "senselessness" or "insensibility"—by the fourth decade of the nineteenth century prisoners made concerted efforts both to specify reasons for the derangement and to paint a clearer picture of the derangement itself. No longer "absent" from their own crimes, the prisoners were now unwilling witnesses to acts that "struck [them] with terror instantly." The *displacement* of the prisoner from intentional actor to unwilling bystander carried fundamental significance for the jurisprudence of partial insanity.

PRISONERS WHO RANTED:
TAKING THE DELUSION SERIOUSLY

I have had great noises in my head for the last four years, and my brains used to go round, and heat-like steams of fire; and as I passed by the houses in the street, flashes used to come by my head; and moreover, I think I am allied to the Royal Family—I have received great homage, when I was young, from people in carriages, and I suppose they took me to be an illegitimate son of the Duke of York; but my mother was not the celebrated Mrs. Clarke—when I went to Paris, I was under the necessity of changing my name; I received similar homage at Paris, and military homage from the soldiers—I have been given to understand I was a descendant of George Rex, who lived at Combe and Delafield's brewing manufactory; I consider myself entitled to the dukedom of Lancaster—when I was at Hicklow, a lady came, very much like my grandfather; I think she was a child of Queen Caroline, the wife of George the Third—she came into the court-yard . . . [and] the night after that, I saw a great flame, which scorched my body; and ever since that lady talked to me I have had a heat over my head; she was talking to me with others through the wall some time—she said my equipage would be ready soon, and I should go to town, and these Royal personages should be looked after; after that I went to shave myself, and as most people make faces when they shave—I had the door open—a gentleman and lady came in, and hurt me tremendously; when I went down to dine there was a chair vacant . . . I concluded that the lady was the cause of the heat in my head, and I had had it ever since.[41]

In addition to their displays of richly detailed delirium and theatrics, trials featuring such "ranters" were distinguished by the attention witnesses gave to the thought-world of the prisoner. Unlike the defendants discussed earlier, whose haunting tales of spirits and unbidden forces were rarely pursued by the court, the delusions of prisoners who took to the witness stand like Lear to the Heath were the occasion for courtroom examination of the reality and strength of the prisoner's beliefs. After William Clark told of his brains going around, royal illegitimacy, "and great flames scorching [his] body," his sister produced a letter from him, reporting that he had "laboured under a delusion about witches and wizards ever since I have corresponded with him." The *OBSP* publisher commented: "The letter being read gave a long and incoherent account of the prisoner's connexion with wizards, and the influence they had over him, and a long history of gipseys, &c.; it bore the Paris post-mark of May 1829. Surgeon Gilbert McMurdo next reported his conversations with the prisoner, concluding that he was indeed insane (to which the prisoner interjected, "He knows nothing about it"). Last to speak was Clark's landlord, who testified that Clark had told him "he was tormented with witches—he told me he fired this shot . . . intending to be taken, that the public might know his troubles concerning these witches." The prisoner ended the trial by protesting (perhaps prophetically): "I think it is a complete imposition—the injury I have received is unimaginable; for example, how would a man like to have his head opened?"[42]

Unlike period medical texts, in which the delusions of the afflicted were never examined, courtroom testimony reveals that in the criminal trial at least, the thought-world of the deranged could move to center stage. In this case, both the prisoner's defense and the testimony that followed invited the jury into the delusional realm of William Clark, a world inhabited by wizards, scorching flames, and vertiginously spinning brains. There is no question that the delusion was "taken seriously," not because an acquittal on the grounds of insanity was returned but because other witnesses paid serious attention to Clark's beliefs. His sister and landlord affirmed the reality of his beliefs; even the medical witness attested to his insanity. Confronting the world of the prisoner from the *inside,* jurors were forced to contemplate the law's conception of intent: willfully chosen behavior informed by the actor's understanding of the events surrounding the crime. The full weight of delusion was felt in trials of these ranters precisely because their understanding of the circumstances surrounding their acts was so profoundly distorted. With or without impelling forces, one could hardly say that such persons *chose* their actions.

A year before Clark's trial, an Old Bailey jury also heard of the existence of just such an overwhelming force in the long and rambling defense uttered by James Sisk, on trial for firing at a guard in the House of Commons. Sisk's external force came in the form of a holy commission to exhort Londoners to repent their sins: "I did what I was commissioned to do by God Almighty." Sisk explained that he had received this assignment while on route to Baltimore: "[T]he idea came into my head that punishment would meet the inhabitants of the whole earth." Upon returning home, the prisoner discovered that the holy commission impelled him to speak. His testimony ended with his reporting having seen "a spot in the sun which has never been seen since the creation of the world, and it is a sure sign that the son of God is coming." Like William Clark's, Sisk's defense contained the suggestion of pronounced involuntariness: "The idea came into my head . . . it would not let me be quiet."[43]

Appearing at the trial of James Sisk was the ubiquitous Gilbert Mc-Murdo, who pronounced the prisoner insane: "[H]e repeated his story to me verbatim as he has today; I put various questions to him, and could not come to the conclusion that it was put on." McMurdo was followed by the prisoner's cousin, who reported Sisk's having spoken "about visions; he said he had recently come from America—that he had been sent with a mission to preach repentance." A final witness reported the prisoner's history of insanity, particularly his "talking of visions, and fancying a conspiracy on his family, to rob him of his property." Recalled to the stand, McMurdo endorsed the medical significance of the prisoner's impairment and suggested a reason for the defendant's change of plans to return from America: "We consider delusions a very common test of insanity; and that of a man's family conspiring against him is one of the most common, and what we are apt to regard as a test of an unsound state of mind."[44]

Whether delusions were "dismissed" or "sanitized" by mad-doctors in the asylum or in print, their significance could not have been lost on the jurors. To the truly insane, the act was not criminal at all but justified—indeed necessary—given a mental world ruled by holy commissions and wizards. When Sisk fired at the guard, he was trying to remove the obstacle to his being able to effect world salvation. When Clark assaulted his victim, he did so "intending to be taken, that the public might know of his troubles concerning these witches." What the jury was able to learn from these "ranters" (in contrast to those who "affirmed" their madness) was how the world looked from inside the derangement—how questions of "knowing right from wrong" had to be framed differently when one's moral compass was magnetized by a will with a *mind* of its own. Erskine's original instruction to the jury in 1800 had opened this line of inquiry, one in which moral and legal transgression were no longer congruent. For the truly insane, Erskine advised, reason had not been driven from its seat but was instead in the embrace of delusion. Now, several decades later, Old Bailey jurors heard of a further embrace, one of impelling forces quite beyond the prisoner's control. In prisoner's defenses, the delusional challenged jurors to enter their world and, in effect, to find their actions willful.

Some prisoners also invited in the judge. In 1805 a young man on trial for attempted murder appeared in the court in a "strait waistcoat" and began the trial by imploring: "My Lord, I wish to be delivered from this encumbrance, then I shall speak as a man; at present I speak as a madman. I am not mad, but can speak the words of truth and soberness."[45] After the constable identified the prisoner as the man responsible for the assault, the defendant abruptly interrupted: "I had something to communicate to His Majesty about Bonaparte."[46] He then launched into a rambling defense of his torment at the hands of imaginary forces, all the time affirming his sanity. Asked by the judge what he knew about Bonaparte, the prisoner answered:

> I would rather not mention it here at present, because you will possibly look upon it as the effect of a disordered brain; I am sober, I speak words of truth; if you read in the Hebrews, you will find it written—A body hast then prepared, Oh Lord; and the same thing was said of him that died at Jerusalem—he is a madman; is not this the carpenter's son . . . What I have to communicate to His Majesty, I will communicate to you in private, if you please not here. I wished to see the Prince of Wales; his insolent porter told me he would not admit a man of my description: I went in disguise.[47]

Ironically, such determined protestations of sanity were the most persuasive "insanity defenses" heard at the Old Bailey. Whether they provided a logical connection between the delusion and the criminal act, whether they vividly portrayed their need to serve a higher power or simply articulated a mental world that, though familiar in its religious and political themes, was sufficiently alien concerning the degree to which biblical and royal persons had penetrated the minds of the prisoner, there is every evidence that the ranters' delusions were taken seriously . . . to the extent that they were themselves coherent. On trial for assault with a pistol, one prisoner in 1830 embarked on a bizarre defense, actually beginning the trial with the following statement: "I acknowledge having fired at him, it was in the defence of the holy name. I called out . . . [t]he mother of our blessed Saviour, the holy church of Rome. I called to her green flags to rise up, and so they will rise, and all the subjects of hell be crushed; it was in defence of her holy name that I fired—thank God . . . [I] would fire on his master in defence of that holy name."[48] The prisoner's landlord told of a morning six weeks earlier when, having arrived to pay his rent, the prisoner "fell down on his knees three times in my shop, and talked incoherently, as he has done today . . . I considered his mind overpowered by Religion." At this point the prisoner interrupted and declared: "What I have to say is, I cried out 'Rose green Loretto, her green flags rise up;' that is, 'Blessed mother Loretto, mother of our church, and goddess rise up'—I said nothing else till the man arrested me, and I fired at him in defence of her name . . . all nations will worship her . . . no heretic that does not believe [in] her will ever see the light of Heaven—I leave it to Almighty God; God knows the best." The *OBSP* publisher added: "The prisoner had interrupted the witnesses several times during the trial with the same sort of language, and whenever insanity was alluded to he always declared he was 'always in his senses.' " The court's only question to Mr. McMurdo was whether the manner was "put on,

[or] a real disordered state of intellect." The judge in the preceding case was likely as perplexed as the twentieth-century reader regarding the identity of "Rose green Loretto" and apparently considered the prisoner's performance to have had a certain element of "chewing the scenery." After the prison surgeon indeed attested to the defendant's insanity, the defendant concluded the trial by declaring: "It was in the execution of my duty as a Christian to destroy that man, and the honour of my church because he is rotten and blind—the holy name, there is no other God but her."[49]

Actually, this prisoner shared with other ranters an explicit denial of madness. Their delusional construction of the world showed that one could be "conscious" and "purposeful" yet totally unmindful of committing any legal harm. Such a mental world suggested the possibility of multiple planes of awareness as well as the very real possibility that multiple forces could animate the will. This is most apparent in those who received holy commissions, but it was also evident in persons who had important business with Bonaparte or vociferously implored green flags to rise up or expressed a mortal fear of wizards. Such prisoners could hardly be described as possessing sufficient understanding of what they were "about" to have willfully chosen their actions. Faced with a host of satanic, religious, and political forces, jurors were forced to look beyond the lay witness's tales of histrionic behavior and even the medical witness's simple declaration of insanity. To directly address the prisoner's ability to distinguish right from wrong and to retain the "will to harm," jurors had to take the prisoner's delusion seriously.

THE EXPRESSION AND EXPERIENCE OF MADNESS

What are the hazards in taking the prisoner's *defense* seriously? After all, if the medical author can be suspected of sanitizing the incoherent rantings of his patients in order to produce a coherent nosology, and if the recovered melancholic's newfound religious salvation may inform his or her interpretation of delusions as the sign of imperfect faith, what is to prevent the historian of psychiatry from wringing the prisoner's defense to find meaning where none either existed or was intended? Further, what was to prevent clever prisoners from counterfeiting madness through the deft employment of allusive imagery and tales of possession? Some prevarication doubtless occurred, although the motivation for such dissembling is unclear. Capital punishment had been removed from all but a few offenses by the late 1830s, and acquittal would have brought indeterminate incarceration "awaiting the King's pleasure." Still, one cannot dismiss the possibility of exaggeration—if not outright deception.

For the rest, the task of discerning the prisoner's meaning is no less daunting, although the language closely paralleled commonly heard phrases in both lay and medical testimony. Far from being silenced, sanitized, or even edited, these prisoners used images that were immediately intelligible to ordinary folk and profoundly significant to the court. How closely their language fit the subjective experience of madness remains an intriguing question. What one can say with full assurance, however, is that by the 1840s the images presented by insanity defendants had muddied the conceptual waters regarding total and partial insanity.

The prisoners' self-proclaimed incapacity to understand the nature and consequences of their actions runs throughout their courtroom statements. With the exception of eight defendants whose verbal outbursts set them apart from the relatively coherent conveyers of the deranged mind, the prisoner's defense from 1760 to 1843 increasingly engaged various philisophico-legal issues relating to mind, purpose, and action. In part, the changes mirror the conceptual maneuvers in the medical literature that assert the existence of partial insanity: lucid intervals, délire partiel, and monomania. Although these "expert" terms are absent from the language of the prisoners, prominently on view are the two variants of partial insanity articulated by Lord Hale in 1736: partial in respect to duration and partial in respect to degree. In the late eighteenth century, prisoners alluded to the periodic sway of insanity as "being out of my wits" and "knowing nothing about it." One prisoner explicitly referred to lunacy and its transitory character ("intervals . . . like the flux and reflux of the tides"), but for a variety of reasons—none of them operating at the time of the trial—most defendants endeavored to distance themselves from the felonious deed with such expressions as "I didn't know where I was" or "[I was] rendered incapable of knowing what I was about." The state of functioning they described stood in stark contrast to the composure with which they delivered their defense. Still, given the success rate of such pleas of derangement, one must conclude that juries were willing to entertain a conception of a major state of distraction (insensibility, witlessness) followed by sufficient insight to permit the prisoner to give a "rational" reason for an irrational act. It seems that "partial in respect of duration" was not partial at all to the jury.[50]

The truly novel element to appear in the last third of this period, however, is the evidence of the second variant of partial insanity: partial in respect of degree. Most prisoners were not alleging that they couldn't *remember* what they had done or were completely oblivious to what they had been "about." They didn't evoke a global feeling of senselessness or insensibility. The image most commonly invoked was that of an unsettled or disordered mind, which left the actor "unconscious" of what he or she was doing. One hears the plaintive defense of those prisoners who couldn't quite understand what they were doing *while* they were doing it. The coupling of "it was like a dream to me" with "I cannot see what intent I had in carrying it out" conjures up the image of someone who has effectively lost control of both thought and action. The specter of forces "bidding" one to kill a beloved brother, coming into one's head, and "not let[ting] me be quiet," "coming over me as I sat by the fire," left the clear impression that the prisoner, though present at the crime, was more witness than perpetrator. Or, as one eighteenth-century judge put it, "mere machine" rather than actor. Theirs may not have been a total madness, but their capacity to understand the nature of what they were doing left them far "younger" than the fourteen-year-old Lord Hale envisioned as the standard for adult culpability.

With firsthand evidence of the signs of delirium and fully formed delusions in the testimony of the ranters, one may be tempted to distinguish the ranters' experience of madness from that of the "affirmers," those who pled insanity, employing imagery that seemed at times exquisitely attuned to the needs of the court. Certainly the former group conformed to contemporary images of classic raving delirium, and in their protestations of sanity they might strike the reader as more sincere than their seemingly more cagey fellow prisoners. Actually, however, the two groups are more alike than one might think. Where the affirmer *testified* about a mind overcome, the ranter demonstrated the actual sway of possession. Where the affirmer *reported* an inability to "get command of [myself]," the ranter conjured up a force that "would not let me be quiet." And where the affirmer *related* that "something came over me," the ranter's list of impelling forces included wizards and witches, Bonaparte, and Rose green Loretto. For all of the ranters' displays, the two groups are united by a continuity of expression regarding human agency and lack of self-control. The affirmers simply cannot be dismissed as reasonably sane prisoners who tailored their expression of madness to the courtroom setting. The images they employed and the constraints they expressed have too much resonance with the world of the ranters, who appeared perfectly oblivious both to the consequences of the legal setting and to the need to adapt their language to legal strictures. The similarity in expression and perhaps in experience returns us to a question posed at the outset: Is the use of conventional language to describe inner torment necessarily a "capitulation"? Can language ever be employed to "retrieve" the experience of pain and mental suffering?

Although histories of law and forensic psychiatry traditionally speculate about the impact of medical evidence on changing legal conceptions of intent and insanity, one is struck with the possibility that the influence might actually proceed in the opposite direction. Is it only a coincidence that prisoners spoke in a language immediately accessible to law? Couldn't one argue that notions of impulse, self-control, and will—so fundamental to Victorian anxiety about social order—were in fact the contemporary names and images that gave meaning to aberrant sensation and "invasion"? Of course, possession by evil spirits and madness as a punishment for imperfect faith had been standard features of mental derangement since at least the Middle Ages. One has only to listen to the content of the ranters' delusions, replete with religious and political demons, to witness the continuity in cultural shaping of psychic torment. Particularly audible in the early to mid-1800s, however, is a secular invasion that the legal culture may well have launched. The mind was under assault not by devils but by mysterious, treacherous forces that flew into the prisoner's mind. That the prisoners' language aped the Victorian fixation on controlling one's impulses is not a coincidence—or, worse, the disingenuous pleading of the manipulative—but rather evidence that the ideal of individual responsibility, so central to the Western conception of culpability, "created" alien forces where there had once been mere insensibility.

Insanity was not only perceived by Victorian culture as evidence of the failure to control the emotions and impulses; it was experienced as such by the sufferer. One understood that one was mad because no conscious purpose could possibly have animated the irrational act. This breakdown of the inner mechanisms of control was only too apparent in the statements "I was bidden to do it," "It would not let me be quiet," "It was like a dream to me." Control of the passions, the foundation of social order, had not merely shaped the *expression* of self-proclaimed madness in court; it had named the *experience* of the internal world.

Conclusion
A MEDICAL QUESTION AT ALL?

$\mathcal{T}$HE WILLING RELINQUISHMENT OF HUMAN AGENCY IN the face of passion's wild beasts marked a prophetic moment in Western conceptions of madness and responsibility. No, "lesion of the will" did not become a standard medical category, and the McNaughtan and Oxford acquittals hardly opened the floodgates to a rush of insanity trials. Yet despite the law's efforts to cling to a cognitive criterion of "knowing right from wrong" as the basis for inferring intent, in lay, medical, and prisoners' testimony, the will had taken on a curious life of its own. Common law had traditionally employed the "will to harm" in a strictly *knowing* sense: one who was able to understand the circumstances surrounding a crime and proceeded to act was assumed to have acted with intent. Persons incapable of distinguishing right from wrong could not appreciate the harm of their behavior, so their actions were not willful in the legal sense. In the 1800s, the will—the legal signifier for "knowing the harm of one's actions"—was reified into an independent element of the psyche that could suffer its own, separate derangement. "Being out of control" was not new to Western minds in the nineteenth century, but crime-bidding spirits flying directly into one's head (and directly into courtroom testimony) certainly were. From lay witnesses and prisoners juries learned of actions impelled by voices and spirits. From medical witnesses they heard of *recognized* states in which the will itself was deranged. Human agency, or rather the limits of human agency, found direct expression in the early to mid-nineteenth century, rendering the determination of culpability uniquely problematic. Acquitting a prisoner for an act he or she was aware of committing but incapable of resisting was qualitatively different from excusing a prisoner who was incapable of understanding what he or she was "about." What role did the new expert witnesses play in the transformation of insanity's meaning?

Testimony given at insanity cases between the years 1760 and 1843

182

clearly reveals that by the 1840s the forensic-psychiatric witness had arrived. Medical witnesses appeared in at least half of all insanity prosecutions and participated in as many as four of five trials animated by violent personal attack. The appearance of medical witnesses also appears to be associated by the mid-nineteenth century with a rise in acquittal rates for both personal and property offenses, although no necessary relation between these two rates is implied. One has no way of predicting the fate of the prisoner's plea without medical testimony. Indeed, having seen how articulate and compelling both the lay witness and the prisoner could be, it really is anybody's guess how much medical witnesses contributed to an acquittal in any one trial. What can be said with confidence is that medical testimony made a significant departure in the early to mid-nineteenth century, simultaneously expanding and refining notions of insanity to include circumscribed derangement and impaired or diseased will.

Beginning in 1812, medical witnesses coupled the familiar concept of delusion with an ineluctable spur to action. Prompted by defense attorneys to assert that delusion would indeed "lead [the prisoner] to any act," forensic-psychiatric witnesses legitimized the notion of human functioning robbed of choice. Grounding the delusion sometimes in somatic disturbance ("a termination of blood to the head," bowel complaints, or heart palpitations) and sometimes in psychological torment (fears that one's mother was drugging one's beer, fears of being poisoned by a spouse), medical witnesses offered the image of individuals so fearful and tormented that they hardly could be described to have acted willfully when they struck out at their supposed tormentors. Occasionally, impaired volition could sit at the center of medical testimony without even the presence of delusion. The will itself was susceptible to a "lesion," propelling the prisoner into atrocious, self-destructive acts that admitted no possible motive. (In fact, the very want of motive revealed this madness to its interpreters.) Most often the will was not directly diseased but had been put into play by a delusion, "that black spot on the mind" that "carries a man quite away." Under such circumscribed intellectual error, the defendant was "not under the moral restraint in which men in general are bound by their conduct." The prisoner was incapable of resisting its force: "the commission of the act [was] placed beyond his moral control." In a mere few decades, medical witnesses had managed to move from beyond the formulaic "I have looked upon him as a man insane" to address directly and persuasively the law's fundamental criterion: a will to harm.[1]

How did the jury hear such testimony? The interest of ordinary folk in the world of the insane was more than a concern to keep pace with that of their credentialed neighbor. Where the eighteenth-century lay witness employed a host of cultural stereotypes to typify a neighbor's physical and conversational antics, the nineteenth-century witness betrayed a curiosity about the actual thought-world of the deluded individual. It was not the prisoner's similarity to a wild beast that interested the neighbors but the power of ideas to subvert the will. Though the prisoner was customarily capable of distinguishing moral good from evil, "when this subject comes across his mind . . . when his mind was on that subject, I conceive he was entirely incapable of knowing what he did." Averred a neighbor in another trial, "[O]n that point, he has always shown some degree of insanity." Whether in the throes of obsessive love, suffering delusions of political victimization, or caught up by spirit-world tempters, the mental realm inhabited by the distracted individual was a continuing source of wonderment for the nineteenth-century lay witness. In the early to mid-nineteenth century, specific forces that *impelled* the prisoner to act were revealed. Captain Folger stripped off his clothes, danced on broken glass, and jumped astride passing whales at the mention of his nemesis's name. Tom Paine appeared to William Whiskard in a dream and told him "he must commit murder." The devil informed the unfortunate Sarah Hughes "you must and you shall kill your child." Where the lay witness was nowhere as explicit as the medical man in naming the will and the emotions, the testimony of neighbors and employers offered an expanding view of what it was like to *be* mad. Beckoning voices, insistent imps from hell, and "violent passions" may not have had the clinical ring of monomania or moral insanity, but they were eminently intelligible when used to impart the experience of madness. Increasingly in the nineteenth century, that experience included a coupling of being "absent in mind" with being "out of control."

The final player in the courtroom drama was the prisoner, who, far from being relegated to a prop as medical witnesses moved to center stage, actually provided the most trenchant images of all. Similar to the testimony of lay and expert witnesses, the prisoner's defense moved beyond generalities of insensibility and senselessness to provide a more tangible view of madness from the inside. Most prisoners did not speak about delusion per se but brought to light the experience of a "mind overcome," of treacherous forces flying into the head, of an inability to "get command" of themselves. "Struck" with "terror" by their acts, "bidden" to commit murder, "unconscious of what [I] was doing," the most articulate of the prisoners gave the jurors a haunting glimpse into unintended criminality. These "reports" about derangement were complemented by the ranters, whose extravagant displays exhibited the full impelling force of a holy commission, wizards, and urgent messages to relay to Bonaparte.

From generalized mental incoherence—an eighteenth-century notion of delirium—to the early to mid-nineteenth-century focus on the will and the inability to retain self-control, the issue that surfaced in courtroom testimony was one of impaired human agency. Centuries of legal opinion had endeavored to define the boundary between sanity and insanity, and between *total* and *partial* insanity, as a question of knowing. The prisoner's "will to harm" was deduced from the cognitive capacity to know right from wrong, to know what he or she was about, to know the events surrounding the criminal acts—including the consequences of such behavior. Instructions to the jury as late as the end of the eighteenth century reveal the enduring force of the criterion of knowing right from wrong and the exclusion of all mental impairment short of a total want of memory and understanding. But what does one do with understanding and even *planning* that flows directly from a fateful misperception of what one and others are "about"? It is perhaps ironic that the most profoundly corrosive element in the law's traditional criterion for assessing intent should be introduced by a lawyer, Thomas Erskine, but it is undeniably clear in retrospect that when jurors were invited into the self-justifying thought-world of the deranged, partial and total insanity became artifacts of an obsolete archaeology of the mind. It was not delusion alone that challenged the traditional defense against "partial insanity" but the impelling force with which delusions were invested. To hold delusory beliefs was one thing; to be "led to any act" they dictated was quite another. Although it was doubtless the medical witness, questioned—indeed, *coached*—by the attorney, who provided the explicit link between profoundly distorted perception and fatefully impelled behavior, juries at the Old Bailey had already heard about alien forces, bidding voices, and invading spirits from lay witnesses and prisoners. Human agency was apparently becoming a scarce commodity in the nineteenth century, and the major casualty, along with impaired volition, seems to have been the law's criterion of knowing right from wrong. Of course, the McNaughtan rules returned, at least officially, to the cognitive criteria, and subsequent trials continued to give lip-service to the issue of knowing right from wrong, but day-to-day courtroom testimony clearly shows that the conception of mental derangement as a question of understanding was fast becoming outdated.

The changes in courtroom testimony and the consequent expansion of the definition of insanity explains why the acquittal rate becomes increasingly problematic as a measure of a community's willingness to absolve allegedly mad prisoners. It is not after all the "fact" of an acquittal that is of concern but the mental state the jury was scrutinizing when it voted to acquit. Moral insanity is a qualitatively different impairment than generalized intellectual delirium, the common eighteenth-century conception of insanity. Had the acquittal rate stayed the same over time, there would remain compelling evidence of the jury's increasing willingness to expand its notions of mental derangement to include direct impairment of the will. Data presented in chapter 1 reveal that the acquittal rate actually *grew* over the course of the nineteenth century, albeit not dramatically. In the context of the changing texture of courtroom testimony and the consequent shifting meaning of insanity, any increase—indeed, the same rate maintained—would signify a considerable alteration in community perspective regarding the nature of madness. Of course, the rate is the crudest of measures and acquires meaning only after actual testimony is scrutinized to reveal the conceptions of the mind that were structuring witness-examination. From lay witnesses, prisoners, and medical experts alike, the jury was beginning to learn in frightening detail how the most normally judicious of people could be reduced, in the words of one judge, to a "mere machine . . . not at all answerable to the laws of God or man for what he has done, any more than the simple knife could be answerable that gave the final blow." By the nineteenth century, this eighteenth-century instruction was describing a prisoner who was only too real.

The tremendous growth in medical participation in insanity trials did not introduce "expert" alien conceptions of human functioning. Witnesses with no medical credentials had earlier alerted the jury that self-control was the real victim of insanity, at least of nineteenth-century insanity. Yet in the deft naming and employment of such notions in medical testimony the professional growth of forensic psychiatry reached a critical stage. Monomania, moral insanity, and delusion functioned in a manner particular to expert testimony. "Lesion of the will" transported Oxford's want of a motive to kill Queen Victoria in his *particular* trial to the *general* case: "[M]oral irregularity is the result of this disease . . . I have had cases under my observation, in which this form of insanity existed." Daniel McNaughtan's derangement was "quite recognized . . . his antecedent delusions lead to one particular crime to another." The undistinguished deranged prisoner also belonged to recognizable populations. Of Thomas Bowler's delusion the jury was told, "Upon all subjects, except the subject of delusion they would think rationally and clearly." Of Elizabeth Wratten's curious "contrivance without consciousness" the jury learned from Dr. David Uwins in 1833, "Among my patients at the Institution, they have gone through the process of reasoning for the object they have in desire, as a sane person would."[2]

As the general physician could explain the signs of death by poison or why a particular head wound was likely to result from a fall rather than a blow from a blunt instrument, the early to mid-nineteenth-century medical witness claimed the existence of discrete species of disease that he alone was competent to apprehend and explain. Referring explicitly to their professional experience and occasionally to the medical literature, the first forensic psychiatrists (rather than "mere" medical witnesses) ventured beyond classifying insanity as intellectual delirium to address separate and independent elements of the psyche: the will and the passions. In terms of professional claims made by a new generation of asylum keepers, they were only keeping pace with their literary brethren. In terms of a more public, untried, and potentially threatening public forum, they were making the boldest of assertions: the existence of a nonintellectualist insanity. One can understand the wary tone in Chief Justice Denman's voice as he asked Dr. Chowne in the trial of Edward Oxford: "Do you conceive this is really a medical question at all which has been put to you?"

One of the most intriguing insights gained from a study of testimony at the Old Bailey is that, for all the dominance they exerted over the courtroom, the judges were clearly the last to know the answer to that question. Lay testimony and the prisoner's defense suggest that the most potent formulation to reach the court was not delirium and an inability to recognize right from wrong but the *surrender* to overpowering passions and forces. Martin Wiener writes that early Victorian social policy was a series of efforts to "constrain and master popular impulsiveness."[3] Whether "popular impulsiveness" was indeed a problem—and given the precipitous rise in nineteenth-century indictable crimes, one could well argue that this was so—it is clear from even the nonmedical testimony at the Old Bailey that unruly impulses were on the minds of the decidedly nonelite as well. Passions were not of course discovered in the early 1800s; it was rather their *autonomous* power that became an article of faith. Depicting the passions as the unruly rabble of the psyche had multiple effects. It lent force and direction to social reformers' efforts to reinforce the rule of law by encouraging citizens to develop habits of self-governance and responsibility. Reifying the passions permitted relatives and prisoners alike to comprehend atrocious deeds as the work of the devil—either religious or secular (that is, Tom Paine). And separating the psyche into passions, will, and intellect enabled medical specialists to propose innovative classifications that could break free of traditional legal strictures of total and partial polarities to address the will directly, sidestepping delusion entirely if they wished.

In retrospect, it seems impossible to overstate how directly psychiatric concepts were informed by the cultural attention to the passions. This is not meant to argue that far from *imposing* medical esoterica on an unsuspecting laity, the mad-doctor simply codified passions à la mode. If what he heard from asylum patients resembled the prisoners' defense so audible in the courtroom, there is every reason to believe that his qualitative reworking of the insanity concept originated in the opportunity the asylum afforded for close and sustained interaction between the keeper and the kept. One need not return to hagiographic "triumphalism"—the notion that a new, enlightened generation of medical specialists was at last able to grasp the true nature of insanity. Rather, one need only place the Victorian psychiatrist directly within mainstream Victorian culture: what other profession better exemplified cultural anxiety about the inculcation of moral habits? Victorian psychiatry was in fact doubly influenced by contemporary conceptions of mental and social health as a function of self-governance. Not only were specialists in mental medicine likely to be influenced by prevailing cultural notions that equated insanity with the rule of the passions, but their patients appear to have experienced their own idiosyncratic derangement as the *invasion* of alien, insistent forces against which they were powerless to struggle. Whether religious or politico-secular, the expressed content of their delusions was eminently based on culture. Medical nosology was therefore not an invention of an overactive professional imagination or the mere enumeration of selected patients who feared a loss of self-control. The relentless cultural focus on the development of inner behavioral controls reveals the Victorian conception of what human nature, left to its devices, would choose for itself or, rather, how long human agency would exist if forced to do battle with the rabble "down below." Psychiatric classifications encompassing and isolating defects of moral control are only the most obvious sign that all was not well with the nation's psyche.

Lesion of the will might strike us today as a risibly materialist rendering of an obviously metaphysical concept, but its introduction into English jurisprudence conceptually cleared the way for successive attempts to limit the citizen's capacity to exercise self-control even as consciousness was retained. Irresistible impulse is only the most obvious indication of its reach. In our own era we have witnessed an array of individuals who are said to have endured victimization outside the range of usual life experiences and who avail themselves of clinically derived syndromes that supposedly account for seemingly criminal actions without criminal responsibility. Child-abuse victims who kill their parents, battered women who mutilate their attackers, and victims of rape who kill their assaulters invite jurors into their world much as those who long ago claimed: "I was bidden to do it." Although the modern-day "syndrome defendant" has more in common with prisoners who plead self-defense than insanity, the similarity in defense dynamics to mid-nineteenth-century prisoners is striking. Now as then clinical specialists are on hand to explain that the particular disorder exists and is recognized. Now as then an alliance has formed between defense counsel and clinical specialist to drive home the point that gnawing fear or deluded conviction can lead to any act. And, ultimately, now as then these concepts did not come drifting curiously across the Atlantic, seizing citizens by surprise. The willingness to entertain states of being, however horrific and singular, that absolve the knowing offender of criminal deeds speaks directly to a larger cultural anxiety about a civilization's capacity to withstand the perfidious forces lying deep within its nature. Although doubtless compassionate and humane, the recognition of such states of being (indeed the mandating of their introduction into contemporary courtroom testimony) carries profound significance for a culture's capacity to articulate standards of behavior— particularly the legal if not moral responsibility to *resist* impulses. As one witnesses the creation of more and more syndromes in American jurisprudence—as each sorrow in personal relationships becomes transformed into a clinical entity that *exists* and is *recognized*—one finds oneself echoing the suspicion and certain worry of the judge in the Oxford trial who was sufficiently prescient to warn against the demonizing of the passions and, by implication, the medicalizing of evil deeds: "Is this really a medical question at all?"

Appendix 1
DECIDING WHEN AND WHERE TO QUANTIFY

In a number of ways the discovery of several hundred trials featuring testimony about mental derangement in the English courtroom presented as many challenges as opportunities. The sheer number and array of witnesses, crimes, and offenders seemed to promise a limitless capacity to quantify key elements in the evolution of the insanity defense in a period that had heretofore yielded accounts of only a handful of famous trials. The decision when and where to quantify is of course initially constrained by the sources—their comprehensiveness and reliability—but in fact is even more conditioned by the sensibility derived from extended familiarity with those sources.

The first question that faces the researcher investigating the historical evolution of the insanity defense concerns the designation of insanity trials. Throughout the eighteenth century and until at least the midpoint of the nineteenth, a formal "plea of insanity" was a courtroom rarity. All trials between the years 1760 and 1843 had to be scrutinized, therefore, because the inclusion only of those ending in "not guilty by reason of insanity" would have deleted cases in which the defense was unsuccessful, as well as insanity acquittals before 1800, which were recorded as simple "not guilty" findings. Several sources of error are possible when the researcher designates "insanity trials" from a formerly undifferentiated universe of prosecutions. First, a case may be overlooked when there are so many to inspect. Although I have no way of knowing how many cases I may have missed, I am confident that I would not have ignored repeated references to madness in the same case. Second, an error might result from the decision to exclude marginal cases—those including references to the defendant as "rather stupid" or "weak in her senses." I agree with Nigel Walker that such descriptions did not amount to a defense of insanity; still, our combined sample doubtless contains judgment calls, as in our decision to include cases in which the prisoner was found "unfit to plead." These are not technically "insanity trials" per se, but the mental state of the accused was clearly at issue, and had his or her fitness for trial not been questioned before the hearing, one suspects that it would have played a prominent role in the defense. The evidence that prompted the court to suspend prosecution would most certainly have resulted in an acquittal, thus making it necessary to include these cases to grasp the proportion of cases that featured mentally deranged offenders relative to all other prisoners readied for trial. Further, these hearings usually included the appearance of medical witnesses, which made them essential for gaining an appreciation of the variety of uses to which expert evidence was put.

Once the universe of 331 trials was enumerated and standard information was deemed retrievable, there was the fundamental decision concerning how best to examine and present the changing courtroom dynamics and the testimony given by witnesses and prisoners. The attempt to discern and display the evolution of new understandings about madness required the construction of data out of dense qualitative narratives. To address some research areas, numerical presentation was feasible and defensible. The *Old Bailey Sessions Papers* (*OBSP*) present trials in a straightforward way: name of the prisoner, victim, type of crime, and the value of items stolen. Usually the occupation of the victim and prosecutor is given, but this is deleted in enough cases to preclude any meaningful comparisons over time. The type of offense is standardly present to permit quantification, and these data are provided in chapter 1, along with an explanation for how offenses were coded into "property" and "personal" offenses. Also easy to quantify are the rates of participation of various witnesses. Even in the severely "compressed" cases, the names and medical designation (if any) of witnesses is given. Verdicts are likewise easy to retrieve, although one must decide how to treat a "not guilty" finding when the qualifier "on the grounds of insanity" is missing. When it was clear that no dispute arose regarding the nature of evidence or identification of the prisoner, insanity appeared to be the sole matter for the jury to deliberate. Consequently, the resulting "not guilty" verdicts were counted as insanity acquittals.

Regardless of how easily verdicts can be retrieved from the *OBSP*, the conceptual usefulness of an acquittal *rate* is not limited to matters of methodological soundness. Any verdict is the result of particular features in a particular trial. How another prisoner might have fared with more articulate lay and medical witnesses and a less vindictive prosecutor is impossible to say. Assembling verdicts into a rate therefore entails a loss of detail about the dynamics that produced any one verdict, although such sacrifice is a necessary cost if one is to examine patterns in contemporary attitudes toward crime and criminal responsibility over time. Acquittal rates in *insanity* trials, however, may be even more problematic because insanity's meaning to courtroom participants in one moment in time is not necessarily its meaning in another. Jury members may be evaluating something very different—madness as physical disease, as mental confusion, as "impulsive will"—when over time they vote to acquit by reason of insanity. Such variation in meaning is hidden by simply computing an acquittal rate; these data must be supplemented by an analysis of insanity's meaning to courtroom participants.

As tempting as it was to construct frequency distributions of terms and images employed by hundreds of lay witnesses, medical personnel, and prisoners, the more familiar I became with the *OBSP*, the more convinced I was that such a display would have been hopelessly reductive and inevitably misleading. The meaning of a concept such as delusion, for example, changes radically when the predominant conception of insanity is one of intellectual confusion than when madness is thought to be a matter of defective impulse control. Delusion has no necessary impelling power in the first instance but assumes authorship of the crime in the second. The context of the testimony, therefore, is fundamental to appreciating how these terms were employed and, one suspects, how they were heard. The one exception I allowed myself was in chapter 4: the enumeration of "causal" elements mentioned by lay witnesses. The proclivity of neighbors and friends to cast their inference in quasi-deterministic episodes was pronounced in one period, and I decided that the time limitation reduced the range of meanings associated with the physical and emotional spurs to action. For the rest, I resolved to present changes in the perception and assessment of derangement over time by searching for themes that surfaced in a particular span of years and examining such shifts in perspective over the study's three periods. I was especially interested in identifying testimony that directly engaged legal issues surrounding intent: the "knowing" component that imputed responsibility.

Purposeful selection carries the inherent risk of reading courtroom testimony with any eye toward presenting a certain construction of social change and then supplying "representative" extracts that would appear to support the case. Such working of the data would have been especially easy because I knew how the story "ended," at least the extent to which all courtroom participants eventually embraced images of impulsive will and defective self-control. Aware of this pitfall, I endeavored to remain alert to the variation within any one period, particularly the continuity of vestigial eighteenth-century notions about madness into the enlightened mid-Victorian courtroom. Given the charges often leveled at sociologists who wander into historical materials, I have been especially sensitive to the hazards of too-ready generalization and reductive, context-free numerism. Quantification and generalization, however, do not separate historians from sociologists. It seems to me that regardless of the disciplinary identification, the researcher who delves into the historical jurisprudence of insanity must remain attentive to how social actors understood both the phenomenon they were negotiating and their role in the decision-making process. To this end, I have endeavored to situate the dawning professional consciousness of the medical witness in the social setting of the courtroom, where conceptual grounding and assertions to skill and insight took root during the process of cross-examination, not before.

Appendix 2

MEDICAL WITNESSES WHO TESTIFIED AT THE OLD BAILEY ABOUT THE MENTAL CONDITION OF THE ACCUSED, 1760–1843

Name	Title mentioned at trial	Year of trial and case number	Comments
Ainsley, Dr.	physician	1812:527 1814:360	Henry Ainsley, 1760–1834. M.D. Cambridge, 1793. FRCP. Phys., St. Thomas's, 1795; resigned, 1800. (Munk)
Barker, Edgar	surgeon	1835:2010	?—1874. Ed., St. Barts. Surg., W. Gen. Disp. MRCS, 1824. FRCS, 1849. LSA, 1823. (Parr)
Barney (Mr.)	surgeon	1790:655	"Surgeon at Sudbury."
Blackman, Charles Thomas		1843–44:43	
Box, Wm. Henry, Esq.	surgeon of the gaol for Middlesex	1828:1349	
Box, Wm. John (Mr.)	assistant surgeon to Newgate	1830:176 1830:1483	
Boyd, Robert (Dr.)	surgeon to Marylebone Infirmary	1841:1071	1808–83. M.D. Edinburgh, 1831. Specialist in insanity. Phys. and Supt., Somerset Co. Asylum, 1848. Wrote many papers on brain diseases. (Munk)
Burns	resident apothecary to St. Luke's Hospital	1840:542	

Appendix 2 (*continued*)

Name	Title mentioned at trial	Year of trial and case number	Comments
Burrows, George [Man]	part owner of madhouse at Hoxton	1812:32	1771–1846. Entered Guy's and St. Thomas's, 1793. Admitted to Corp. Surg., Soc'y Apoth. (n.d.). Org'd Ass'n Surg.-Apoth. Eng. and Wales (chairman). Opened insane asylums at Chelsea (1816); The Retreat (1823). Created Doctor, Univ. St. Andrews, 1824.
Campbell, John	physician at Finsbury Dispensary	1837:1674	"Lives in Weymouth Street, Portland-place."
Chambers, John	surgeon	1842–43:1011	?—1846. Surg.'s mate, hosp. staff, MRCS, 1809. FRCS, 1844. LSA, 1844. Long list of med./mil. posts. (Parr)
Chapman (Mr.)	surgeon	1760:261	?—Samuel. M.D. Aberdeen, 1763. Lic., Coll. Phys., 1765.
Chowne (Dr.)	physician to Charing-Cross Hospital	1840:1877	1791–1870. William Dingle. M.D. Edinburgh (n.d.). Est'd London, 1833. Charing-Cross Hosp. his main interest; 1 of 4 orig. mgrs. of its med. school. "Physician to Charing-Cross" at time of testimony, specialty seems to have been obstetrics. Frequent contrib. to med. journals; lectured on med. jurisprudence. (Munk)
Clark, James Fernandez	surgeon	1840:1877	1788–1870. M.D. Edinburgh, 1817. Lic., Coll. Phys., 1826. Phys., St. Barts. Wrote memoir of John Conolly. (Munk)
Coleman, Thomas (Mr.)	navy surgeon	1784:943	Warranted, 1778. (MR '83)

Appendix 2 (*continued*)

Name	Title mentioned at trial	Year of trial and case number	Comments
Combes (Dr.)		1780:415	?Charles Combe, M.D. 1743–1817 (Glasgow, 1784). Obstetrician, Coll. Phys., 1784.
Conolly, John	physician to Hanwell Lunatic Asylum	1840:1877 1843:847	1794–1866. M.D. Edinburgh [Diss.: "De statu mentis in insania et melancholia"]. Joined Med. and Chirurgical Soc'y London; active, Soc'y Diffusion Useful Knowledge.
Cook, William	surgeon	1842,3:2897	
Coombe (Dr.)	physician	1816:211	Consulted on case with the late Dr. Simmons. (same as Combes?)
Crawford, John	Lecturer, medical jurisprudence, Andersonian University, Glasgow	1843:874	[Munk has a "Mervyn Archdale Nott Crawford" (1807–1891)]
Dalton, Jsph. (Mr.)	surgeon	1822:811	"Lives at Carey-street, Lincoln's Inn fields."
Davies, John Birt	physician	1840:1877	1799–1878. M.D. Edinburgh, 1822. FRCP, 1859. Phys., Gen. Disp. Birmingham; chair, forensic med. "for many years," Birmingham's Royal School of Med. and Surgery. Elected city's 1st coroner, 1839 (presided over thousands of inquests until 1875). (Munk)
Day, Henry	surgeon	1837:550	1814–1881. Ed. at Guy's, qualified 1835. Treated lunatics in private practice. Expert microscopist. Published clinical histories. "I live at Acton."

Appendix 2 (*continued*)

Name	Title mentioned at trial	Year of trial and case number	Comments
de Castro, Benjamin		1789:494	With brother Daniel Jacob, likely members of prominent de Castro Sarmento family, Portuguese Jews who emigrated to London in 1720–21.
de Castro, Daniel Jacob		1789:494	
Diggan (Mr.)	surgeon	1780:325	Diggins, apoth. in St. Albans St. (MR'83)
Douglas, James (Dr.)	surgeon at Glasgow	1843:874	
Drewry, Edward	surgeon	1841–42:1766	
Fenner, John	surgeon	1828:1349	"Resides at Pentonville."
Fisher, John	surgeon at Newgate	1841,2:1766	1788?–1876. Ed., St. George's & Westminster. Surg., Bow-Street patrol, 1821. 1st surg.-in-chief, Metropolitan Police Force, 1829. FRCS, 1844. Hon. M.D., Univ. Erlangen. "Attended Newgate to see the prisoner in consequence of an appointment." (Parr)
Fuller, Henry	surgeon	1835:806	"Lives in Hackney road."
Gardner, Samuel	surgeon	1842–43:2856	"I live in Edgeware Road."
Goodyear, Wm. Fred	apothecary to Marylebone Infirmary	1819:1417	
Gosner (Mr.)	apothecary to Bethlem Hospital	1784:943	John Gozna. Apoth., Bethlem, 1772–96. Collected stat. data on insane used by Haslam.
Gouldsmith, John	surgeon	1841:2608	In partnership with Joseph McCrea.
Halifax, Thomas	apothecary	1833:1304	"Apothecary at Woolrich." M.D. Edinburgh.

Appendix 2 (*continued*)

Name	Title mentioned at trial	Year of trial and case number	Comments
Harding (Mr.)	surgeon	1839:1577	1808–1883. John F., MRCS, 1835. FRCS, 1852. LSA, 1835. Studied at St. Barts. Examining surg., Infant Orphans. Appt'd to attend Newgate.
Hart Myers, Jos. (Dr.)	physician	1789:494	?–1823. b. New York. M.D. Edinburgh, 1779. Phys., Portuguese Hosp., General Disp., and Hosp. for German and Dutch Jews (n.d.) "I live on John Street, America-Square."
Haslam, John	apothecary to Bethlem	1813:11	1764–1844. Apoth., Bethlem, 1795–1816. M.D. Hosp. Aberdeen, 1816. LRCP. Wrote books on madness, med. jurisprudence, as well as criticism, comic pieces. Removed from Bethlem after parliamentary inquiry on the state of care of the insane.
Hayes, James	surgeon	1838:499	"Lives in Newgate Street."
Hodgkin (Dr.)	physician	1840:1877	"Lecturer on morbid anatomy, I have written some works on pathological anatomy and the promotion of health."
Hodson (Mr.)	"medical professor"	1809:605	"Attends the compter." Hodson, surg. or apoth. at Preston. (MR'83)
Houghton (Mr.)	surgeon	1827:1613	Saw prisoner on his return from Warburton's [madhouse].
Hunter, John	surgeon	1840:2316	"Lives in Hart-Street, Bloomsburg."

Appendix 2 (*continued*)

Name	Title mentioned at trial	Year of trial and case number	Comments
Hutchenson, Wm.	physician to Royal Lunatic Asylum at Glasgow	1843:874	d. 1869. Wm. Barclay Hutchenson. MRCSA, 1829. FRCS, 1852. L, 1830. St. Barts. Med. officer attending the Founding Hosp.
Hyatt (Mr.)	surgeon and apothecary	1812:527	Active in Ealing.
Key, Charles Aston	surgeon of Guy's Hospital	1843:874	b. 1793. Apprenticed to father, 1810. Ed., Guy's 1814. Ass't Surg., Guy's, 1821. Surg. to Prince Albert, 1847. MRCS, 1821; one of orig. 300 Fellows. FRCS, 1843. 1st (1823) to successfully ligature subclavian artery for cure of axillary aneurysm. (Parr)
Langley, John	surgeon and apothecary	1842–43:2856	
Lee, Henry (Dr.)	physician	1828:41	M.D. Edinburgh. Lic., Coll. Phys., 1819. Phys., Gen. Disp. Birmingham, 1831. Bachelor Med. 1831, Caius Coll., Cambridge. Settled in London. "Lives at N. 10, Howland Street, Fitzroy Square." d. 1869.
Leo, Luis (Dr.)		1798:470 1801:446	b. 1753. M.D. Active in Sephardic community: "Dr. Leo of Houndsditch."
Lesley (Mr.)	surgeon and apothecary	1813:884	Two possibles: (1) John. Regimental surg., Coldstream Regiment, 3d warrant, 1779. (2) Leslie, William. Navy surgeon, warrant, 1781.
Lowndes, Francis	"medical gentleman"	1805:457	Wrote 2 books on med. electricity. (BL Cat.)

Appendix 2 (*continued*)

Name	Title mentioned at trial	Year of trial and case number	Comments
Mayberry, Chas.	surgeon	1822:1070	
McClewer, Wm.	surgeon	1843:874	"I practice in London . . . accompanied Dr. Monroe and Sir Alexander Morison to Newgate on four occasions."
M'Crea, Joseph	surgeon	1841:2608	In partnership with John Gouldsmith.
McMurdo, Gilbert (Mr.)	surgeon of Newgate	1830:176+ 16 other trials	1799–1869. MRCS 1824, FRCS 1843, one of orig. 300 fellows. FRS 1839. Surg. to Newgate Jail at a salary. Ass't. Surg.: Royal Opthalmic H., Moorfields 1830. (Parr)
Miller (Dr.), Patrick		1830:177	b. 1782. DMI Edinburgh, 1804. Extra-Lic., Coll. Phys., St. Thomas's Lunatic Asylum, 1822. Son of Dr. Matthew Stewart, prof. of math, Univ. of Edinburgh. Ed. Edinburgh by his maternal uncle, Dugald Stewart. (Munk) Accompanied McMurdo to visit prisoners.
Monro, Edward Thomas (Dr.)		1828:1349 1841:2608 1843:874	d. 1856. M.D. Oxford, 1814, FCP 1816. Like 3 generations of his family, devoted himself to treating insanity and was phys. to Bethlem. "I live in Harley Street."
Monro (Dr.)		1780:415	1715–91. John. Phys., Bethlem. Oxford, 1747. M.D. by dipl., 1787. Son T. Monro appointed his asst. at Bethlem.
Morison, Alexander		1843:874	1779–1866. DMI, Edinburgh 1799.

Appendix 2 (*continued*)

Name	Title mentioned at trial	Year of trial and case number	Comments
Morison, Alexander (*continued*)			Appointed inspecting phys., lunatic asylums in Surrey, 1810. Elect phys., Bethlem, 1835. LCP, 1808. FCP 1841. "For many successive years he delivered a course of lectures on mental diseases, and by them, his writings did much to extend knowledge of this difficult department of practice." Wrote 3 books. (Munk)
Nelson (Mr.)	navy surgeon	1835:842	Two possibles: (1) John D. MRCS 1839, FRCS 1858, LSA 1840. Ed. London Hosp. Surg. to Queen Adelaide's Lying In Hospital. Fellow, Obstetrical Soc'y. (2) Thomas, 1768–1848. Surg.-accoucher, 1787. DMI Edinburgh, 1799. LCP, 1800.
Nevly, William	apothecary at St. Luke's	1813:11	
North, John (Mr.)	surgeon	1819:1417	1790–1873. MRCS, 1809. FRCS, 1843; one of orig. 300 Fellows. Spec. midwifery and diseases of women and children. Lect., Westminster Hosp. School and Middlesex Hosp. Wrote med. pubs. Co-ed., *London Med. and Phys. J.* (Parr)
O'Donnell, John A.	apothecary	1785:599	
Olding (Mr.)	assistant surgeon of the gaol	1839:2355	

Appendix 2 (*continued*)

Name	Title mentioned at trial	Year of trial and case number	Comments
Parkin, Henry	surgeon in the Royal Marines	1835:1119	1779–1849. M. of the Surgeon's Co., 1796. M.D. Aberdeen, 1810. FRCS, 1843; one of orig. 300 Fellows. Surg., Royal Navy (Royal Marines) Inspector of Fleet Hosp. for 50 yrs. Lived in Cornwall.
Pascal, Francis, Rogers	surgeon	1818:776	
Perry, Sebastian	physician	1839:1786	
Ramsden, William	surgeon	1796:512	
Rayner, Frederick	surgeon	1840:2316	"Surgeon at Uxbridge."
Rayner, Wm.	surgeon	1840–2316	"Surgeon at Uxbridge."
Reynolds, Thomas	apothecary at Charing-Cross Hospital	1784:971	Active at Charing-Cross.
Scudamore, Chas., Sir	M.D.	1840–41:39	1779–1849. (3d son of med. practitioner in Kent.) DMI Glasgow, 1814. LCP, 1814. Knighted, 1829. Phys., Buxton Bath Charity. Wrote on rheumatism, diagnoses of diseases of the chest, gout, pulmonary consumption.
Self, James	surgeon	1835–36:216	
Simmons, Samuel Foart	physician to St. Luke's Hospital	1785:599 1806:32	b. 1750. M.D. Leyden, 1776, LRCP, FRCP, FRS. Phys., Westminster Gen. Disp., 1780–81, St. Luke's 1781–1800. Treated George III, 1813. Compiled *Med. Reg. 1779*.
Sims	doctor	1803:580	Two possibles: (1) James Sims. 1741–1820. DMI Leyden LCP. Phys., Gen. Disp. One of founders, London Med.

Appendix 2 (*continued*)

Name	Title mentioned at trial	Year of trial and case number	Comments
Sims (*continued*)			Soc'y. Wrote "A Discourse on the Best Method of Prosecuting Medical Inquiries." (DNB) (2) John Sims. d. 1831. M.D. Edinburgh, 1774, LCP, 1779. Phys., Surrey Disp., charity for delivering married women at home.
Sutherland, A. R. (Dr.)	physician to St. Luke's	1813:11	d. 1861. M.D. Edinburgh, 1805. LRCP. Phys., St. Luke's, 1811–36.
Taylor, Samuel	surgeon and apothecary	1840,1:39	"Lives in High-Street, Kensington."
Turner (Dr.)	doctor	1814:360	?Thos. M.D. Trinity Coll., Cambridge, 1804. Ass't phys., St. Thomas's, 1800. Appointed to 1st metropolitan commission on lunacy; later an early member of Board of Commissioners in Lunacy. (Munk)
Uwins, David (M.D.)	physician	1833:1304	b. 1780–1837. DMI Edinburgh, 1803. LCP, 1807. Wrote widely published "Treatise on Those Disorders of the Brain and Nervous System Which Are Usually Considered and Called Mental" (1833). Contrib. med. arts. to *Gregory's Ency.* and 2 arts. on insanity and madness to *Q. Rev.* (July 1816). (Munk)
Wakefield (Mr.)	surgeon to the House of Correction	1834:1654	
Waldron (Mr.)	surgeon	1814:746	"Attends Giltmur-street compter."

Appendix 2 (*continued*)

Name	Title mentioned at trial	Year of trial and case number	Comments
Waller, William	"a medical man"	1798:113	
Want, John	surgeon	1816:293	"Lives in North Crescent, Bedford Square. I have had some experience in the diseases of the mind."
Warburton, Thos.		1805:637 1812:527	Testified that he was med. man at Hoxton and earlier at St. Luke's. Son, John Warburton. M.D. Cambridge, 1820. FCP, 1821. Devoted himself to study of treatment of insanity. Phys., St. Luke's, 1829.
Ward, Stephen Henry	medical student at London Hospital	1839:2101	1819–80. M.D. London (Hospital). FRCP, 1870. Phys., Seaman's Hosp., 1859. City of London Hosp. for Diseases of the Chest. Examiner, Soc'y Apoth. Pres., Hunterian Soc'y.
Webb, Thos.	surgeon of the House of Correction, Coldbath Fields	1805:637 1812:527 1819:1417	Surg., Clerkenwell Prison.
Williams, James, Sr.		1804:25	
Williams, James, Jr.		1804:25	
Willis	doctor	1800:315	1718–1807. Francis. M.D. Oxford, 1759. Son, John Willis, also M.D. Family owned private madhouse and were active in treatment of George III.
Winslow, Forbes	surgeon	1843:43	"Author of a work on insanity": *The Plea of Insanity in Criminal Cases* (London, 1843), and *The Principles of Phrenology* (1832).

Notes

INTRODUCTION

1. Stirn has not escaped the notice of historians of suicide. The prisoner achieved considerable fame by poisoning himself at the trial and by leaving a dramatic note on the prison wall naming "Lucifer" as his tormentor. See Michael MacDonald and Terence R. Murphy, *Sleeping Souls: Suicide in Early Modern England* (Oxford: Clarendon Press, 1990), esp. 211–12, 284.

2. Indictments are an excellent historical source for examining the activity of the grand jury but not necessarily for estimating the *universe* of crime. As many researchers have noted, indictments record the incidence of crime only after the victim has decided to prosecute, the committing magistrate has determined to prepare the charge for the grand jury's deliberation, and the grand jury returns an indictment. Several stages removed from the actual crime, indictments are not likely to yield an accurate picture of the *universe* of criminal activity in eighteenth-century England. Interestingly, this insight is not new. The "dark area" of crime was conceptualized as early as the nineteenth century: the extent of offensivity that did not make its way into the official record by way of indictments, jail-delivery lists, and depositions. See J. M. Beattie, "Towards a Study of Crime in Eighteenth-Century England: A Note on Indictments," in Paul Fritz and David Williams, eds., *The Triumph of Culture: Eighteenth-Century Perspectives* (Toronto: A. M. Hakkert, 1972), 299–314.

3. The "Old Bailey" was the popular name for the Justice Hall adjoining Newgate Prison, the principal jail for Middlesex and London counties. By the mid-eighteenth century, there were eight sessions per year at the Old Bailey. Outside London, the most serious crimes were tried before the judges at the assizes. The Old Bailey was the equivalent of the assize court. In 1834, the Old Bailey was enlarged and housed in the new Central Criminal Court. The anomalies of prosecution in London and Middlesex counties are reviewed in J. H. Baker, "Criminal Courts and Procedure at Common Law, 1550–1800," in J. S. Cockburn, ed., *Crime in England, 1550–1800* (Princeton: Princeton University Press, 1977), esp. 30–31.

4. Thomas Rogers Forbes, *Surgeons at the Bailey: English Forensic Medicine to 1878* (New Haven: Yale University Press, 1985), 15–23.

5. Langbein has scrutinized the historical credibility of the *OBSP* by employing the shorthand trial notes of Sir Dudley Ryder, who presided during the decade of the 1750s. When the judge's notes have been set against the trial narratives, the papers have been deemed reliable. Langbein, "Shaping the Eighteenth-Century Criminal Trial: A View from the Ryder Sources," *University of Chicago Law Review* 50 (1983): esp. 6–26.

6. The relatively amorphous nature of a defense "case" was not particular to insanity trials; the usual trial of the Old Bailey could hardly be said to feature a fully articulated case, or even an articulate version of the case as such. This degree of legal preparation and attention to evidence and proof would await the coming of a lawyer, permitting the full range of adversarial tactics: opening and closing statements, capacity to address the jury, and so on. That he could examine and cross-examine witnesses was not an inconsiderable aid to the defense, but it hardly amounted to mounting a defense "case."

7. For an enlightening interchange between the accused and "his" attorney that reveals this narrow role, see Langbein, "Shaping," 130:

> *Court:* Prisoner, what have you to say for yourself? . . . You hear you are charged with having divers kinds of goods in your lodgings. What account can you give how you came by them?
> *Prisoner:* My counsel will speak for me.
> *Counsel:* I can't speak that for you, you must speak yourself.

8. Langbein, "Shaping," 123.

9. Mr. Garrow is identified as *prisoner's counsel* (italics in original) in 1786. *Old Bailey Sessions Papers* (hereafter, *OBSP*), case 591, 6th sess., 868.

1. Crime, Punishment, and the Jury

1. For a comprehensive overview of research in eighteenth-century crime and criminality, the criminal trial, punishment, and criminal legislation, see Joanna Innes and John Styles, "The Crime Wave: Recent Writing on Crime and Criminal Justice in Eighteenth-Century England," *Journal of British Studies* 25 (October 1986): 380–435. Classic works in eighteenth-century crime and social history include E. P. Thompson, *Whigs and Hunters: The Origin of the Black Act* (London: Allen Lane, 1975); Douglas Hay, Peter Linebaugh, and E. P. Thompson, eds., *Albion's Fatal Tree: Crime and Society in Eighteenth-Century England* (New York: Pantheon, 1975); and John Brewer and John Styles, eds., *An Ungovernable People: The English and Their Law in the Seventeenth and Eighteenth Centuries* (New Brunswick, N.J.: Rutgers University Press, 1980). The most widely cited research on eighteenth-century offenders and offenses includes J. M. Beattie, "Crime and the Courts in Surrey, 1736–1753," in J. S. Cockburn, ed., *Crime in England, 1550–1800* (Princeton: Princeton University Press, 1977), 155–86; J. M. Beattie, "The

Pattern of Crime in England, 1660–1800," *Past and Present* 62 (1974): 47–95; George Rudé, *Criminal and Victim: Crime and Society in Early Nineteenth-Century England* (Oxford: Clarendon Press, 1985); and Clive Emsley, *Crime and Society in England, 1750–1900* (London: Longman, 1987). The social composition of the jury and its supposed effects on decision-making are discussed in Peter J. King, " 'Illiterate Plebians, Easily Misled': Jury Composition, Experience, and Behavior in Essex, 1735–1815," in J. S. Cockburn and Thomas A. Green, eds., *Twelve Good Men and True: The Criminal Trial Jury in England, 1200–1800* (Princeton: Princeton University Press, 1988), 254–304; Douglas Hay, "War, Dearth and Theft in the Eighteenth Century: The Record of the English Courts," *Past and Present* 95 (1982): 117–60; J. M. Beattie, "London Juries in the 1690s," in Cockburn and Green, eds., *Twelve Good Men,* 214–53; and Douglas Hay, "The Class Composition of the Palladium of Liberty: Trial Jurors in the Eighteenth Century," in Cockburn and Green, eds., *Twelve Good Men,* 305–57. The socio-economic characteristics of prosecutors (victims of the offenses) are examined in Peter J. King, "Decision-Makers and Decision-Making in the English Criminal Law, 1750–1800," *Historical Journal* 27, no. 1 (1984): 25–58; Brewer and Styles, *Ungovernable People;* and David Philips, *Crime and Authority in Victorian England: The Black Country, 1835–1860* (London: Croom Helm, 1977). On "jury lawlessness" see Thomas Andrew Green, *Verdict According to Conscience: Perspectives on the English Criminal Trial, 1200–1800* (Chicago: University of Chicago Press, 1985), esp. 356–63.

2. Each of these features of the eighteenth-century criminal trial are discussed extensively by John H. Langbein in "The Criminal Trial before the Lawyers," *University of Chicago Law Review* 45 (Winter 1978): 263–316, and Langbein, "Shaping the Eighteenth-Century Criminal Trial: A View from the Ryder Sources," *University of Chicago Law Review* 50 (Winter 1983): 1–136.

3. For a discussion of the legislative policy that resulted in the profusion of capital statutes relating to larceny specifically, see Leon Radzinowicz, *A History of the English Criminal Law and Its Administration from 1750,* vol.1: *The Movement for Reform* (London: Stevens & Sons, 1948), esp. 3–49.

4. These Enlightenment principles were first articulated in Cesare Beccaria, *An Essay on Crimes and Punishments* (London: F. Newbery, 1775).

5. Langbein, "Shaping," esp. 37–41; King, "Decision-Makers," esp. 42–51; Green, *Verdict According to Conscience,* esp. 280–84.

6. The debate over the extension of the Royal Pardon sits at the center of a much larger concern with the supposed political purposes of the eighteenth-century criminal law, which includes Radzinowicz's analysis of the operation of the "The Prerogative of Mercy" (*History,* esp. 107–37), and Hay's interpretation of the ideological purpose of conjoining terror and mercy to strengthen ruling class hegemony ("Property, Authority and the Criminal Law," in Hay et al., eds., *Albion's Fatal Tree,* esp. 17–63). Hay's analysis has been critiqued by John Langbein in "Albion's Fatal Flaws" (*Past and Present* 98 [1983]: 96–120) in part by employing King's analysis ("Decision-

Makers") of the social background of victim/prosecutors and the criteria for pardons extracted from judicial petitions.

7. Originally employed by the medieval church to retain ecclesiastical jurisdiction over clerics, by 1705 this privilege was extended to nonclerics. Michael Ignatieff, *A Just Measure of Pain: The Penitentiary in the Industrial Revolution, 1750–1850* (London: Penguin, 1978), 18. See also Langbein, "Shaping," 37–41.

8. Langbein, "Albion's Fatal Flaws," 117.

9. Although research has demonstrated the class origins of jurors in and around London, determining the effect of social position in a jury's disposition to convict has proved elusive. All researchers agree that petit juries were drawn from the upper tier of society (usually the upper third) but disagree regarding how heavily their verdicts reveal class bias or even "ruling-class" ideology. King ("Decision-Makers") concludes that juries in Surrey represent the "middling sort," though this is a middling sort of the decidedly property-holding. They appeared to share interests with those above and below them depending on the nature of the offense. Hay ("Class Composition") studied juries in Staffordshire, noting that three-quarters of the local citizenry were too poor to be chosen; more than half the population did not meet the property qualification. Hay concludes that juries were "prosecution-oriented," but since King's research has also demonstrated the modest social standing of most prosecutors, one might infer that juries were representing a rather broad range of "interests." Beattie ("Crime and the Courts") found jurors in late seventeenth-century London to be men of considerable wealth and rank, though somewhat below the highest levels of both. He emphasizes the continuity in functioning connecting jury service to other forms of local governance and does not hazard a guess regarding whose interests juries actually represented.

10. Langbein contends that partial verdicts were, in a sense, sentencing decisions, usually having the effect of lessening the disposition from death to transportation ("Albion's Fatal Flaws," 106). Originating in the early seventeenth century, the idea of transporting convicts to colonies had become much more popular by the late 1600s and expanded considerably in the eighteenth century. See John H. Langbein, *Torture and the Law of Proof: Europe and England in the Ancien Régime* (Chicago: University of Chicago Press, 1976), 39–44.

11. Green, *Verdict According to Conscience,* 274, 280.

12. King, "Illiterate Plebians," 255.

13. Green, *Verdict According to Conscience,* 378–83.

14. On common law's disposition regarding children and the insane, see Nigel D. Walker, *Crime and Insanity in England,* vol. 1: *The Historical Perspective* (Edinburgh: Edinburgh University Press, 1968), 26–29.

15. Most reduced charges occurred in years with high food prices and low crime rates. See Hay, "War, Dearth," 155.

16. P. J. King, "Decision-Makers."

17. Although recent scholarship has narrowed the focus somewhat to the trial jury and the exercise of "pious perjury," the range of discretionary decisions in eighteenth-century criminal justice was extremely broad. These include the victim, who had to decide whether to prosecute; the magistrate, who decided to go forward with the prosecution and jail the accused; the grand jury, which indicted; the trial jury, which could acquit or find a partial verdict, and finally the judge, who could recommend a pardon.

18. MacDonald and Murphy document the evolution of another insanity "plea" in their study of coroners' juries investigating suicides during the period 1500–1800. The authors determined that by the end of the eighteenth century the determination of lunacy—a finding of non compos mentis—included increasingly less severe states of mental distraction, which led them to infer a growing acceptance of "mental disease" as a cause of suicide. As MacDonald and Murphy suggest, the increasing frequency of lunacy findings implies a "secularization" of suicide in which philosophers and physicians appeared to have played a role. The nature of this role remains unclear, since medical appearances at coroners' inquests are mentioned but not systematically explored in terms of the level of participation or how the testimony was received. The medical testimony was clearly a matter of legal concern, as seen in the protests lodged against the "lenient interpretation of psychiatric evidence." Medical participation was usually restricted to hearings concerning suicides of well-to-do persons, yet lunacy verdicts were also returned for decidedly non-elite victims, prompting the authors to conclude that "it was difficult to condemn people who suffered misfortunes that might befall anyone" (Michael MacDonald and Terence Murphy, *Sleepless Souls: Suicide in Early Modern England* [Oxford: Clarendon Press, 1990], esp. 57–58, 125–40).

Further, MacDonald and Murphy speculate on the significance of the jurors' social position for rendering a verdict at the coroner's inquest. These men of middling status occupied a middle ground between, on one hand, the received opinion of the educated and the powerful, and on the other, local society which viewed self destruction through its own moral concerns and cultural meanings. According to the authors, coroners' verdicts increasingly revealed the existence of "tolerant and secular attitudes to suicide" (344).

19. Quoted in Emsley, *Crime and Society,* 48. See also Langbein, "Criminal Trial," and Rudé, *Criminal and Victim.*

20. For an overview of the changing dynamics in crimes of personal violence, see Laurence Stone, "Interpersonal Violence in English Society, 1300–1980," *Past and Present* 101 (1983): 22–33.

21. This point is made in Joel P. Eigen, "Intentionality and Insanity: What the Eighteenth-Century Juror Heard," in William F. Bynum, Roy Porter, and Michael Shepherd, eds., *The Anatomy of Madness,* vol. 2: *Institutions and Society* (London: Tavistock, 1985), 40.

22. For a discussion of Robert Peel's efforts at law consolidation and the abo-

lition of capital punishment for most forms of felony, see Radzinowicz, *History,* esp. 1:567–85.

23. Rudé, *Criminal and Victim,* 50–64.
24. Rudé, *Criminal and Victim,* 63.
25. King, "Illiterate Plebians," 254–55.
26. G. R. Elton offers still more reasons to question what an acquittal rate signifies. Were the prisoners falsely accused in the first place? Were juries acquitting from compassion or under some type of pressure? See "Introduction: Crime and the Historian," in J. S. Cockburn, *Crime in England,* 12.
27. King, "Illiterate Plebians," 255.
28. Beattie, "Crime and the Courts," 174–77.
29. Occasionally in the late 1700s one reads a judge's instruction that "care should be taken" of this prisoner (following a finding of "not guilty"), and twice the jury supplemented its acquittal with "believing him to be deranged" or "insensible at the time." The provisions of the 1800 act mandating secure confinement for prisoners who received a "special verdict" are discussed in chapter 2. In the years immediately following the Hadfield verdict and the passage of the Criminal Lunatics Act, acquittals at the Old Bailey were accompanied with the instruction "detained awaiting the King's pleasure."
30. Eigen, "Intentionality and Insanity," 41.
31. It was not unusual for a jury to be composed of many members who had served before. Additionally jurors in London served as a panel for the entire session—30 to 40 trials at a time. The phenomenon of juror experience, and its supposed effect on likely verdicts and ability to remain independent from the judge are explored in King, "Illiterate Plebians"; Beattie, "London Juries"; and Hay, "Class Composition."
32. This issue is explored in chapter 6.
33. It needs to be stressed here that for *individual* cases in which medical witnesses appeared, the chances for acquittal always exceeded the overall rates for that period. The problem of course is that without a "control trial"— one which repeated the prosecution without the mad-doctor—there is no way to gauge the influence of, and weight conferred on medical testimony. Medical witnesses, fearful of courtroom humiliation, might have selected only those cases with the most manifest and unambiguous signs of madness, as occasions to make a court appearance.
34. See Green's discussion of the social background of the criminal as focal point of critics of the death penalty (*Verdict According to Conscience,* 378–79).
35. Green, *Verdict According to Conscience,* 383.

2. INSANITY

1. See, e.g., Henri de Bracton, *De legibus et consuetudinibus Angliae,* ed. George E. Woodbine (New Haven: Yale University Press, 1915); Matthew Hale, *The History of the Pleas of the Crown* (London: E. & R. Nutt, 1736),

esp. 30–37; William Blackstone, *Commentaries on the Laws of England* (Oxford: Clarendon Press, 1869), esp. vol. 4; William Holdsworth, *A History of English Law* (London: Methuen, 1903); James Fitzjames Stephen, *A History of the Criminal Law of England,* vol. 2 (London: Macmillan, 1883), esp. 94–114, 124–86. Nigel Walker has unearthed several cases involving insanity offenders in the Middle Ages. See *Crime and Insanity in England,* vol. 1: *The Historical Perspective* (Edinburgh: Edinburgh University Press, 1968), 18–26. The most comprehensive review of the celebrated eighteenth- and nineteenth-century insanity trials may be found there (52–103). For research on individual trials, see Jacques M. Quen, "James Hadfield and Medical Jurisprudence of Insanity," *New York State Journal of Medicine* 69 (1969): 1221–26; Richard Moran, "The Origin of Insanity as a Special Verdict: The Trial for Treason of James Hadfield (1800)," *Law and Society Review* 19 (1985): 487–519; Moran, *Knowing Right from Wrong: The Insanity Defense of Daniel McNaughtan* (New York: Free Press, 1981); and Moran, "The Punitive Uses of the Insanity Defense: The Trial for Treason of Edward Oxford (1840)," *International Journal of Law and Psychiatry* 9 (1986): 171–90.

2. *OBSP,* 1787, case 158, 1st sess., 228.

3. *OBSP,* 1787, case 158, 1st sess., 229.

4. For a discussion of the centrality of intention to the issue of criminal responsibility, see Hyman Gross, *A Theory of Criminal Justice* (New York: Oxford University Press, 1979). The relation between intention and insanity is discussed in Joel Peter Eigen, "Intentionality and Insanity: What the Eighteenth-Century Juror Heard," in William F. Bynum, Roy Porter, and Michael Shepherd, eds., *The Anatomy of Madness,* vol. 2: *Institutions and Society* (London: Tavistock, 1985), 34–51.

5. Robert H. Dreher, "Origin, Development, and Present Status of Insanity as a Defense to Criminal Responsibility in the Common Law," *Journal of the History of the Behavioral Sciences* 3 (1967): 47–57.

6. Quoted in Walker, *Crime and Insanity,* 26.

7. For a discussion of the centrality of human reason to Bracton's construction of the insane as "brutis," see Anthony Platt and Bernard Diamond, "The Origins and Developments of the 'Wild Beast Concept' of Mental Illness and Its Relation to Theories of Criminal Responsibility," *Journal of the History of the Behavioral Sciences* 1 (1965): esp. 360–65.

8. Quoted in Platt and Diamond, "Origins and Development," 358.

9. E. Coke, *Third Part of the Institutes of the Laws of England* (Philadelphia: Alexander Towar, 1836). On the comparable issues in imputing responsibility to the insane and the young, see Walker, *Crime and Insanity,* 40–41. The author's earliest source for the application of the "knowing right from wrong" standard to youthful offenders is from Michael Dalton, a contemporary of Coke: "[I]f one that is *'non compos mentis,'* or an ideot, kill a man, this is no felony, for they have not knowledge of Good and Evil, nor can have a felonious intent, nor a will or mind to do harm" (*The Country Justice* [London, 1618]).

10. The restrictive attention paid to understanding as opposed to self-control was a particular feature of the law until at least the early nineteenth century. Eighteenth-century insanity is still a matter of impaired *understanding,* not an inability to restrain one's will.
11. Hale, *History of the Pleas,* 30.
12. Hale, *History of the Pleas,* 31.
13. Hale, *History of the Pleas,* 36.
14. For a comprehensive account of Arnold's trial, see Walker, *Crime and Insanity,* 53–57. For successive mistranslations of Bracton's thirteenth-century use of *brutis,* see Platt and Diamond, "Origins and Developments."
15. The trial has taken on considerable ideological significance in an effort to examine the political symbolism of Ferrers's trial and public execution. See, e.g., Douglas Hay, "Property, Authority, and the Criminal Law," in Douglas Hay, Peter Linebaugh, and E. P. Thompson, eds., *Albion's Fatal Tree: Crime and Society in Eighteenth-Century England* (New York: Pantheon, 1975), 33–36.
16. Quoted in Walker, *Crime and Insanity,* 62.
17. Walker, *Crime and Insanity,* 60–62.
18. *OBSP,* 1784, case 388, 4th sess., 548.
19. *OBSP,* 1790, case 655, 7th sess., 799.
20. The "directed verdict" is discussed in John Langbein, "The Criminal Trial before the Lawyers," *University of Chicago Law Review* 45 (Winter 1978): esp. 284–330.
21. *OBSP,* 1784, case 388, 4th sess., 546.
22. *OBSP,* 1784, case 388, 4th sess., 549.
23. *OBSP,* 1786, case 591, 6th sess., 874–76.
24. *OBSP,* 1787, case 4, 1st sess., 10; *OBSP,* 1784, case 388, 6th sess., 547, 546.
25. *OBSP,* 1787, case 4, 1st sess., 10. The rejection of "spirits" as part of a defense does not seem to have been a uniform practice in the 1700s. For a review of the provisions for drunkenness in common law, see Walker, *Crime and Insanity,* 177–81.
26. *OBSP,* 1786, case 591, 6th sess., 874.
27. *OBSP,* 1786, case 360, 4th sess., 600.
28. *OBSP,* 1786, case 591, 6th sess., 874–75.
29. *OBSP,* 1786, case 591, 6th sess., 876.
30. *OBSP,* 1786, case 591, 6th sess., 876–77.
31. Quoted in Moran, "Origin," 499.
32. Quoted in Moran, "Origin," 503. Erskine's conviction concerning the inextricable connection linking the delusion to the specific act committed was precise and uncompromising. Delusion was not "evidence" of insanity in and of itself. By the mid-1830s, medical psychologists would take issue both with the necessary link between delusion and the act and with the need to find delusion at all.
33. Nigel Walker surmises that "Dr. Creighton" was indeed Alexander Crichton, author of *Inquiry into the Nature and Origin of Mental Derangement*

(London: T. Cadell, Junior, and W. Davies, 1798). "Creighton" had visited Hadfield in detention and testified in the trial that the prisoner answered "irrationally" when any questions were put to him on the "subject of his lunacy . . . [I]t requires that the thoughts which have relation to his madness should be awakened in his mind, in order to make him act unreasonably" (Walker, *Crime and Insanity*, 76; see 74–81 for his analysis of the Hadfield trial). Further commentary on Hadfield may be found in Quen, "James Hadfield."

34. Although the story about the jury gaping at Hadfield's exposed skull has become part of the lore of the trial, Moran writes that he was unable to find any evidence that such a scene actually took place. In the history of insanity, the spectre of Hadfield's exposed brains has taken its place next to the image of Pinel striking off the inmates' chains at Bicêtre, a hospital in Paris that housed mad people.

35. Hale, *History of the Pleas*, 30.

36. For a discussion of the importance of delusion to medical testimony particularly, see Joel Peter Eigen, "Delusion in the Courtroom: The Role of Partial Insanity in Early Forensic Testimony," *Medical History* 35 (1991): 25–49.

37. *OBSP,* 1812, case 433, 5th sess., 272.

38. *OBSP,* 1812, case 433, 5th sess., 267.

39. *OBSP,* 1812, case 433, 5th sess., 270.

40. *OBSP,* 1812, case 433, 5th sess., 273.

41. *OBSP,* 1812, case 433, 5th sess., 273.

42. *OBSP,* 1786, case 360, 4th sess., 602–3.

43. *OBSP,* 1796, case 512, 7th sess., 823.

44. *OBSP,* 1786, case 591, 6th sess., 874–77.

45. Walker believes that the jurors' actions could be explained in two ways. Perhaps they concluded that the madman knew and intended what he was doing in only a limited context. Alternatively, they may have thought that he was unable to appreciate the wrongfulness of his action because his "moral sense was impaired" (*Crime and Insanity*, 40–41).

3. Insanity and Medical Psychology

1. Roy Porter, *Mind-Forg'd Manacles: A History of Madness in England from the Restoration to the Regency* (London: Athlone Press, 1987).

2. G. S. Rousseau, e.g., explores the utility (and social exclusivity) of the "language of nerves" for members of the eighteenth-century elite who sought to ensure their class position in an era when an aristocratic title no longer secured rank. His analysis leads one to suspect a reciprocal relation between medical views and the social aspirations of the gentry. Such a relation may tempt one to challenge Porter's notion that psychiatry was "shaped from below" since the class position of the romantically nervous might have been more exalted than the neighborhood physic's. Yet Porter's point is well taken: psychiatry as a body of opinion was not imposed on an unsuspecting

citizenry but was rather fashioned out of folk beliefs, perhaps even given direction by the mobility aspirations of the soi-disant gentry. G. S. Rousseau, "Towards a Semiotics of the Nerve: The Social History of Language in a New Key," in Peter Burke and Roy Porter, eds., *Language, Self, and Society: A Social History of Language* (Cambridge: Polity Press, 1991), 213–75.

3. The opinions one finds in medical texts are of course speculations about "general" psychology that are applied to medical settings. They are not, in any simple sense, schools of *medical psychology*. Indeed, one must use the term "school" advisedly as well, since in this context all that is implied is a cluster of individuals who drew on shared assumptions or wrote in reference to a common intellectual ancestor. It is nonetheless true that the late Georgian and early Victorian period witnessed the emergence of several quite discernible models employed to understand madness. With care, one can parcel out the array of opinions to conceptually discrete approaches, or schools.

4. The notion that madness has a "true nature" has been dismissed as "essentialism" by the current generation of social scientists who have posited a "social construction" of insanity. Although one can hardly question the charge that extreme subjectivity attends efforts to define the (true) nature of madness, the equally extreme relativism of the social construction school has at times bordered on the absurd, refusing to consider the aberrant thought processes and deranged behavior of those "labeled" mad. Diagnostic categories supposedly reveal (only) the anxieties of reason or the inability of bourgeois culture to deal with "nonconformists." One wonders if such glib pronouncements have been informed by firsthand investigation of the "labeling process" or the study of historical sources that might illuminate how the bourgeois audience "consigned eccentricity" to the asylum. While conceding that clinical classification of mental disorders has been anything but exact, it is still intriguing to read of the continuity of diagnostic imagery associated with melancholia, from the ancient Greeks to the early nineteenth century, despite the rather substantial transformation in "audience." See Stanley W. Jackson, *Melancholia and Depression: From Hippocratic Times to Modern Times* (New Haven: Yale University Press, 1986).

5. Although Galen is normally credited with the fourfold typology of humors and temperaments, Hippocrates, Aristotle, and Aretaeus were also attentive to the relation of body fluids and disease. For a review of medical thought regarding humoralism in ancient Greece and Rome, see Jackson, *Melancholia*, 3–45. Bruce Haley also reviews Galen's ideas and their role in the Victorian conception of healthy functioning in *The Healthy Body and Victorian Culture* (Cambridge: Harvard University Press, 1978).

6. Humoralism is the first in a long series of theories about "the mind/body problem." Early modern people inherited from Greek philosophy (not to say Christianity) the conviction that the soul and the body were distinct entities, a conception of human functioning that challenged generations of deep thinkers to speculate about precisely how the two "communicated"

with each other. To not-so-deep thinkers, the obvious effects of alcohol, the reality of blushing, and the arousal of certain private body parts provided unambiguous indication that the human being was a unity. Nowhere was this belief more evident than in the conviction that organic corruption was at the root of mental disturbance. Medical theorists and laypersons alike seized on head injuries, burning fevers, or excesses of wine as causes of delirium. Since the mind, immaterial and indivisible, was forced to function in the physical structure it inhabited, if the body was diseased, perturbed, or unsettled, the effects on the mind's functioning were thought to be self-evident. For a comprehensive survey of stages in conceptualizing the dualism of mind and body, see C. A. Van Peursen, *Body, Soul, Spirit: A Survey of the Body-Mind Problem* (London: Oxford University Press, 1966). The centrality of physicalist renderings of derangement to the medical approach to insanity is examined in Roger Smith, *Trial by Medicine: Insanity and Responsibility in Victorian Trials* (Edinburgh: Edinburgh University Press, 1981), esp. 40–56, and most recently by Andrew Scull, *The Most Solitary of Afflictions: Madness and Society in Britain, 1700–1900* (New Haven: Yale University Press, 1993), esp. 216–31.

7. There is a vast seventeenth- and eighteenth-century literature on nerves, sensory input, and the brain. Major figures in the debate include Boerhaave, who asserted a "hydraulick" model, picturing nerves as hollow tubes filled with animal spirits; Thomas Willis, the first theorist to state unequivocally that the soul was limited to the brain—thus underscoring the nerves' fundamental role as the conduit of sensory input; and William Cullen, who declared all diseases to be nervous conditions because all were mediated through the nerves. See, e.g., William Cullen, *Nosology; or, A Systematic Arrangement of Diseases* (Edinburgh: C. Stewart, 1800). An overview of the debate concerning nervous sensation and ideation can be found in Porter, *Mind-Forg'd Manacles*. For a discussion of Willis's singular importance to Locke, see G. S. Rousseau, "Nerves, Spirits and Fibres: Towards Defining the Origins of Sensibility, with a Postscript 1976," *Blue Guitar* 2 (1976): 125–53.

8. The curious interface of philosophy and psychology relative to the nerves is discussed by G. S. Rousseau, "Psychology," in G. S. Rousseau and Roy Porter, eds., *The Ferment of Knowledge: Studies in the Historiography of Eighteenth-Century Science* (Cambridge: Cambridge University Press, 1980), see esp. 163–78.

9. John Locke, *An Essay Concerning Human Understanding* (1690), ed. John Yolton (London: Everyman, 1961).

10. Locke's conception of a mind molded by experiences played a pivotal role in the Enlightenment belief that people were capable of being shaped to effect the goals of both social and political reform. Although Locke was enormously influential in the late eighteenth century, several prominent medical psychologists espoused an overtly anti-Lockean conception of human thought. A decidedly elitist conception of human malleability, which "em-

braced cultural refinement at the expense of [progressive] scientific values," is described in Akihito Suzuki, "An Anti-Lockean Enlightenment? Mind and Body in Early Eighteenth-Century English Medicine," in Roy Porter, ed., *Medicine and the Enlightenment* (Amsterdam: Rodopi, 1994), 1–24. For a comprehensive survey of the importance of Locke's "association of ideas" for a generation of British medical psychologists, see Robert Hoeldtke, "The History of Associationism and British Medical Psychology," *Medical History* 11 (1967): 46–65.

11. John Monro, e.g., took vociferous exception to William Battie's characterization of insanity as "deluded imagination." "Is deluded imagination a significant characterization for the naked wanderer, for e.g.? [T]hose who recover describe it no otherwise than a total suspension of every rational faculty." Only a global disturbance could explain the "otherness" of the mad: the confused speech, the flightiness of ideas, the hallucinations and delusions. For an expanded discussion of Monro's differences with Battie, see *Remarks on Dr. Battie's Treatise on Madness* (London: John Clarke, 1758).

12. *OBSP,* 1784, case 211, 2d sess., 257.

13. G. E. Berrios, "Delirium and Confusion in the Nineteenth Century: A Conceptual History," *British Journal of Psychiatry* 139 (1981): 439–49. See also H. Werlinder, *Psychopathy: A History of the Concepts; Analysis of the Origin and Development of a Family of Concepts in Psychopathology* (Uppsala: ACTA Universitatis Upsaliensis, 1978), 26–28.

14. David Hartley, *Observations on Man, His Frame, His Duty, and His Expectations* (London: S. Richardson, 1749).

15. *A Treatise on Madness* (London: John Clarke, 1758), 5–6, 24–25.

16. *Observations on the Nature, Kinds, Causes and Prevention of Insanity* (London: Richard Phillips, 1806), 47–52.

17. *Observations on the Nature,* 135.

18. Robert Burton, *The Anatomy of Melancholy,* vol. 3 (New York: Hurd & Houghton, 1874), 365–450; Jackson, *Melancholia and Depression.*

19. Arnold, *Observations,* 88.

20. John Johnstone, *Medical Jurisprudence of Madness* (Birmingham: J. Belcher, 1800), 23. Johnstone is unusual in distinguishing madness from delirium. Most medical writers used one term or the other to signify mental derangement.

21. George Edward Male, *Elements of Juridical or Forensic Medicine: For the Use of Medical Men, Coroners and Barristers* (London: E. Cox & Son, 1818), 202.

22. Not all clinical experience confirmed Arnold's separation of delirium into "ideal" and "notional" varieties. Alexander Crichton, for example, claimed that in his own case histories, it was clear that "one and the same individual has both erroneous notions and erroneous ideas" [i.e., sensations]. Crichton, *An Inquiry into the Nature and Origin of Mental Derangement* (London: T.

Cadell Junior and W. Davies, 1798), 22. Crichton testified at the trial of James Hadfield.

23. John Haslam, *Observations on Madness and Melancholy: Including Practical Remarks on Those Diseases; Together with Cases: And an Account of the Morbid Appearances on Dissection* (London: J. Callow, 1809), quotations on 46–47, 45; Haslam, *Medical Jurisprudence as It Relates to Insanity, According to the Law of England* (London: C. Hunter, 1817), quotation on p. 18.

24. Hartley, *Observations on Man*, 56.

25. James Mill, *Analysis of the Phenomena of the Human Mind* (London: Baldwin and Craddock, 1829).

26. For a discussion of cerebral localization in eighteenth- and nineteenth-century medical psychology, see Robert M. Young, *Mind, Brain, and Adaptation in the Nineteenth Century* (Oxford: Clarendon Press, 1970).

27. The notion that the mind housed innate faculties capable of performing discrete functions dates at least to Aristotle and has been the subject of speculative medical thought ever since. A comprehensive survey of the various schools of thought contained within faculty psychology can be found in J. A. Fodor, *The Modularity of Mind: An Essay on Faculty Psychology* (Cambridge: MIT Press, 1983).

28. See, e.g., the discussion of the organs of "larceny" and of "murder" in Charles Augustus Blode, *Dr. F. J. Gall's System of the Functions of the Brain* (1807); George Combe and Andrew Combe, *On the Functions of the Cerebellum by Drs. Gall, Vimont, and Broussais* (Edinburgh: Machlachlan & Stewart, 1838), 162–67; Andrew Combe, *Observations on the Mental Derangement; Being an Application of the Principles of Phrenology to the Elucidation of the Causes, Symptoms, Nature and Treatment of Insanity* (Boston: Marsh, Cape & Lyon, 1834); and Forbes Winslow, *The Principles of Phrenology as Applied to the Elucidation and Cure of Insanity, an Essay Read at the Westminster Medical Society, January 14th, 1832* (London: S. Highley, 1832). On the importance of evidence of monomania to the arguments of phrenology, see Roger Cooter, "Phrenology and British Alienists, ca. 1825–45," in Andrew Scull, ed., *Madhouses, Mad-Doctors, and Madmen: The Social History of Psychiatry in the Victorian Era* (Philadelphia: University of Pennsylvania Press, 1981), 58–104.

29. David Uwins, physician to Peckham Asylum, was a prominent voice in the phrenology movement. He also testified at the Old Bailey in 1833 in an intriguing forgery case examined in chapter 6. His writings on phrenology include *A Treatise on Those Disorders of the Brain and the Nervous System, Which Are Usually Considered and Called Mental* (London: Renshaw and Rush, 1833), and *Remarks on Nervous and Mental Disorder with Special Reference to Recent Investigations on the Subject of Insanity* (London: Thomas and George Underwood, 1830).

30. J. G. Spurzheim, *Observations of the Deranged Manifestations of the Mind, or Insanity* (London: Baldwin, Craddock, and Joy, 1817), 70.

31. Combe and Combe, *On the Functions of the Cerebellum*, 166–67.

32. By dint of Reason, Gall maintains, man's motives are independent of the propensities and faculties he shares with animals. He can distinguish truth from error, the just from the unjust. For Gall's views on criminal responsibility, "illusive liberty," and free agency, see the *Weekly Medico Chirurgical and Philosophical Magazine,* 14 June 1823, 289–97; 21 June 1823, 305–10; 5 July 1823, 337–40; and 12 July 1823, 353–57.

33. *Weekly Medico Chirurgical and Philosophical Magazine,* 7 June 1823, 275.

34. Attention to innate faculties, propensities, and instincts in no way compromised a discussion of human agency; indeed, proper socialization was thought to be critical for the development of self-control. Gall's ideas sat at the center of a progressive agenda which looked to religion, education, law, and moral codes to influence the "natural activities of the faculties." See Roger Cooter, *The Cultural Meaning of Popular Science* (Cambridge: Cambidge University Press, 1985), esp. 169–98.

35. Winslow, *Principles of Phrenology,* 25. Winslow makes this observation in the context of the proper role for the medical witness: not to decide "on the abstract question of insanity, but upon the *degree* of impairment."

36. For a comprehensive review of phrenology's popularity, see Cooter, *Cultural Meaning.* One of Cooter's most intriguing discoveries is that, for all its questionable scientific underpinnings, phrenology derived strongest professional support—as measured by representation on membership lists—from medical men.

37. Alexander Morison, e.g., accompanied lectures on mental derangement with drawings of individuals in various states of insanity, explaining that "repetition of the same ideas and emotions, and the consequent repetition of the same movements of the muscles of the eyes, and of the face give a particular expression" (*Outlines of Lectures on Mental Diseases* [London: Longman, Rees, Orme, Brown and Green, and S. Highley, 1826], 125).

38. See Spurzheim, *Observations of the Deranged,* 72–73.

39. Pinel's account of his surprise at discovering madness among inmates who gave no "evidence of any lesion of the understanding, but who were under the domination of instinctive and abstract fury" may be found in *A Treatise on Insanity, in Which Are Contained the Principles of a New and More Practical Nosology of Maniacal Disorder That Has Been Offered to the Public, Exemplified by Numerous and Accurate Historical Relations of Cases from the Author's Public and Private Practice,* trans. D. D. Davis (Sheffield: W. Todd, 1806). Pinel's formulation of manie sans délire found its intellectual roots in the Enlightened salon of Madame Helvétius, as revealed in the role he accords the passions and the imagination in the determination of behavior. The most comprehensive analysis of the French school of *médecine mentale* can be found in Jan Goldstein, *Console and Classify: The French Psychiatric Profession in the Nineteenth Century* (Cambridge: Cambridge University Press, 1987). The *clinical* root of Pinel's thinking was a matter of professional conviction, stemming from his belief that medical insight could be gained only through repeated and sustained conversation with and observation of

the mad, not by resorting to "inherited medical systems." See Dora B. Weiner, "Mind and Body in the Clinic: Philippe Pinel, Alexander Crichton, Dominique Esquirol, and the Birth of Psychiatry," in G. S. Rousseau, ed., *The Languages of Psyche: Mind and Body in Enlightenment Thought* (Berkeley: University of California Press, 1990), 331–402. On the significance of the conceptual break in the medical theorizing on insanity which Pinel and his followers effected, see Werlinder, *Psychopathy.*

40. J. E. D. Esquirol, *Mental Maladies: A Treatise on Insanity,* trans. E. K. Hunt (Philadelphia: Lea and Blanchard, 1845), 351. According to G. E. Berrios, monomania was a version of the partial insanity concept (except, of course, that it was full-blown derangement as long as the afflicted's mind was turned to the delusion). See Berrios, "Obsessional Disorders during the Nineteenth Century: Terminological and Classificatory Issues," in W. F. Bynum, R. Porter, and M. Shepherd, eds., *The Anatomy of Madness: Essays in the History of Psychiatry,* vol. 1: *People and Ideas* (London: Tavistock, 1985), 166–87. See also Goldstein, *Console and Classify,* 155–58.

41. Esquirol, *Mental Maladies,* 351.

42. Raymond de Saussure, "The Influence of the Concept of Monomania on French Medico-Legal Psychiatry (from 1825 to 1840)," *Journal of the History of Medicine* 1 (1946): 377, quotation on 373.

43. Quoted in Saussure, "Influence of the Concept of Monomania," 372–73.

44. Quoted in Saussure, "Influence of the Concept of Monomania," 372.

45. The most thorough discussion of the conceptual origin of "lesion of the will" can be found in François Leuret, "Review of Elias Regnault, *Degré de compétence,*" *Annales d'hygiène publique et de médecine légale* 1 (1829), and in two publications by Charles-Chrétien-Henri Marc: *Annales d'hygiène publique et de médecine légale* 10 (1833): 357–474, and *Dé la folie, considérée dans ses rapports avec les questions médico-judiciares,* pt. 1 (Paris: J. B. Ballière, 1840).

46. Marc, *De la folie,* 88.

47. Referring to Pinel's manie sans délire and Prichard's moral insanity (see below), Esquirol wrote: "The understanding is more or less affected; were it not thus, the insane would permit themselves to be controlled by their understanding, and would discover their views were false, and their actions, unusual and strange" (*Mental Maladies,* 321).

48. Goldstein, *Console and Classify,* esp. 155–89.

49. The disaggregation of the mind and the resulting autonomy of intellect, will, and emotion in nineteenth-century novels is explored in Simon Durang, "The Strange Case of Monomania: Patriarchy in Literature, Murder in *Middlemarch,* Drowning in *Daniel Deronda,*" *Representations* 23 (Summer 1988): esp. 86–87.

50. Berrios suggests that once a "semantic steady state" has been reached in descriptive psychopathology, clinical language will endure until the following conditions obtain: (1) the cognitive aims of the "community of users" or "thought collective" change direction, (2) the "psychopathological object

itself undergoes transformation beyond permissible limits," or (3) the "controlled interaction between object and language generates further scientific growth" ("Descriptive Psychopathology: Conceptual and Historical Aspects," *Psychological Medicine* 14 [1984]: 303–13).

51. Although Goldstein provides rich testimonials of medical men who recanted their earlier statements regarding the existence of monomania, one still searches for primary materials that will enable the historian to examine Berrios's other criteria: changes in the psychopathological "object" itself, and shifting dynamics in the opportunity for close observation and scrutiny. Certainly the change in professional association between the keepers and the kept could well have led to an assault on the "semantic steady state" as well. For a review essay of Goldstein's thesis, see Joel Peter Eigen, "A Mania for Diagnosis: Unraveling the Aims of Nineteenth-Century French Psychiatrists," *Journal of the History of the Human Sciences* 2 (1989): 241–51.

52. See Goldstein, *Console and Classify,* 189–96; see also Berrios, "Obsessional Disorders," 170–71.

53. James C. Prichard, *A Review of the Doctrine of a Vital Principle as Maintained by Some Writers on Phrenology: With Observations on Physical and Animal Life* (London: Sherwood, Gilbert and Piper, 1829), 176.

54. James C. Prichard, *A Treatise on Insanity and Other Disorders Affecting the Mind* (London: Sherwood, Gilbert and Piper, 1835), 12.

55. Prichard, *Treatise on Insanity,* 12, 95.

56. On nineteenth-century Scottish thought, see Hoeldtke, "History," 55–63; G. P. Brooks, "The Faculty Psychology of Thomas Reid," *Journal of the History of the Behavioral Sciences* 12 (1976): 65–77; and Frank M. Albrecht, "A Reappraisal of Faculty Psychology," *Journal of the History of the Behavioral Sciences* 6 (1970): 36–40.

57. Conolly, *An Inquiry Concerning the Indications of Insanity with Suggestions for the Better Protection and Care of the Insane* (London: John Taylor, 1830), 113, 155, 225.

58. James C. Prichard, *On the Different Forms of Insanity in Relation to Jurisprudence, Designed for the Use of Persons Concerned in Legal Questions Regarding Unsoundness of Mind* (London: Hippolyte Ballière, 1842), 17.

59. The ambiguity regarding the state of the intellects is not surprising given the similarities between monomania and moral insanity as conceptual terms. Werlinder, e.g., refers to Prichard's notion of moral insanity as a variant of Esquirol's monomania. Esquirol compared moral insanity to his *monomanie affective,* revealing how much he considered the "moral" in moral insanity to symbolize nonintellectualist passion. Werlinder, *Psychopathy,* 48.

60. Again, part of the confusion regarding occluded consciousness may originate in moral insanity's French heritage, specifically the concept lesion of the will. In monomania, we have noted, the intellects are not scrambled but "overridden." Does this leave them, like the car-struck pedestrian, flattened in the street yet conscious? Or does it leave the sufferer "without a clue what hit

him"? This was no idle topic for abstract speculation: on the "integrity of the intellects" the question of intention rested.

61. Martin J. Wiener, *Reconstructing the Criminal: Culture, Law, and Policy in England, 1830–1914* (Cambridge: Cambridge University Press, 1990), esp. 14–45.

62. See Roger Smith, *Trial by Medicine: Insanity and Responsibility in Victorian Trials* (Edinburgh: Edinburgh University Press, 1981), esp. 38–40.

63. For the Victorians, the proper cultivation of physical and mental habits was thought to be essential for both physical and moral well-being. There is a pivotal role for the will in this conceptualization, for its influence works to unify body and mind, producing a wholeness which, to the Victorians, symbolized health. Not only does the will work to preserve a balance between body and mind, it also becomes an active agent in the mental process itself: analyzing and selecting objects of consciousness, permitting the mind to rise to the level of abstraction, ultimately distinguishing between vice and virtue. One has only to consider the thought process when asleep to appreciate the effects of a weakened, selective will: the impaired capacity to distinguish between sensory products relayed *to* the mind, and unreal images created *in* the mind. When the Victorians compared dreams to delusion, the common element occasioned by the suspension of the will was clear and compelling: an inability to distinguish fantasy from reality. On the Victorians' attitude toward the will and its role in the maintenance of mental and physical health, see Haley, *Healthy Mind,* esp. 62–68.

64. Delusion fit particularly well with this cognitive conception of insanity precisely because it stressed the individual's understanding of what he was doing. Even though good evidence might exist of an elaborately confused picture of reality, Roger Smith cautions that the misperception had to be of a certain quality to answer the law's fundamental concern—namely, "[D]id [the prisoner] know that he was committing an offence against the laws of god and nature?" For a comprehensive analysis of medical psychology's conceptualization of insanity as a physical disease, see Smith, *Trial by Medicine,* 40–56. On the incommensurate discourses of medicine and law, see Roger Smith, "Scientific Thought and the Boundary of Insanity and Criminal Responsibility," *Psychological Medicine* 10 (1985): 15–23.

4. THE LAY WITNESS'S TESTIMONY

1. MacDonald, *Mystical Bedlam: Madness, Anxiety, and Healing in Seventeenth-Century England* (Cambridge: Cambridge University Press, 1981), 113.

2. *OBSP,* 1798, case 554, 8th sess., 602; 1814, case 746, 7th sess., 392; 1824, case 867, 5th sess., 311.

3. *OBSP,* 1823, case 619, 4th sess., 231.

4. *OBSP,* 1828, case 119, 1st sess., 50.

5. *OBSP,* 1814, case 701, 7th sess., 372; 1822, case 811, 5th sess., 330.

6. *OBSP,* 1825, case 1116, 6th sess., 432.

7. *OBSP,* 1841–42, case 1766, 8th sess., 341.

8. *OBSP,* 1833, case 1304, 7th sess., 732.

9. *OBSP,* 1833, case 892, 5th sess., 470. Another reference to a prisoner clothed in rags can be found in 1829, case 716, 4th sess.

10. MacDonald, *Mystical Bedlam.*

11. *OBSP,* 1828, case 2, 1st sess., 4.

12. *OBSP,* 1806, case 399, 6th sess., 360; *OBSP,* 1841–42, case 2752, 11th sess., 1122; *OBSP,* 1794, case 627, 6th sess., 1334; see also *OBSP,* 1801, case 558, 6th sess., 410.

13. *OBSP,* 1829, case 716, 4th sess., 333; *OBSP,* 1811, case 433, 5th sess., 259.

14. *OBSP,* 1828, case 119, 1st sess., 48.

15. *OBSP,* 1785, case 644, 6th sess., 936–41; *OBSP,* 1826, case 1090, 6th sess., 431.

16. *OBSP,* 1797, case 542, 7th sess., 531.

17. *OBSP,* 1784, case 388, 4th sess., 539.

18. *OBSP,* 1786, case 591, 6th sess., 872.

19. *OBSP,* 1785, case 599, 6th sess., 812.

20. *OBSP,* 1784, case 971, 8th sess., 1302.

21. *OBSP,* 1765, case 145, 2d sess., 86.

22. *OBSP,* 1794, case 211, 4th sess., 527.

23. *OBSP,* 1787, case 494, 5th sess., 608; *OBSP,* 1787, case 4, 1st sess., 9.

24. *OBSP,* 1785, case 644, 5th and 6th sess., 935. There were also those prisoners who gave "contrary" answers, these being seen as not "rational" responses. See *OBSP,* 1794, case 627, 8th sess., 1335, and *OBSP,* 1798, case 554, 8th sess., 603.

25. *OBSP,* 1801, case 558, 6th sess., 409.

26. *OBSP,* 1806, case 399, 6th sess., 360.

27. *OBSP,* 1800, case 315, 4th sess., 278.

28. *OBSP,* 1806, case 399, 6th sess., 361.

29. *OBSP,* 1789, case 494, 5th sess., 606. This interchange is discussed in chapter 5.

30. *OBSP,* 1815, case 723, 6th sess., 335.

31. *OBSP,* 1838, case 499, 4th sess., 412.

32. *OBSP,* 1805, case 457, 6th sess., 411.

33. *OBSP,* 1825, case 506, 3d sess., 214.

34. *OBSP,* 1813, case 11, 1st sess., 11. For other cases that include political themes, see 1815, case 45, 1st sess., 25, and 1830, case 176, 1st sess., 88–91.

35. *OBSP,* 1790, case 328, 3d sess., 365–66.

36. *OBSP,* 1805, case 457, 6th sess., 412.

37. *OBSP,* 1784, case 211, 2d sess., 257.

38. *OBSP,* 1805, case 457, 6th sess., 412.

39. *OBSP,* 1785, case 644, 6th sess., 941.

40. *OBSP,* 1822, case 811, 5th sess., 330.

41. *OBSP,* 1802, case 314, 4th sess., 236.

42. *OBSP,* 1769, case 500, 7th sess., 383. See also 1842/3, case 1011, 5th sess., 859 ("He has been quite a different man to what he was before").
43. *OBSP,* 1838, case 499, 4th sess., 413.
44. *OBSP,* 1838, case 499, 4th sess., 411.
45. *OBSP,* 1798, case 274, 5th sess., 276.
46. *OBSP,* 1800, case 362, 5th sess., 325.
47. *OBSP,* 1787, case 158, 1st sess., 226.
48. *OBSP,* 1840, case 1862, 9th sess., 458. See also 1839, case 2101, 9th sess., 542 ("he did not appear at all to know what he was doing").
49. *OBSP,* 1828, case 119, 1st sess., 50.
50. *OBSP,* 1835, case 866, 5th sess., 815–16.
51. The first, 1760–1800, begins with the trial of Earl Ferrers and ends with the prosecution of James Hadfield. Thomas Erskine's construction of delusion in 1800 marked the first attempt to question the meaning of "total insanity," which had been invoked specifically at the Ferrers trial and in subsequent instructions to jurors at least until the end of the century. With Hadfield's acquittal, the possibility that forms of derangement short of total insanity would be considered by the jury seemed to signify an important demarcation point for considering the flow of courtroom testimony. The nineteenth-century cases are further divided in two, 1801–1829 and 1830–1843, with the final fourteen years constituting a separate period because of the exponential growth in medical witnesses.
52. *OBSP,* 1780, case 325, 6th sess., 451.
53. Although an explicit reference to madhouse confinement was unusual in eighteenth-century courtroom testimony, by the early 1800s, lay witnesses increasingly commented on the prisoner's history of incarceration in both public and private asylums. Institutions mentioned included Mile's, Bethnal Green, Bedford, and most often St. Luke's. Only once was such a reference made to support the inference of madness: "I have every reason to believe he is not in a right state of mind, for he has been confined as a lunatic" (*OBSP,* 1824, case 48, 1st sess., 23). Instead, family members invoked the necessity of confinement to support their assertion that the prisoner had been simply out of control. See 1822, case 658, 4th sess., 286; 1834, case 1654, 8th sess., 826; 1828, case 1776, 7th sess., 833; 1837, case 721, 5th sess., 689. On the desirability of jailing a prisoner previously confined in an asylum, see the letter sent by John Conolly, physician to Hanwell Asylum, to the defendant's mother, 1841, case 1326, 7th sess., 38–39.
54. *OBSP,* 1803, case 463, 5th sess., 363.
55. *OBSP,* 1803, case 463, 5th sess., 363–65.
56. *OBSP,* 1827, case 1613, 6th sess., 627.
57. *OBSP,* 1833, case 815, 4th sess., 399.
58. *OBSP,* 1833, case 815, 4th sess., 399, 400, 402.
59. *OBSP,* 1831, case 555, 3d sess., 303.
60. *OBSP,* 1835, case 1996, 11th sess., 790.
61. *OBSP,* 1838, case 499, 4th sess., 412.

62. *OBSP*, 1768, case 247, 3d sess., 134.

63. *OBSP*, 1804, case 25, 1st sess., 28.

64. *OBSP*, 1839, case 587, 4th sess., 489.

65. *OBSP*, 1834, case 72, 1st sess., 67. See also 1808, case 656, 7th sess., 437 ("About two years ago he received news from Gibraltar that his friends all died in the flames; that turned his head rather lunatic.")

66. *OBSP*, 1842–43, case 1011, 5th sess., 859.

67. *OBSP*, 1836, case 1159, 7th sess., 29–30.

68. *OBSP*, 1833, case 1366, 7th sess., 772.

69. *OBSP*, 1833, case 1366, 7th sess., 772.

70. *OBSP*, 1808, case 656, 7th sess., 437–38.

71. *OBSP*, 1808, case 656, 7th sess., 437.

72. *OBSP*, 1837, case 550, 4th sess., 522; *OBSP*, 1833, case 815, 4th sess., 399. Not all lay witnesses, however, appealed to "common understandings" about madness. "Madmen may frequently have a design of forethought and malice," averred a witness in 1760, concluding his testimony with the caveat: "this was only my opinion" (*OBSP*, 1760, case 261, 7th sess., 269–74). His comment is noteworthy in two respects. First, it appears that from the beginning of this period, insane persons could be thought capable of deliberate, premeditated acts. Second, such a qualifier is found only in lay testimony. When mad-doctors testified in court, their opinion was grounded not in personal or "cultural" understanding but in professional experience, increasingly gained in the asylum.

73. *OBSP*, 1802, case 314, 4th sess., 235.

74. *OBSP*, 1787, case 4, 1st sess., 7–8.

75. *OBSP*, 1823, case 619, 4th sess., 229.

76. *OBSP*, 1843, case 2856, 12th sess., 1003.

77. *OBSP*, 1798, case 113, 2d sess., 144.

78. *OBSP*, 1833, case 1304, 7th sess., 735.

79. *OBSP*, 1803, case 463, 5th sess., 364; 1815, case 723, 6th sess., 337; 1799, case 274, 5th sess., 276.

80. *OBSP*, 1839, case 2101, 9th sess., 542.

5. Medical Testimony in Insanity Trials, I

1. *OBSP*, 1785–86, case 599, 6th sess., 823.

2. *OBSP*, 1785–86, case 599, 6th sess., 822.

3. *OBSP*, 1785–86, case 599, 6th sess., 822.

4. *OBSP*, 1785–86, case 599, 6th sess., 823.

5. In the words of John Henry Wigmore, the witness must speak as a knower, not a guesser. He must see an action, not merely believe it took place (*Evidence in Trial at Common Law*, vol. 7 [Boston: Little, Brown, 1985], 2).

6. Bushell's case (1671), quoted in Learned Hand, "Historical and Practical Considerations Regarding Expert Testimony," *Harvard Law Review* 15

(1901): 45. See also James Bradley Thayer, *A Preliminary Treatise on Evidence at the Common Law* (Boston: Little, Brown, 1898), esp 194– 97.

7. Hand, "Historical and Practical," 43.

8. Hand, "Historical and Practical," 42–43. On the role of medical evidence in coroners' inquests, see Thomas Rogers Forbes, "Crowner's Quest," *American Philosophical Society Transactions* 68, pt. 1 (1978): 5–50. Anne M. Crowther and Brenda White investigate the evolution of medical evidence in Scottish law in *On Soul and Conscience: The Medical Expert and Crime* (Aberdeen: Aberdeen University Press, 1988).

9. Hand, "Historical and Practical," 50.

10. Thomas Rogers Forbes, *Surgeons at the Bailey: English Forensic Medicine to 1878* (New Haven: Yale University Press, 1985), 36–37. See also Catherine Crawford, "The Emergence of English Forensic Medicine: Medical Evidence in Common Law Courts, 1730–1830" (D.Phil., Oxford University, 1987).

11. Forbes, *Surgeons,* 38.

12. Crawford provides an excellent analysis of the emergence of the chirurgiens jurés in "Emergence," esp. 152–56. The slow development of English forensic medicine is examined in D. J. Gee, "The English Medical Witness— Why So Late?" *Medicine, Science and Law* 33 (1993): 11–20. On the Continent, medical testimony often concerned legal cases regarding paternity, infanticide, inheritance, annulment of marriage, and murder. On medical jurisprudence in Prussia, see Johanna Geyer-Kordesch, "Natural Law and Medical Ethics in the Eighteenth Century," in Robert Baker, Dorothy Porter, and Roy Porter, eds., *The Codification of Medical Morality: Historical and Philosophical Studies of the Formalization of Western Medical Morality in the Eighteenth and Nineteenth Centuries,* vol. 1: *Medical Ethics and Etiquette in the Eighteenth Century* (Dordrecht: Kluwer, 1993), 123–39.

13. Crawford, "Emergence," 168.

14. The fear of exposure to public ridicule at the hands of rude attorneys and the judiciary is a constant theme in nineteenth-century medical texts. "'Oh,' say the gentlemen of the robe, (who have lately been so free with medical character, and so exceedingly witty on medical professors), you are a 'mad doctor' are you? We are not then surprised that you should come forward with your apologetic pen, on the present crisis, and we may easily anticipate the context of your present pamphlet" (David Uwins, *Remarks on Nervous and Mental Disorder with Special Reference to Recent Investigations on the Subject of Insanity* [London: Thomas and George Underwood, 1830], 5). Michael Alberti, professor of medicine at the University of Halle, expressly referred to the dangers of courtroom cross-examination for medical witnesses in particular and for the credibility of medical science in general. The sixth volume of his *System of Medical Jurisprudence* (1747) addresses the question of expert testimony in terms of medical honor, authority, and competence—the witness is instructed to admit to medical doubt and ambiguity when it exists. For a discussion of Alberti's work, see Geyer-Kordesch, "Natural Law," esp. 133–36.

15. Crawford, "Emergence," 222.

16. Review of Paris and Fonblanque's *Medical Jurisprudence,* quoted in Crawford, "Emergence," 253.

17. J. G. Smith, *The Principles of Forensic Medicine* (London: T. and G. Underwood, 1821); J. A. Paris and J. S. M. Fonblanque, *Medical Jurisprudence* (London: W. Phillips, 1823); Robert Christison, *Syllabus of the University Course of Lectures on Medical Jurisprudence* (Edinburgh: J. Balfour, 1826).

18. Forbes, *Surgeons,* 21. See also Forbes, "Crowner's Quest"; "Inquests in London and Middlesex Homicides, 1673–1782," *Yale Journal of Biological Medicine* 50 (1977): 207–20; and "Coroner's Inquests in the County of Middlesex, England, 1819–1842," *Journal of the History of Medicine and Allied Sciences* 32 (1977): 379–94.

19. Forbes, *Surgeons,* 49–165.

20. John Haslam, *Medical Jurisprudence as It Relates to Insanity According to the Laws of England* (London: C. Hunter, 1817), 15–19.

21. Haslam, *Medical Jurisprudence,* 60, 61.

22. J. M. Pagan, *The Medical Jurisprudence of Insanity* (London: Ball, Arnold, 1840), 23.

23. *British and Foreign Medical Review* (July 1840): 129–54, quotations on 144, 143, 140.

24. Erskine had introduced delusion into English law during the trial of James Hadfield. These questions regarding the connection of delusion to the crime were voiced in a review essay of J. C. Prichard, *On the Different Forms of Insanity in Relation to Jurisprudence Designed for the Use of Persons Concerned in Legal Questions Regarding Unsoundness of Mind* (London: Hippolyte Baillière, 1842), in *British and Foreign Medical Review* (July 1843): 81–87.

25. Prichard, *On the Different Forms,* 16, 17, 85, quoted in *British and Foreign Medical Review* (July 1843).

26. Prichard, *On the Different Forms,* 82, quoted in *British and Foreign Medical Review* (July 1843).

27. Forbes Winslow, *The Plea of Insanity in Criminal Cases* (London: H. Renshaw, 1843), 34.

28. Winslow, *Plea of Insanity,* 60, 76, 75. On the Henriette Cornier trial, see Jan Goldstein, *Console and Classify: The French Psychiatric Profession in the Nineteenth Century* (Cambridge: Cambridge University Press, 1987), esp. 165–66, 178, 180, 184–85.

29. Winslow, *Plea of Insanity,* vii, vi, 73.

30. Wigmore, *Evidence in Trial,* 44.

31. The lectures were offered by Alexander Morison. Between 1825 and 1843, his total audience is said to have numbered fewer than 150 (Andrew T. Scull, "From Madness to Mental Illness: Medical Men as Moral Entrepreneurs," *Archives européens sociologie* 16 [1975]: 242, n. 85).

32. *OBSP,* 1833, case 1304, 7th sess., 733.
33. Crawford, "Emergence," 35–38.
34. *OBSP,* 1813, case 11, 1st sess., 14.
35. *OBSP,* 1805, case 457, 6th sess., 412.
36. *OBSP,* 1774, case 129, 2d sess., 74.
37. *OBSP,* 1835, case 806, 5th sess., 815.
38. *OBSP,* 1800, case 315, 4th sess., 278.
39. *OBSP,* 1822, case 811, 5th sess., 331.
40. *OBSP,* 1789, case 494, 5th sess., 605. The de Castros were part of a notable lineage of Jewish physicians who emigrated from Spain. Their story is told in Richard Barnett, "Dr. Jacob de Castro Sarmento and the Sephardim in Medical Practice in Eighteenth-Century London," *Transactions of the Jewish Historical Society of England* 27 (1982): 84–114. (Dr. Hart Myers, who also testified in this case, is mentioned in Barnett's article.)
41. *OBSP,* 1789, case 494, 5th sess., 605.
42. *OBSP,* 1789, case 494, 5th sess., 605.
43. *OBSP,* 1789, case 494, 5th sess., 606.
44. *OBSP,* 1784, case 943, 8th sess., 1259.
45. *OBSP,* 1805, case 637, 7th sess., 556.
46. *OBSP,* 1812, case 32, 1st sess., 23–24.
47. *OBSP,* 1833, case 815, 4th sess., 402.
48. *OBSP,* 1833, case 1304, 7th sess., 736.
49. "Professional acquaintance" appears to have slid precipitously in the third period. Actually, the numbers had not dropped so much, but the medical witness category had been all but swamped by Gilbert McMurdo, who made one-third of all court appearances in the "Prison or Jail Interview" category. Although certainly fewer in number, the asylum physicians are highly noticeable when they do appear and evince ongoing professional association of great importance, as revealed in the content of their courtroom testimony (see chapter 6).
50. Roy Porter, *Mind-Forg'd Manacles: A History of Madness in England from the Restoration to the Regency* (London: Athlone Press, 1987), esp. 169–75.
51. *OBSP,* 1831, case 397, 2d sess., 197.
52. *OBSP,* 1833, case 1304, 7th sess., 736.

6. MEDICAL TESTIMONY IN INSANITY TRIALS, II

1. *OBSP,* 1780, case 325, 6th sess., 451; *OBSP,* 1785, case 599, 6th sess., 822.
2. *OBSP,* 1784, case 943, 8th sess., 1259.
3. *OBSP,* 1785, case 599, 6th sess., 822.
4. *OBSP,* 1784, case 971, 8th sess., 1303.
5. *OBSP,* 1796, case 512, 7th sess., 823.
6. *OBSP,* 1812, case 527, 6th sess., 331–33.
7. *OBSP,* 1812, case 527, 6th sess., 333.

8. Ainsley's deft avoidance of the "either-or" choice he was given was not the first time a medical witness decided to enlarge the possible range of mental functioning. A Dr. Luis Leo, who, in answering a question that forced him to speculate whether a prisoner stole spoons in a "lucid interval" or in a "moment of insanity," chose to answer: "He could do it in the paroxysm of mania." Whether this phrase was an intriguing foreshadowing of the concept of "reasoning mania" we have no way of knowing, but what is important for the early stages of professional consciousness in the courtroom is the instance of a medical witness insisting on defining his own terms, not following the dialogue imposed by the lawyer. Further, Leo was expanding the meaning of "manic" to include artful and not simply frantic behavior. The lay observer might conclude that the prisoner had returned to rationality because of the skill with which he pursued his objective. It was an insane pursuit, however, not a lucid interval. See *OBSP*, 1801, case 446, 5th sess., 319–20.

9. *OBSP*, 1812, case 527, 6th sess., 339.

10. *OBSP*, 1842–43, case 2857, 12th sess., 1006.

11. *OBSP*, 1812, case 527, 6th sess., 337.

12. *OBSP*, 1784, case 388, 3d sess., 546; *OBSP*, 1812, case 527, 6th sess., 333.

13. "I did so misconduct myself in a way of total absence of thought, never contemplating such a crime" (*OBSP*, 1827, case 217, 1st sess., 98).

14. *OBSP*, 1827, case 1613, 7th sess., 628.

15. *OBSP*, 1828, case 1349, 6th sess., 624.

16. *OBSP*, 1822, case 811, 5th sess., 331.

17. *OBSP*, 1833, case 1304, 7th sess., 733.

18. *OBSP*, 1833, case 1304, 7th sess., 733.

19. *OBSP*, 1833, case 1304, 7th sess., 734.

20. For Gall's views on partial alienation, see the *Weekly Medico-Chirurgical and Philosophical Magazine,* 26 July 1823, 2–3.

21. Joel Peter Eigen, "Delusion in the Courtroom: The Role of Partial Insanity in Early Forensic Testimony," *Medical History* 35 (1991): 25–49. By citing this earlier work I appear to be breaking a self-imposed rule regarding the construction of frequency distributions of the *elements* of courtroom testimony. This paper was completed when I believed that such egregious positivism was warranted. The computations are accurate, and I suppose I could defend the table by reminding the reader that the period covered is sufficiently limited to narrow the possible range in delusion's meaning. Still, there is the possibility that medical witnesses were using the term differently, so I would suggest taking the profusion of delusion with a grain of salt.

22. *OBSP*, 1841, case 2608, 12th sess., 935.

23. *OBSP*, 1830, case 176, 1st sess., 91.

24. *OBSP*, 1840–41, case 39, 1st sess., 20–21.

25. *OBSP*, 1840–41, case 39, 1st sess., 24.

26. *OBSP*, 1840–41, case 39, 1st sess., 23–24.

27. *OBSP*, 1838, case 499, 4th sess., 413–14.

28. Although mental disturbance associated with childbirth was seen as a discrete disease based in organic disturbance, its basis in law was ambiguous because of its obvious temporary duration. Periodic insanity had always been suspect as a sufficiently debilitating condition: one could not be sure of the mental state of the accused at the moment of the crime. As Shelley Day points out, "Temporary derangement was not a reason for a pardon, much less a defence that could lead to an acquittal" ("Puerperal Insanity: The Historical Sociology of a Disease" [D.Phil., Cambridge University, 1985], 80). Still, in chapter 2, I mention a trial in 1668 in connection with Hale's analysis of "temporary and complete insanity," which centered on the issue of infanticide. In this case the jury did acquit, although it seems clear that the "honest and virtuous deportment of the woman" provided a critical context for the plea of insanity. Any sign of prevarication, any "social circumstance" suggesting a rational motive to destroy the child presumably would have compromised the prisoner's credibility. Even if the prisoner was convicted, sentences in infanticide cases as early as the late sixteenth century could be commuted, owing, one suspects, to the mental state of the prisoner. But this was not a consistent outcome, nor was it grounded in any codified legal ruling (Day, "Puerperal Insanity," 121). Nigel Walker has located a Scottish case in which a prisoner convicted of infanticide was saved by royal mercy, although he was unable to find a similar case of clemency in the English courtroom (*Crime and Insanity in England,* vol. 1: *The Historical Perspective* [Edinburgh: Edinburgh University Press, 1968], 127).

29. Day, "Puerperal Insanity," 157.

30. Day provides an excellent review of the medical perspectives of the derangement thought to be associated with parturition in "Puerperal Insanity," esp. 153–99.

31. Day, "Puerperal Insanity," 111. The range of mental states thought to accompany childbirth and its aftermath provided considerable latitude to medical witnesses: "[S]he was not aware what she was doing, or if she was . . . she was incapable of controlling her actions" (121). An institutional framework already existed for expert opinion in criminal trials centering on infanticide. Medical men had traditionally played an important role in coroners' inquests called to determine the circumstances that surrounded the death of an infant. See Roger Smith, *Trial by Medicine: Insanity and Responsibility in Victorian Trials* (Edinburgh: Edinburgh University Press, 1981), esp. 143–50.

32. *OBSP,* 1840, case 1877, 9th sess., 504–5.

33. James C. Prichard, *On the Different Forms of Insanity in Relation to Jurisprudence Designed for the Use of Persons Concerned in Legal Questions Regarding Unsoundness of Mind* (London: Hippolyte Baillière, 1842), 69. In this passage Prichard is discussing the similarity between monomania and moral insanity.

34. In 1822, Prichard specifically mentioned puerperal mania in regard to impulsive will: "[A] blind impulse without reason . . . she is perfectly aware of

the atrocity of the deed she is so powerfully impelled to" (cited in Day, "Puerperal Insanity," 162).

35. *OBSP,* 1840, case 1877, 9th sess., 507.

36. *OBSP,* 1840, case 1877, 9th sess., 508.

37. *OBSP,* 1840, case 1877, 9th sess., 506.

38. *OBSP,* 1840, case 1877, 9th sess., 509–10.

39. *OBSP,* 1840, case 2316, 11th sess., 823. The prisoner's statement of utter helplessness in the face of "blind influence" reminds one of quotations from French texts used by Marc to substantiate the existence of a lesion of the will. Marc cited a patient of Leuret's: "Je ne puis m'en empêcher, c'est plus fort que moi" (Charles-Chretien-Henri Marc, *De la folie, considerérée dans ses rapports avec les questions médico-judiciaires,* pt. 1 [Paris: J. B. Baillière, 1840], 88).

40. *OBSP,* 1842–43, case 2857, 12th sess., 1006.

41. *OBSP,* 1841, case 2608, 12th sess., 932–33.

42. Erskine's original instruction regarding delusion was that it must be the immediate precipitator to the crime. Mere proof of delusion did not exculpate; the connection between the delusion and the act had to be obvious. According to the attorney, the "act must be the immediate, unqualified offspring of [the] disease." The setting for Erskine's comments is provided in chapter 2.

43. *OBSP,* 1842–43, case 874, 5th sess., 756–59.

44. *OBSP,* 1842–43, case 874, 5th sess., 760.

45. *OBSP,* 1842–43, case 874, 5th sess., 761.

46. *OBSP,* 1842–43, case 874, 5th sess., 763.

47. James Cowles Prichard, *A Treatise on Insanity and Other Diseases Affecting the Mind* (London: Sherwood, Gilbert & Piper, 1835), 94.

48. *OBSP,* 1840, case 1877, 9th sess., 505.

49. The expansion of medical treatment to include both traditional physical remedies and the newer, moral treatment has constituted an active area of scholarship in the history of psychiatry not least because of the direct threat moral treatment was thought to pose to medical control of the asylums. Goldstein's account of French psychiatry is particularly geared to Pinel's ability to incorporate the "console" function into treatment (*Console and Classify: The French Psychiatric Profession in the Nineteenth Century* [Cambridge: Cambridge University Press, 1987], esp. 197–230). In England, the moral treatment movement was symbolized most dramatically in the York Retreat, whose history, rationale, and regimen are the subject of Anne Digby's *Madness, Morality and Medicine: A Study of the York Retreat, 1796–1914* (Cambridge: Cambridge University Press, 1985). Andrew Scull examines the threat such efforts at moral treatment posed to English psychiatrists in "Mad-Doctors and Magistrates: English Psychiatry's Struggle for Professional Autonomy in the Nineteenth Century," *Archives européens sociologie* 27 (1976): 279–305.

50. *OBSP,* 1841, case 1766, 8th sess., 339–40.

51. Quoted in John Henry Wigmore, *Evidence in Trial at Common Law,* vol. 7 (Boston: Little, Brown, 1985), 4.

52. Stanley W. Jackson, *Melancholia and Depression: From Hippocratic Times to Modern Times* (New Haven: Yale University Press, 1986). A recent examination of a particular European delusion can be found in Gill Speak, "An Odd Kind of Melancholy: Reflections on the Glass Delusion in Europe (1440–1680)," *History of Psychiatry* 1 (1990): 191–206.

53. Goldstein, "Console and Classify," 162–96.

7. The Prisoner's Defense

1. *OBSP,* 1813, case 11, 1st sess., 14.

2. On the attorney's role, see the Introduction.

3. According to Ingram, "Any degree of access to the patient's language is denied by the intervention of the language of sanity." His review of the literature leads him to conclude that the utterances of the mad have been "sanitized" and thus reflect conventional cultural discourse, which values rational communication above all (*The Madhouse of Language: Writing and Reading Madness in the Eighteenth Century* [London: Routledge, 1991], quotations on 8, 127; see esp. 1–34).

4. For Monro's rejection of the notion of madness as deluded imagination, see John Monro, *Remarks on Dr Battie's Treatise on Madness* (London: John Clarke, 1758). Haslam's views can be found in *Observations on Insanity with Practical Remarks on the Disease, and an Account of the Morbid Appearances on Dissection* (London: F. C. Rivington, 1798).

5. Ingram's differences with Foucault can be found in *Madhouse,* 5–10. For Foucault's views on the impossibility of retrieving the experience of madness, see *Folie et déraison: Histoire de la folie a l'âge classique* (Paris: Plon, 1961), vii.

6. Roy Porter, *Mind-Forg'd Manacles: A History of Madness in England from the Restoration to the Regency* (London: Athlone Press, 1987), 236.

7. Several case histories published in the eighteenth century reveal something of the thought-world of the patient, as reported by the mad-doctor. See William Pargeter, *Observations on Maniacal Disorders* (Reading, 1792), 31–63. For a case of a "female maniac with a facility to versification" see William Perfect, *Annals of Insanity Comprising a Selection of Curious and Interesting Cases in the Different Species of Insanity, Lunacy, or Madness, with the Modes of Practice, as Adopted in the Treatment of Each,* 3d ed. (London: Murray and Highley, 1803), 49–58. Wild fancies on religious matters are chronicled on 87–92. Delusions offered on 330–35, including the case of the baker at Ferrara who believed he was made of butter and had to give up his vocation lest he melt. These delusions could occasionally be lethal. Perfect reports the case of a man who believed he was so enormous that he could not go through the door of his apartment. His physicians gave orders that he should be forcibly led through it, but he cried out as he was forced along "that the

flesh was torn from his bones, and that his limbs were broken off, of which terrible impression he died in a few days, accusing those who conduct[ed] him with being his murderers" (*Annals of Insanity,* 335).

8. John Perceval, *Perceval's Narrative* (London: E. Wilson, 1838), 1131–34.

9. Perceval, *Perceval's Narrative,* 173.

10. The "Wild Beast Test" is discussed in chapter 2. For a full description of the case that animated the test and the judge's comments, see Nigel D. Walker, *Crime and Insanity in England,* vol. 1: *The Historical Perspective* (Edinburgh: Edinburgh University Press, 1968), 53–57.

11. Nigel Walker, *Crime and Insanity in England,* vol. 1: *The Historical Perspective* (Edinburgh: Edinburgh University Press, 1968), 62.

12. Such statements reminds one of Perceval's comment: "I had not power to restrain my will" (*Perceval's Narrative,* 58).

13. *OBSP,* 1830, case 177, 1st sess., 92.

14. With so many defenses to scan, there was an obvious temptation to try to quantify the prisoners' images and metaphors. The only terms that surfaced with any regularity were "senselessness" and "insensibility," discussed below in the text. There were other constructions regarding "not knowing what I was about" and "not remembering what I did" and in time, repeated phrases having to do with the mind and consciousness, but the context in which these terms surfaced changed over time, so that any frequency distribution would give a false idea of the predominance and waning influence of any one phrase as the years progressed. Instead, I have opted to continue the format of earlier chapters, separating the time span into three periods and selecting those trials that feature innovations in the prisoner's defense. The context is the key to grasping the significance of the emergence of these themes. My method was to look at the testimony as it evolved and to select those narrative extracts that reveal significant shifts in the defendants' expressions of derangement.

15. *OBSP,* 1760, case 78, 3d sess., 86; *OBSP,* 1767, case 247, 3d sess., 134.

16. *OBSP,* 1764, case 403, 6th sess., 242; *OBSP,* 1771, case 275, 4th sess., 203; emphasis added.

17. G. S. Rousseau, "Nerves, Spirits, and Fibres: Towards Defining the Origins of Sensibility, with a Postscript in 1976," *Blue Guitar* 2 (1976): 125–53.

18. *OBSP,* 1769, case 366, 6th sess., 314.

19. Quoted in Ingram, *Madhouse,* 70.

20. *OBSP,* 1792, case 110, 1st sess., 276.

21. *OBSP,* 1797, case 456, 6th sess., 443.

22. *OBSP,* 1802, case 594, 7th sess., 398.

23. According to both Coke and Blackstone, drunkenness aggravated the offense. As Nigel Walker points out, however, Coke belonged "to a comparatively sober age." The availability by the middle 1700s of cheap and powerful liquor from Scotland and the Continent made drunkenness a daily occurrence and sight. The prisoners studied here were doubtless appealing to the drinking habits of the jurors. Walker found one case where drinking

was clearly the prisoner's defense, and as it turns out, an effective one: "[I was] so drunk I could not see through a story ladder." In the early nineteenth century, a judge could instruct the jury that it could take drinking into account in determining the extent of malice in the prisoner's act: whether premeditated or done "with sudden heat and impulse." If sudden, the "intoxication of the accused could properly be taken into consideration." This case was later overruled, although jurors were told they could take intoxication into account in deciding between a murder or a manslaughter conviction in other trials of the 1830s (Walker, *Crime and Insanity,* 177–81).

24. *OBSP,* 1767, case 302, 5th sess., 193.
25. *OBSP,* 1784, case 943, 8th sess., 1259.
26. *OBSP,* 1798, case 494, 7th sess., 536.
27. *OBSP,* 1815, case 784, 7th sess., 363.
28. *OBSP,* 1810, case 753, 7th sess., 461.
29. *OBSP,* 1808, case 389, 5th sess., 275.
30. *OBSP,* 1827, case 1613, 7th sess., 627.
31. *OBSP,* 1827, case 217, 1st sess., 98.
32. *OBSP,* 1815, case 1784, 7th sess., 363.
33. *OBSP,* 1829, case 461, 2d sess., 216. (Defense given in written form.)
34. *OBSP,* 1833, case 619, 3d sess., 296.
35. *OBSP,* 1837, case 1089, 6th sess., 1009.
36. *OBSP,* 1827, case 1394, 6th sess., 541.
37. Porter, *Mind-Forg'd Manacles,* 180–82.
38. Early nineteenth-century studies in neurophysiology had considerable implications for insanity because human movements were increasingly described in "automatic" terms. On the obvious lack of mental control attendant to hysterical and epileptic seizures, see Roger Smith, *Trial by Medicine: Insanity and Responsibility in Victorian Trials* (Edinburgh: Edinburgh University Press, 1981), 46–56.
39. *OBSP,* 1841–42, case 1975, 8th sess., 499.
40. *OBSP,* 1840, case 2316, 11th sess., 824.
41. *OBSP,* 1831, case 555, 3d sess., 303.
42. *OBSP,* 1831, case 555, 3d sess., 303.
43. *OBSP,* 1830, case 176, 1st sess., 90.
44. *OBSP,* 1830, case 176, 1st sess., 91.
45. *OBSP,* 1805, case 637, 7th sess., 555.
46. *OBSP,* 1805, case 637, 7th sess., 555.
47. *OBSP,* 1805, case 637, 7th sess., 555–56.
48. *OBSP,* 1830, case 177, 1st sess., 91.
49. *OBSP,* 1830, case 177, 1st sess., 92, 91.
50. That prisoners who manifested this sort of partial insanity were acquitted really does not violate Hale's criterion of "perfect" or total insanity. As discussed earlier, a certain ambiguity attends his classic delineation of partial insanity. Lord Hale clearly believed that a partial insanity such as melancholia—partial in respect of degree—should not qualify for exculpation. The

other sense of "partial"—that is, duration—is left open to interpretation. Lunatics "in the heights of their distemper . . . the person that is absolutely mad for a day, killing a man in that distemper, is equally not guilty, as if he were mad without intermission" (Matthew Hale, *The History of the Pleas of the Crown* [London: E. & R. Nutt, 1736], esp. 30–31). The *OBSP* therefore reveal numerous examples of this sort of "partial insanity," usually referred to as senselessness, which constituted a successful prisoner's defense.

CONCLUSION

1. *OBSP,* 1843, case 874, 5th sess., 763, 759, 760, 762.
2. *OBSP,* 1840, case 1877, 9th sess., 504–05; *OBSP,* 1843, case 874, 5th sess., 757–59; *OBSP,* 1812, case 527, 6th sess., 333; *OBSP,* 1833, case 1304, 7th sess., 733.
3. Martin J. Weiner, *Reconstructing the Criminal: Culture, Law, and Policy in England, 1830–1914* (Cambridge: Cambridge University Press, 1990), 38.

Index